BART SIMPSON™
PRINCE of PRANKS

TITAN BOOKS

BART SIMPSON: PRINCE OF PRANKS

Collects Bart Simpson Comics 38, 39, 40, 41, 42

Published in the UK by Titan Books, a division of Titan Publishing Group,
144 Southwark St., London, SE1 0UP, under licence from Bongo Entertainment, Inc.

FIRST EDITION: MAY 2011

ISBN 9780857681492

4 6 8 10 9 7 5 3

Publisher: Matt Groening
Creative Director: Bill Morrison
Managing Editor: Terry Delegeane
Director of Operations: Robert Zaugh
Art Director: Nathan Kane
Art Director Special Projects: Serban Cristescu
Production Manager: Christopher Ungar
Assistant Art Director: Chia-Hsien Jason Ho
Production/Design: Karen Bates, Nathan Hamill, Art Villanueva
Staff Artist: Mike Rote
Administration: Ruth Waytz, Pete Benson
Intern: Max Davison
Legal Guardian: Susan A. Grode
Trade Paperback Concepts and Design: Serban Cristescu
Cover: Kevin Newman and Serban Cristescu

Contributing Artists:
Serban Cristescu, Chuck Dixon, Nathan Hamill, Jason Ho, James Lloyd,
Nina Matsumoto, Kim Narsete, Kevin Newman, Phyllis Novin, Phil Ortiz, Andrew Pepoy,
Mike Rote, Robert Stanley, Steve Steere Jr., Chris Ungar, Carlos Valenti,
Art Villanueva, Ken Wheaton

Contributing Writers:
James W. Bates, Tom Beland, John Delaney, Tony DiGerolamo,
Brian Houlihan, Amanda McCann, Jesse Leon McCann, Tom Peyer,
Mary Trainor, Patric Verrone, Chris Yambar

Printed in Spain

CONTENTS

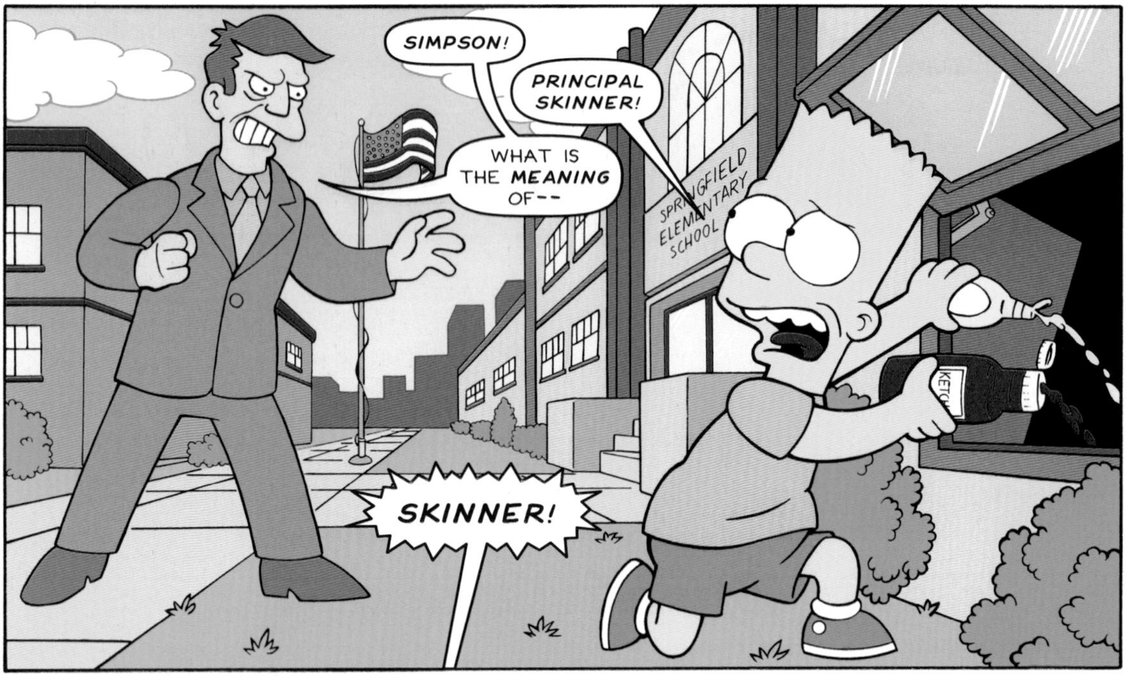
SIMPSON!
PRINCIPAL SKINNER!
WHAT IS THE MEANING OF--
SPRINGFIELD ELEMENTARY SCHOOL
KETCH
SKINNER!

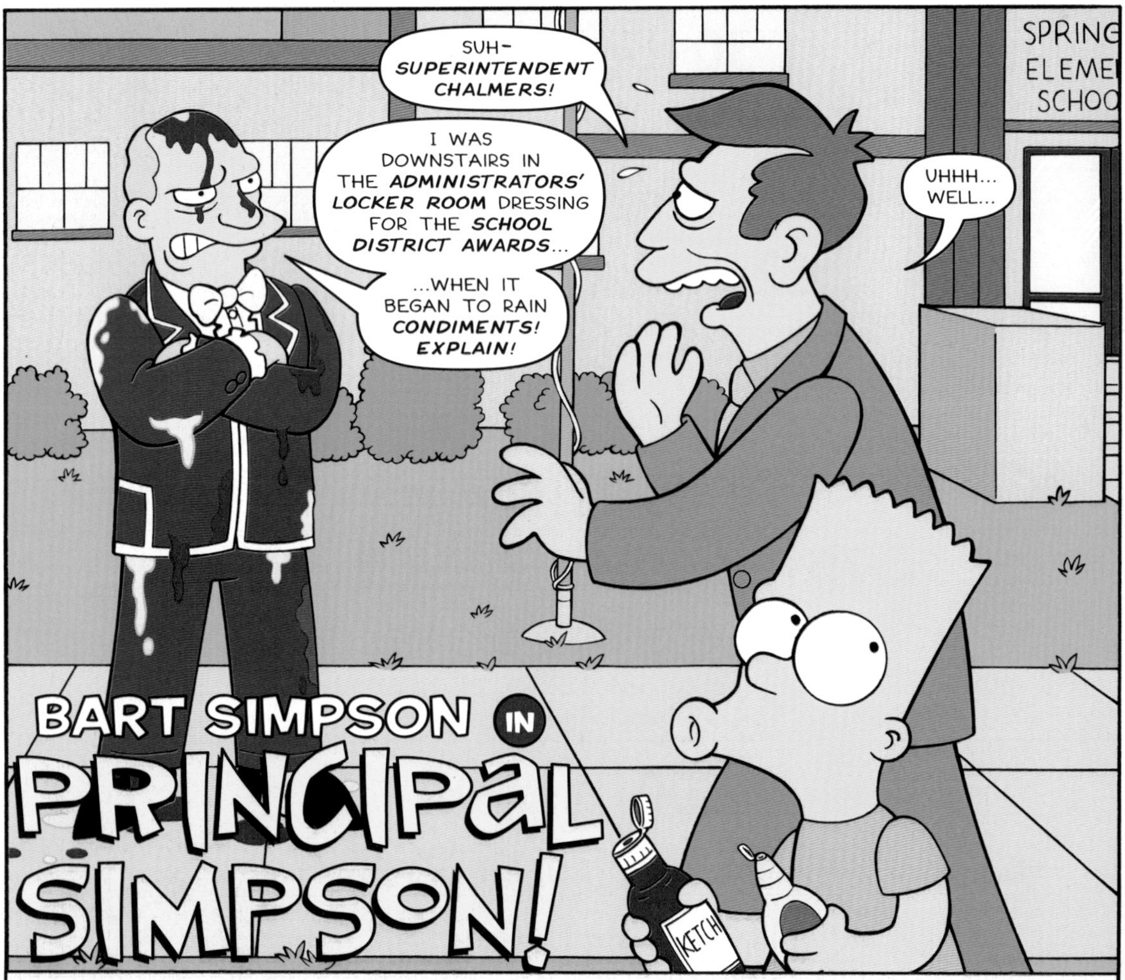
SUH-SUPERINTENDENT CHALMERS!
I WAS DOWNSTAIRS IN THE ADMINISTRATORS' LOCKER ROOM DRESSING FOR THE SCHOOL DISTRICT AWARDS...
...WHEN IT BEGAN TO RAIN CONDIMENTS! EXPLAIN!
UHHH... WELL...
BART SIMPSON IN
PRINCIPAL SIMPSON!
KETCH

TOM PEYER SCRIPT | **MIKE DECARLO** PENCILS | **KEN WHEATON** INKS | **ROBERT STANLEY** COLORS | **KAREN BATES** LETTERS | **BILL MORRISON** EDITOR

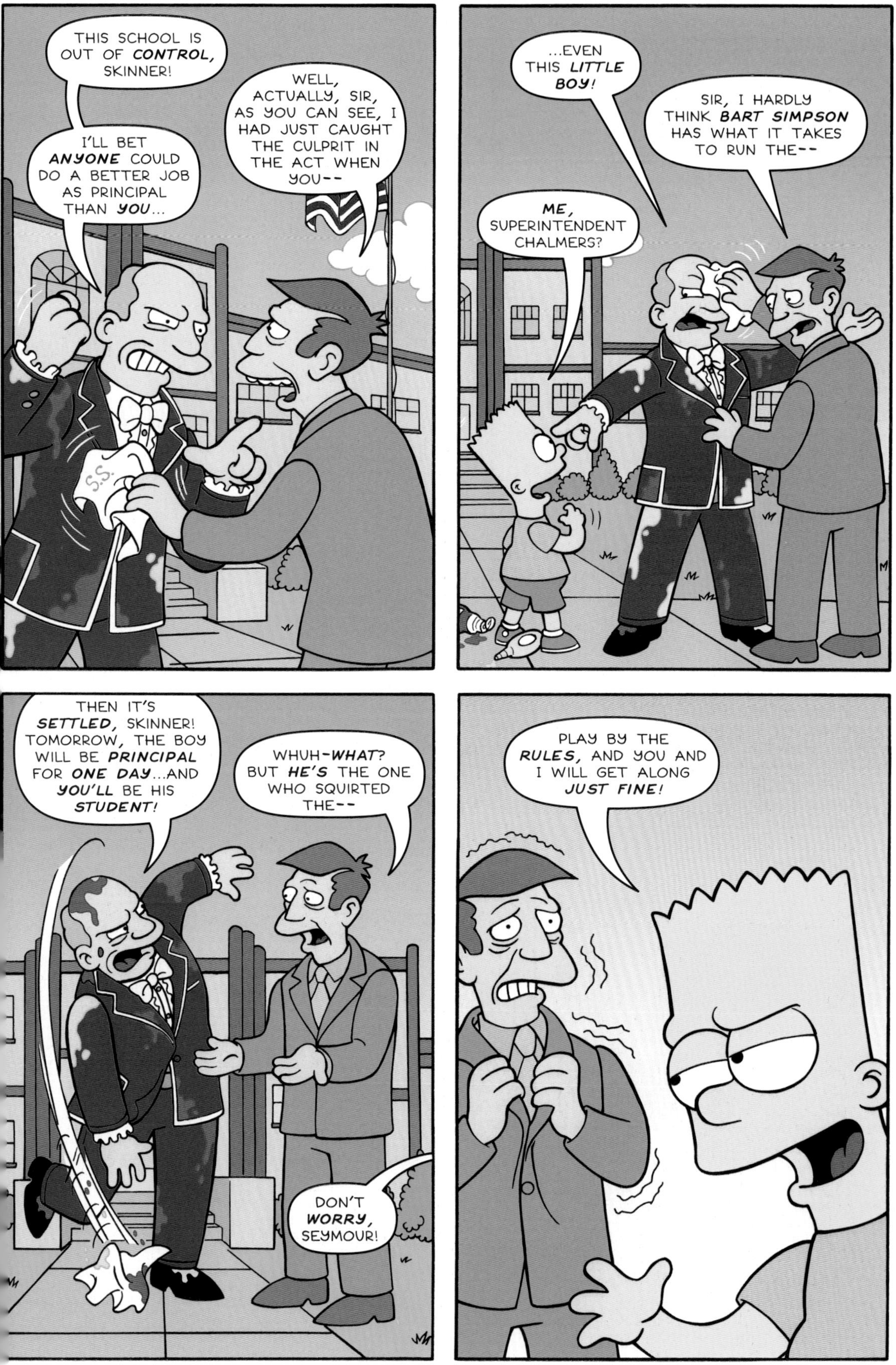
THIS SCHOOL IS OUT OF **CONTROL,** SKINNER!
I'LL BET **ANYONE** COULD DO A BETTER JOB AS PRINCIPAL THAN **YOU**...
WELL, ACTUALLY, SIR, AS YOU CAN SEE, I HAD JUST CAUGHT THE CULPRIT IN THE ACT WHEN YOU--
S.S.
...EVEN THIS **LITTLE BOY!**
SIR, I HARDLY THINK **BART SIMPSON** HAS WHAT IT TAKES TO RUN THE--
ME, SUPERINTENDENT CHALMERS?
THEN IT'S **SETTLED,** SKINNER! TOMORROW, THE BOY WILL BE **PRINCIPAL** FOR **ONE DAY**...AND **YOU'LL** BE HIS **STUDENT!**
WHUH-**WHAT?** BUT **HE'S** THE ONE WHO SQUIRTED THE--
DON'T **WORRY,** SEYMOUR!
PLAY BY THE **RULES,** AND YOU AND I WILL GET ALONG **JUST FINE!**

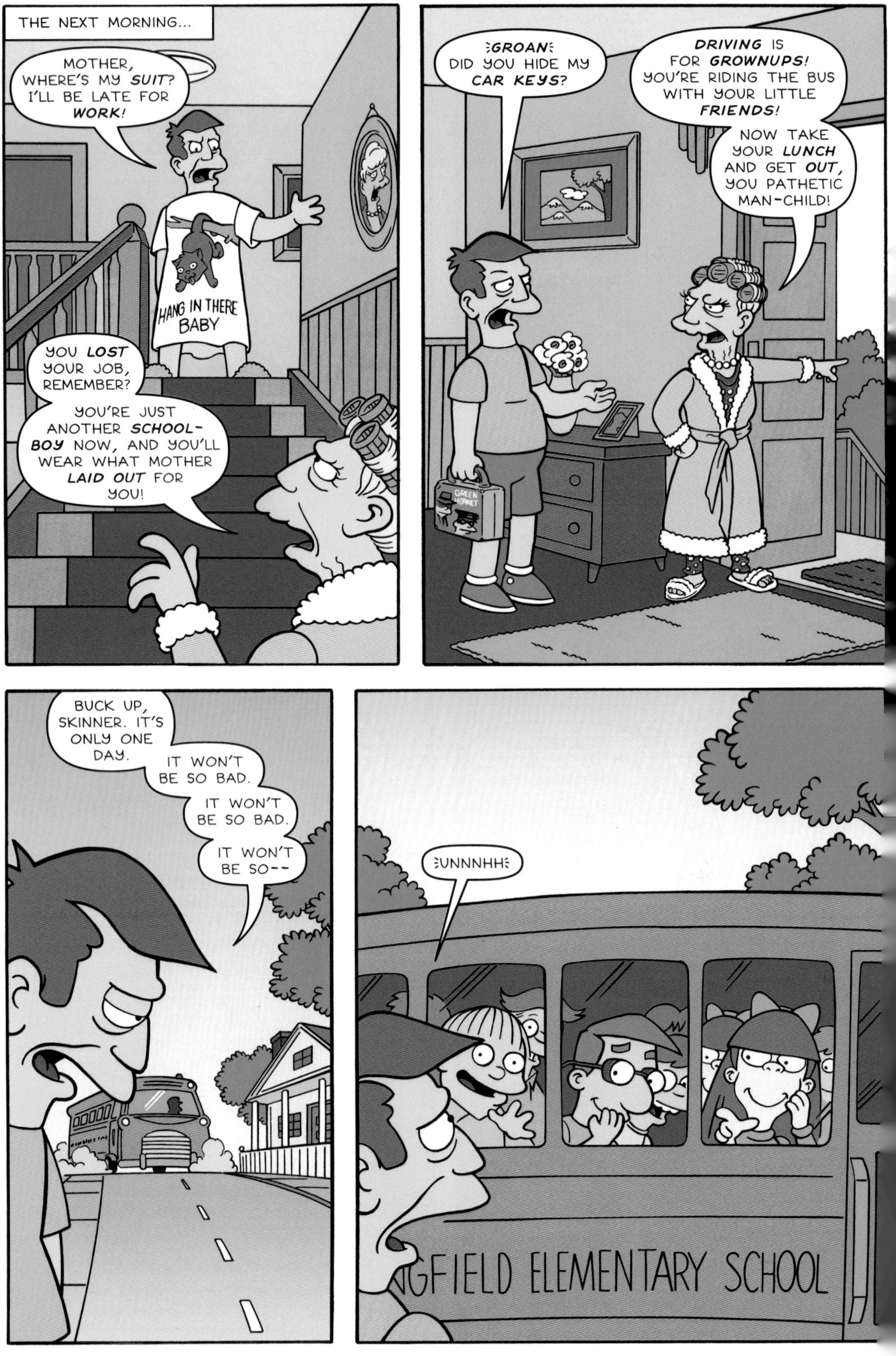
THE NEXT MORNING...
MOTHER, WHERE'S MY SUIT? I'LL BE LATE FOR WORK!
HANG IN THERE BABY
YOU LOST YOUR JOB, REMEMBER?
YOU'RE JUST ANOTHER SCHOOL-BOY NOW, AND YOU'LL WEAR WHAT MOTHER LAID OUT FOR YOU!
GROAN DID YOU HIDE MY CAR KEYS?
DRIVING IS FOR GROWNUPS! YOU'RE RIDING THE BUS WITH YOUR LITTLE FRIENDS!
NOW TAKE YOUR LUNCH AND GET OUT, YOU PATHETIC MAN-CHILD!
GREEN HORNET
BUCK UP, SKINNER. IT'S ONLY ONE DAY.
IT WON'T BE SO BAD.
IT WON'T BE SO BAD.
IT WON'T BE SO--
UNNNHH
GFIELD ELEMENTARY SCHOOL

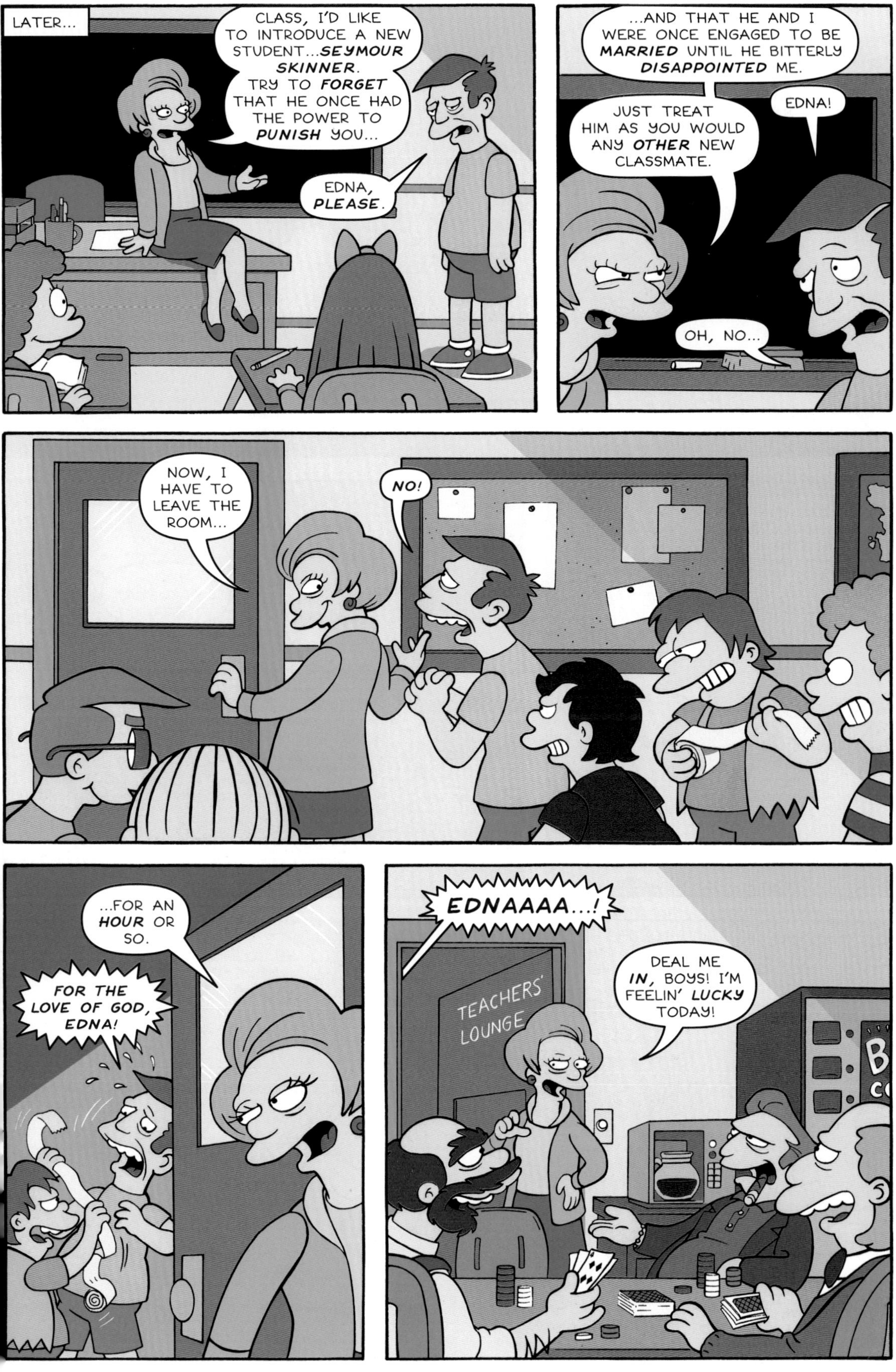
LATER...
CLASS, I'D LIKE TO INTRODUCE A NEW STUDENT...SEYMOUR SKINNER. TRY TO FORGET THAT HE ONCE HAD THE POWER TO PUNISH YOU...
EDNA, PLEASE.
...AND THAT HE AND I WERE ONCE ENGAGED TO BE MARRIED UNTIL HE BITTERLY DISAPPOINTED ME.
JUST TREAT HIM AS YOU WOULD ANY OTHER NEW CLASSMATE.
EDNA!
OH, NO...
NOW, I HAVE TO LEAVE THE ROOM...
NO!
...FOR AN HOUR OR SO.
FOR THE LOVE OF GOD, EDNA!
EDNAAAA...!
TEACHERS' LOUNGE
DEAL ME IN, BOYS! I'M FEELIN' LUCKY TODAY!

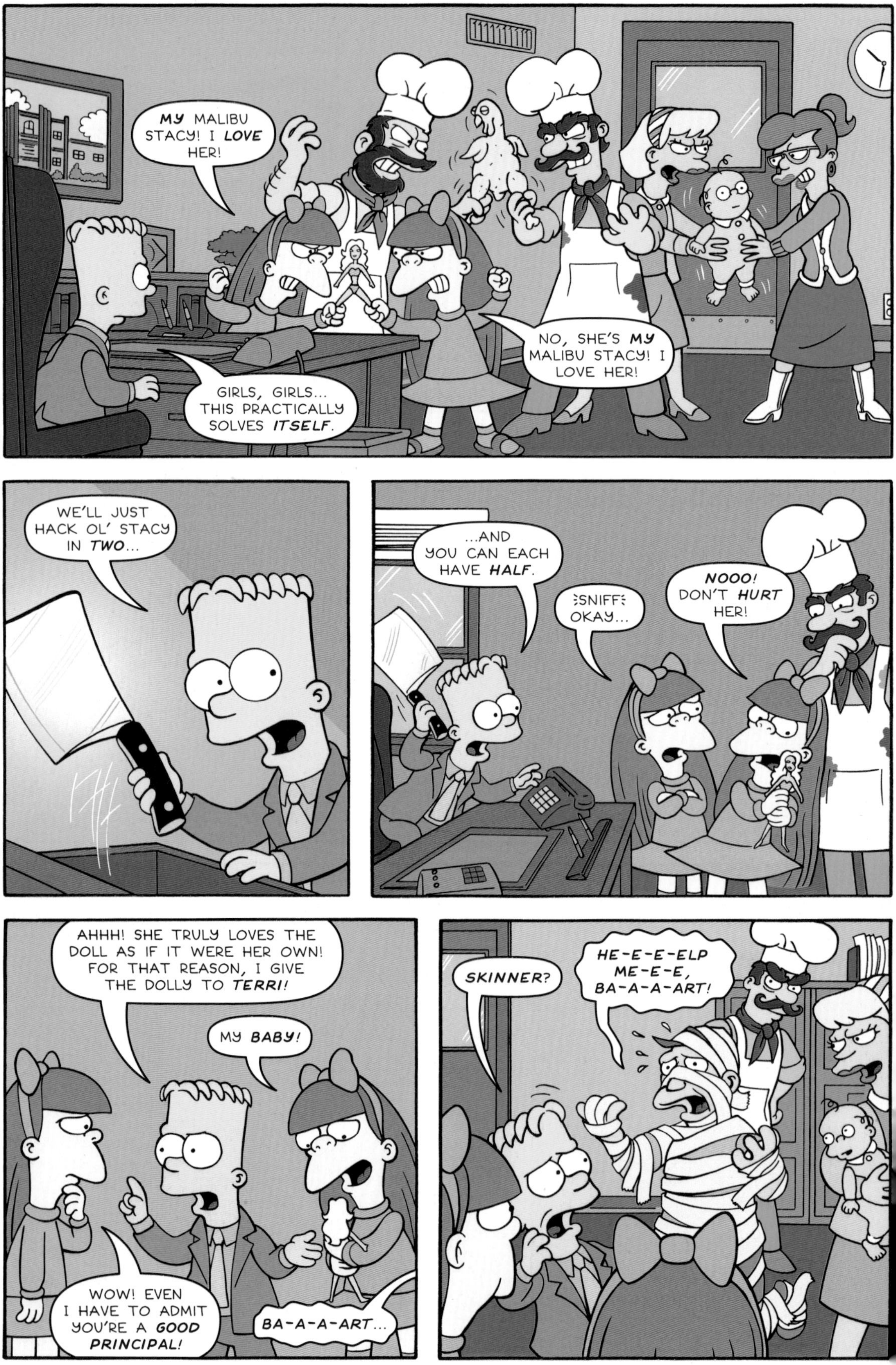
MY MALIBU STACY! I LOVE HER!
NO, SHE'S MY MALIBU STACY! I LOVE HER!
GIRLS, GIRLS... THIS PRACTICALLY SOLVES ITSELF.
WE'LL JUST HACK OL' STACY IN TWO...
...AND YOU CAN EACH HAVE HALF.
SNIFF OKAY...
NOOO! DON'T HURT HER!
AHHH! SHE TRULY LOVES THE DOLL AS IF IT WERE HER OWN! FOR THAT REASON, I GIVE THE DOLLY TO TERRI!
MY BABY!
WOW! EVEN I HAVE TO ADMIT YOU'RE A GOOD PRINCIPAL!
BA-A-A-ART...
SKINNER?
HE-E-E-ELP ME-E-E, BA-A-A-ART!

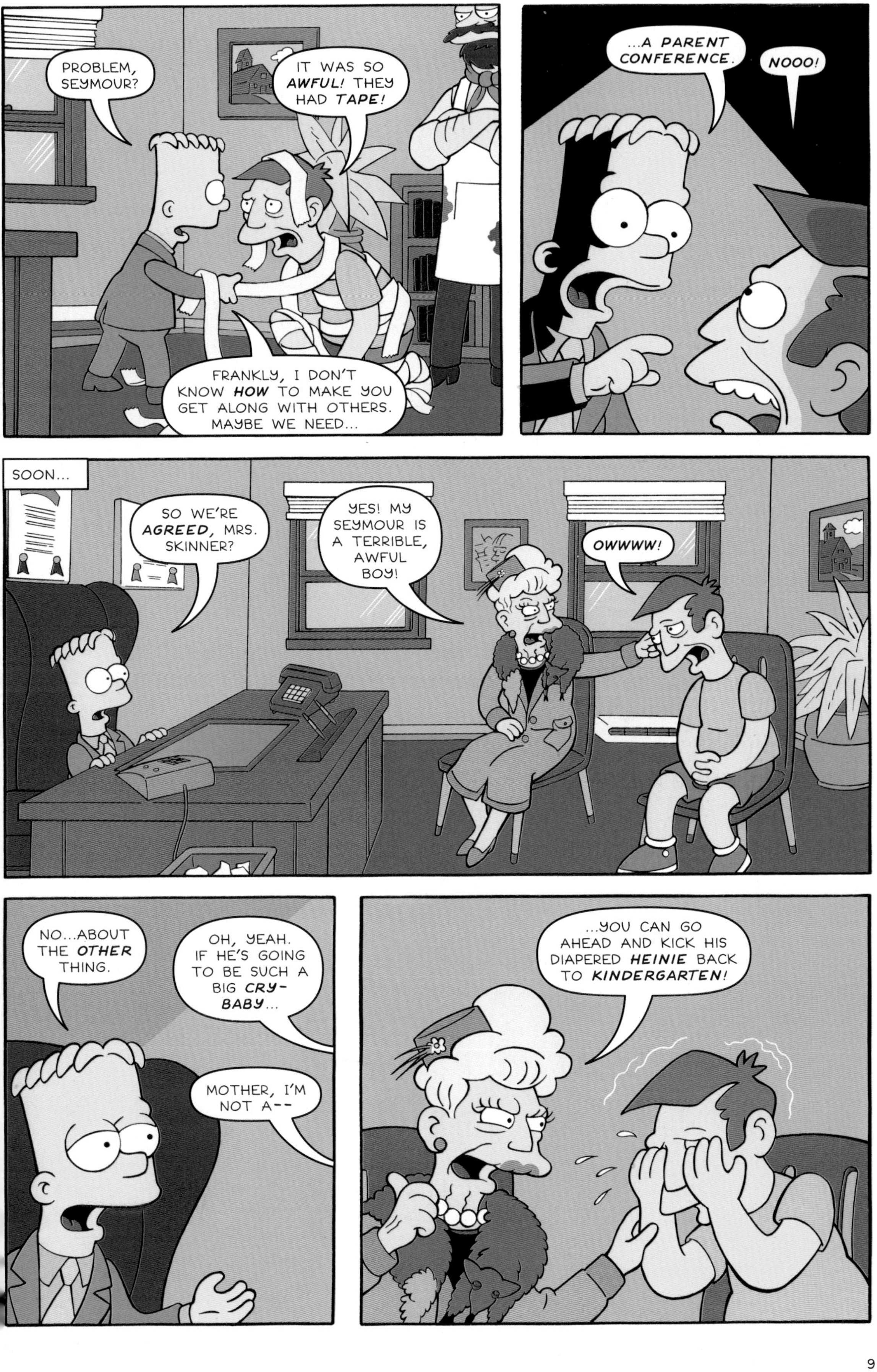
PROBLEM, SEYMOUR?
IT WAS SO AWFUL! THEY HAD TAPE!
FRANKLY, I DON'T KNOW HOW TO MAKE YOU GET ALONG WITH OTHERS. MAYBE WE NEED...
...A PARENT CONFERENCE.
NOOO!
SOON...
SO WE'RE AGREED, MRS. SKINNER?
YES! MY SEYMOUR IS A TERRIBLE, AWFUL BOY!
OWWWW!
NO...ABOUT THE OTHER THING.
OH, YEAH. IF HE'S GOING TO BE SUCH A BIG CRY-BABY...
MOTHER, I'M NOT A--
...YOU CAN GO AHEAD AND KICK HIS DIAPERED HEINIE BACK TO KINDERGARTEN!

I AM NOT TOO BIG FOR KINDER...
I AM NOT TOO BIG FOR KINDERG...
I AM NOT TOO BIG FO...
I AM NOT TOO BIG FOR K...
I AM NOT TOO BIG FOR KINDE...
I AM...OR KIND...
I AM...OR KIN...
I M...

THE SIIIIMP-SUUUNS...

BRI-I-I-ING

GARTEN
GARTEN
GARTEN
GARTEN
GARTEN
GARTEN
GARTEN

♫ PUMMM- ♫ PUM-PUM-PUM- ♫ PUMMM ♫

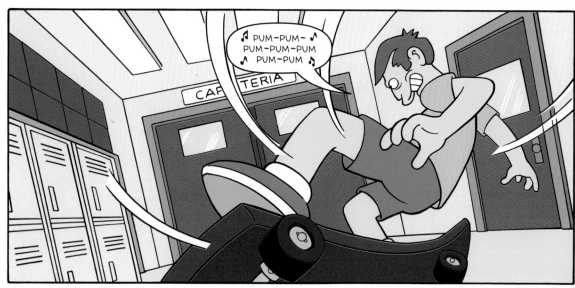

♫ PUM-PUM- ♫ PUM-PUM-PUM ♫ PUM-PUM ♫

CAFETERIA

MY, BUT BLACKBOARD-WRITING IS GOOD FOR SHAKING OFF THE BLUES!

I CAN'T WAIT TO DIG INTO THIS TEMPTING FOODSTUFF AT A TABLE FULL OF BOISTEROUS...

...CLASSMATES.

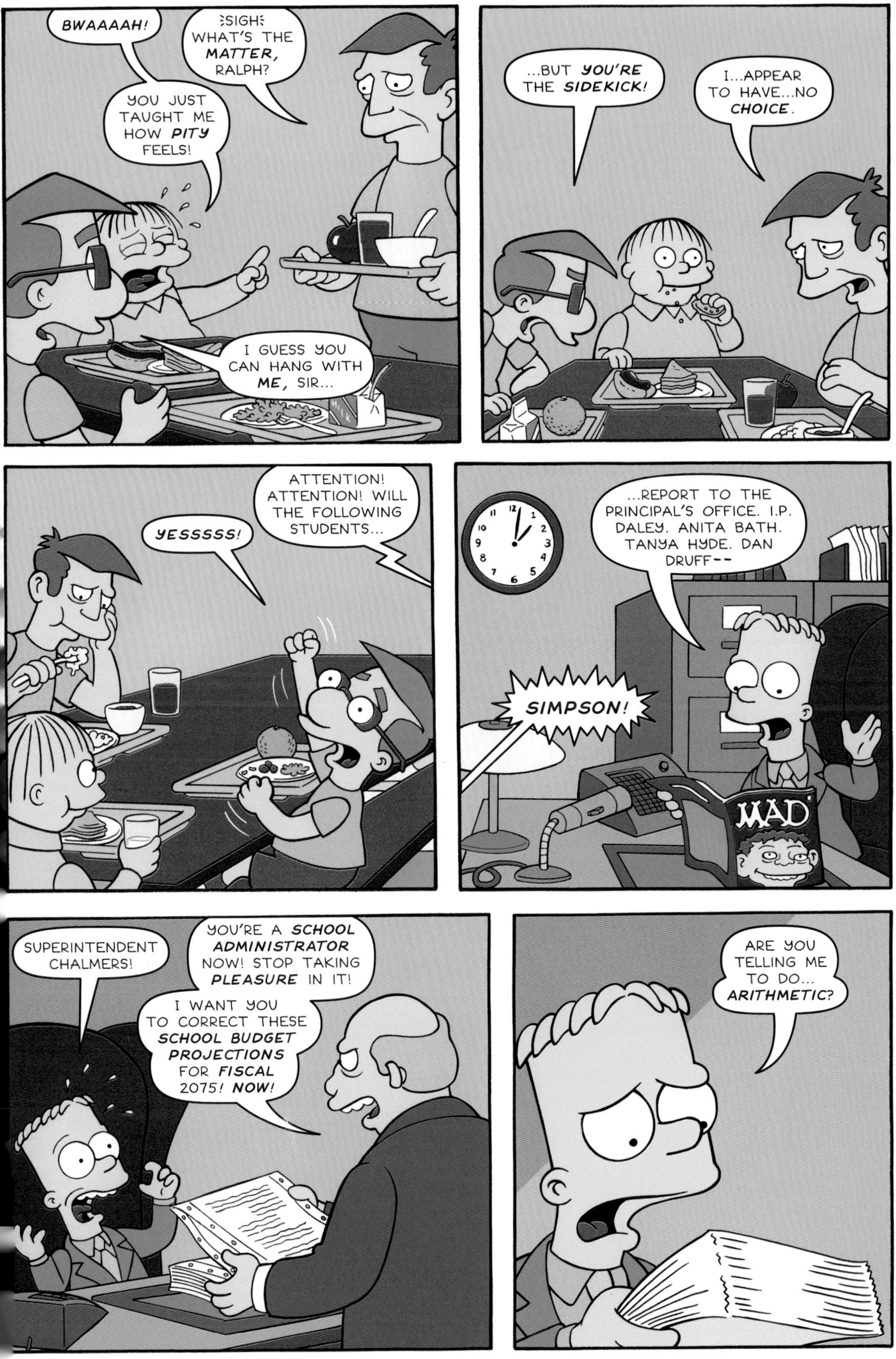
BWAAAAH!
:SIGH: WHAT'S THE MATTER, RALPH?
YOU JUST TAUGHT ME HOW PITY FEELS!
I GUESS YOU CAN HANG WITH ME, SIR...
MILK
...BUT YOU'RE THE SIDEKICK!
I...APPEAR TO HAVE...NO CHOICE.
YESSSSS!
ATTENTION! ATTENTION! WILL THE FOLLOWING STUDENTS...
...REPORT TO THE PRINCIPAL'S OFFICE. I.P. DALEY. ANITA BATH. TANYA HYDE. DAN DRUFF--
SIMPSON!
MAD
SUPERINTENDENT CHALMERS!
YOU'RE A SCHOOL ADMINISTRATOR NOW! STOP TAKING PLEASURE IN IT!
I WANT YOU TO CORRECT THESE SCHOOL BUDGET PROJECTIONS FOR FISCAL 2075! NOW!
ARE YOU TELLING ME TO DO... ARITHMETIC?

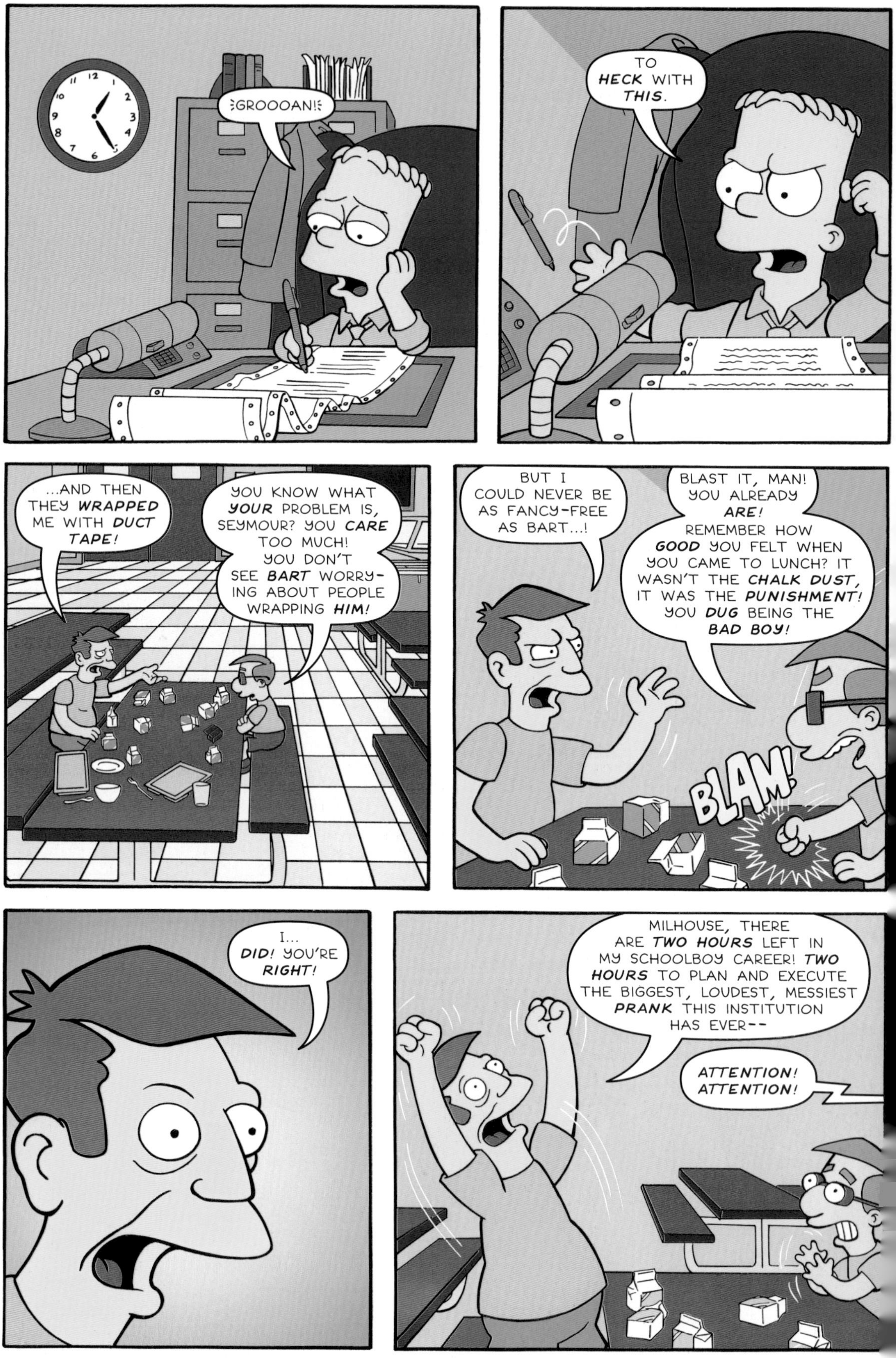
GROOOAN!
TO HECK WITH THIS.
...AND THEN THEY WRAPPED ME WITH DUCT TAPE!
YOU KNOW WHAT YOUR PROBLEM IS, SEYMOUR? YOU CARE TOO MUCH! YOU DON'T SEE BART WORRYING ABOUT PEOPLE WRAPPING HIM!
BUT I COULD NEVER BE AS FANCY-FREE AS BART...!
BLAST IT, MAN! YOU ALREADY ARE! REMEMBER HOW GOOD YOU FELT WHEN YOU CAME TO LUNCH? IT WASN'T THE CHALK DUST, IT WAS THE PUNISHMENT! YOU DUG BEING THE BAD BOY!
BLAM!
I... DID! YOU'RE RIGHT!
MILHOUSE, THERE ARE TWO HOURS LEFT IN MY SCHOOLBOY CAREER! TWO HOURS TO PLAN AND EXECUTE THE BIGGEST, LOUDEST, MESSIEST PRANK THIS INSTITUTION HAS EVER--
ATTENTION! ATTENTION!

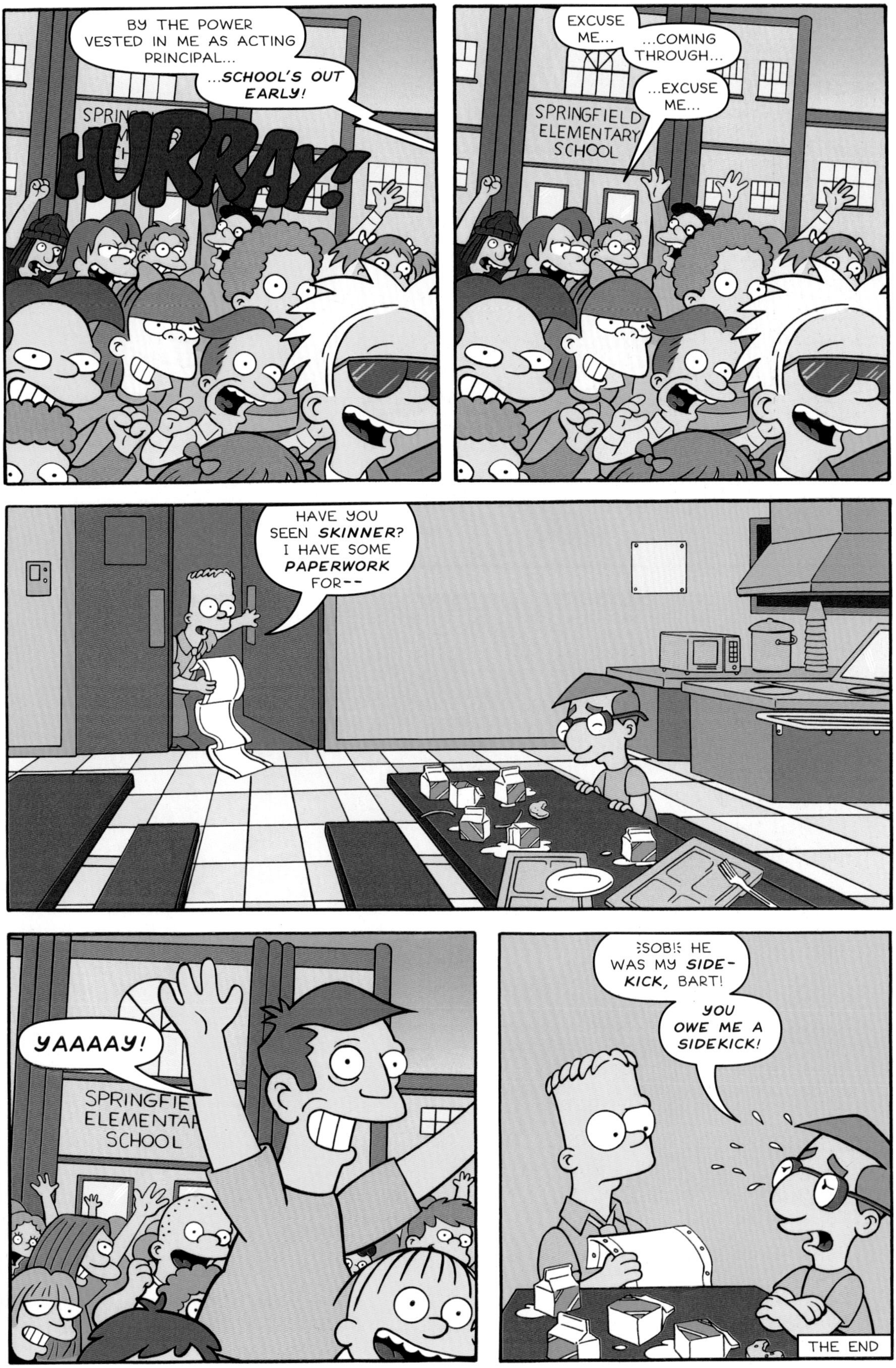
BY THE POWER VESTED IN ME AS ACTING PRINCIPAL...
...SCHOOL'S OUT EARLY!
HURRAY!
EXCUSE ME...
...COMING THROUGH...
...EXCUSE ME...
SPRINGFIELD ELEMENTARY SCHOOL
HAVE YOU SEEN SKINNER? I HAVE SOME PAPERWORK FOR--
YAAAAY!
SPRINGFIE ELEMENTAR SCHOOL
SOB! HE WAS MY SIDE-KICK, BART!
YOU OWE ME A SIDEKICK!
THE END

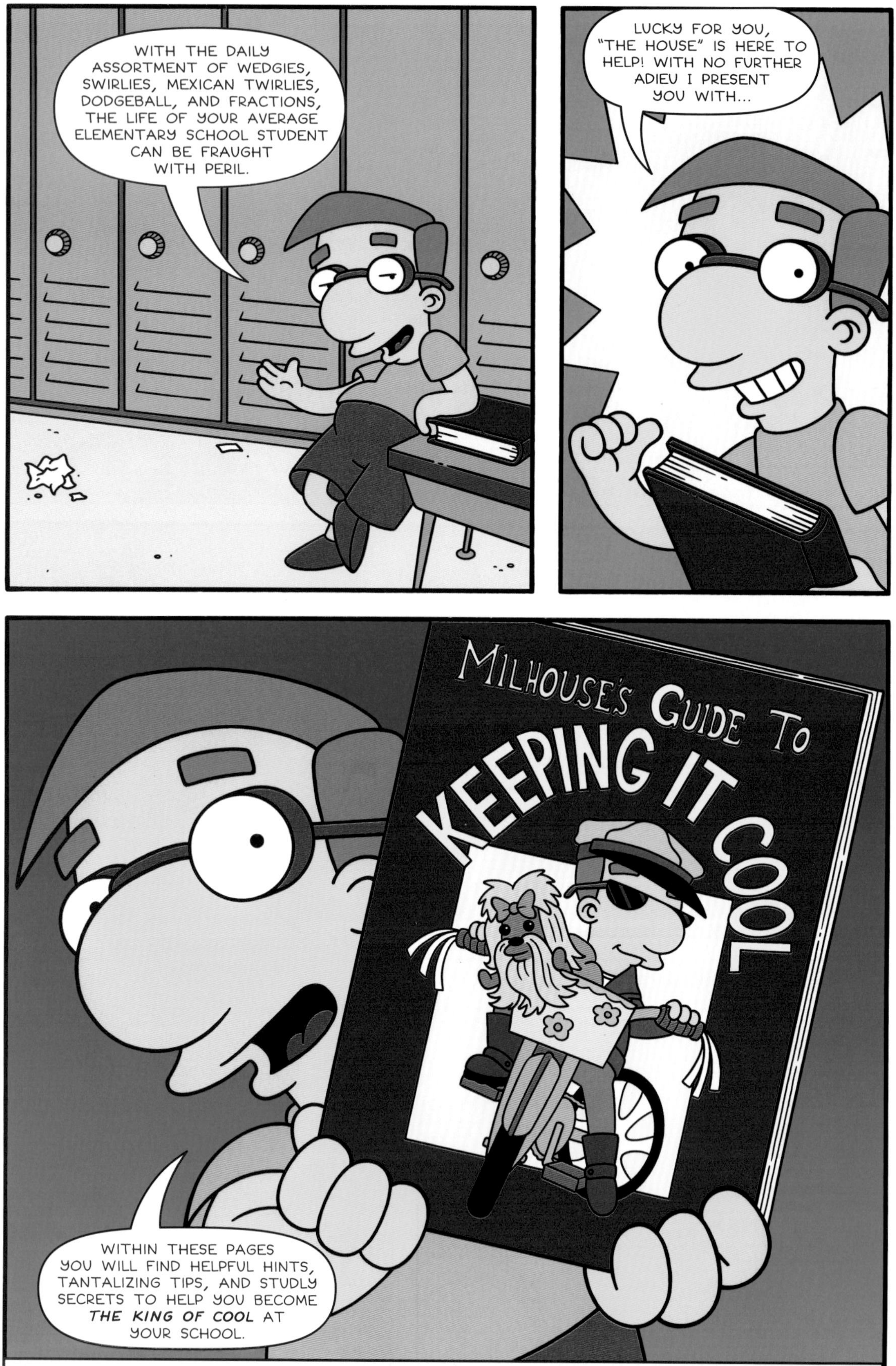
WITH THE DAILY ASSORTMENT OF WEDGIES, SWIRLIES, MEXICAN TWIRLIES, DODGEBALL, AND FRACTIONS, THE LIFE OF YOUR AVERAGE ELEMENTARY SCHOOL STUDENT CAN BE FRAUGHT WITH PERIL.
LUCKY FOR YOU, "THE HOUSE" IS HERE TO HELP! WITH NO FURTHER ADIEU I PRESENT YOU WITH...
MILHOUSE'S GUIDE TO
KEEPING IT COOL
WITHIN THESE PAGES YOU WILL FIND HELPFUL HINTS, TANTALIZING TIPS, AND STUDLY SECRETS TO HELP YOU BECOME ***THE KING OF COOL*** AT YOUR SCHOOL.

BRIAN HOULIHAN SCRIPT	***NINA MATSUMOTO*** PENCILS	***MIKE ROTE*** INKS	***ART VILLANUEVA*** COLORS	***KAREN BATES*** LETTERS	***BILL MORRISON*** EDITOR

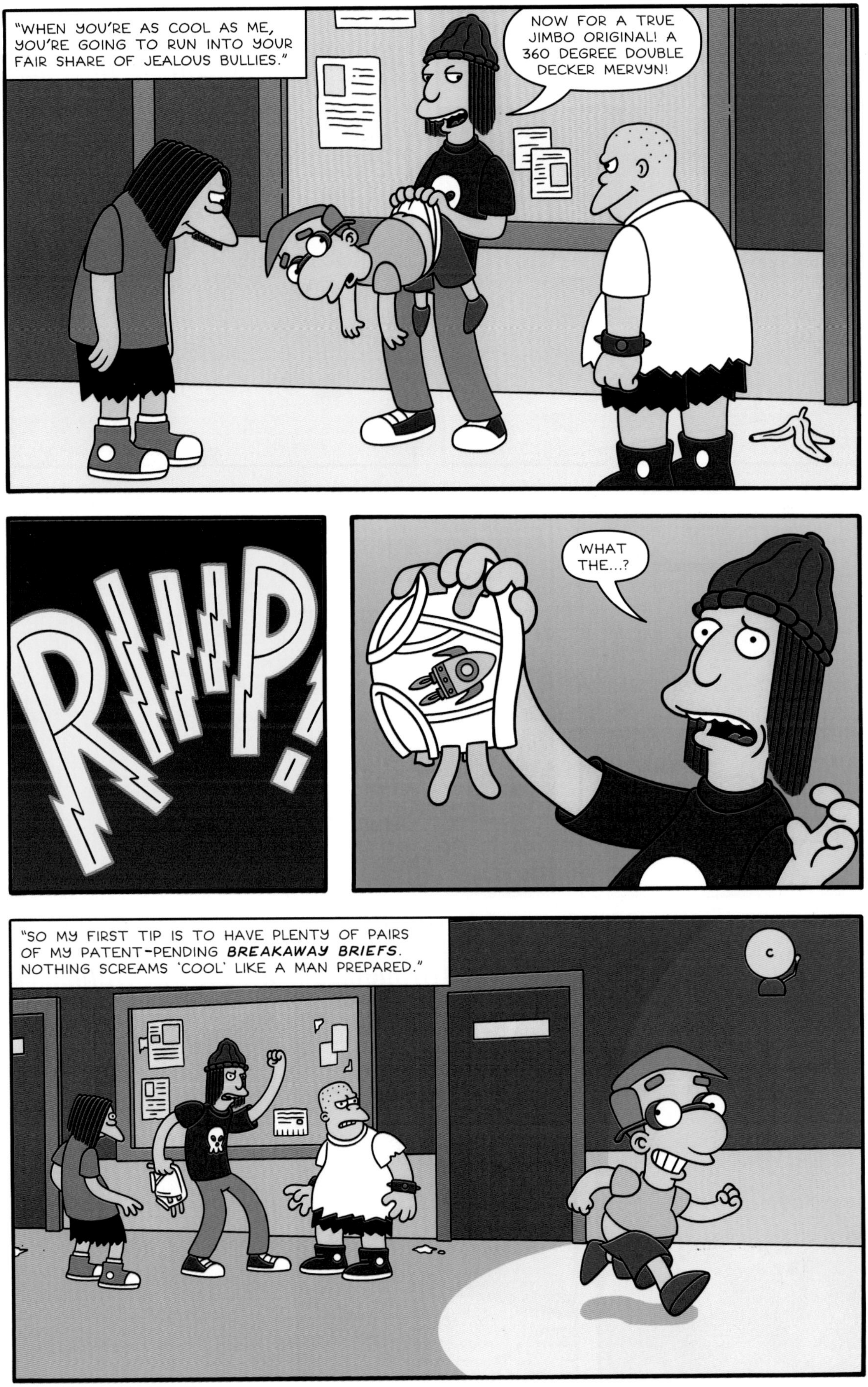
"WHEN YOU'RE AS COOL AS ME, YOU'RE GOING TO RUN INTO YOUR FAIR SHARE OF JEALOUS BULLIES."
NOW FOR A TRUE JIMBO ORIGINAL! A 360 DEGREE DOUBLE DECKER MERVYN!
RIIIP!
WHAT THE...?
"SO MY FIRST TIP IS TO HAVE PLENTY OF PAIRS OF MY PATENT-PENDING ***BREAKAWAY BRIEFS***. NOTHING SCREAMS 'COOL' LIKE A MAN PREPARED."

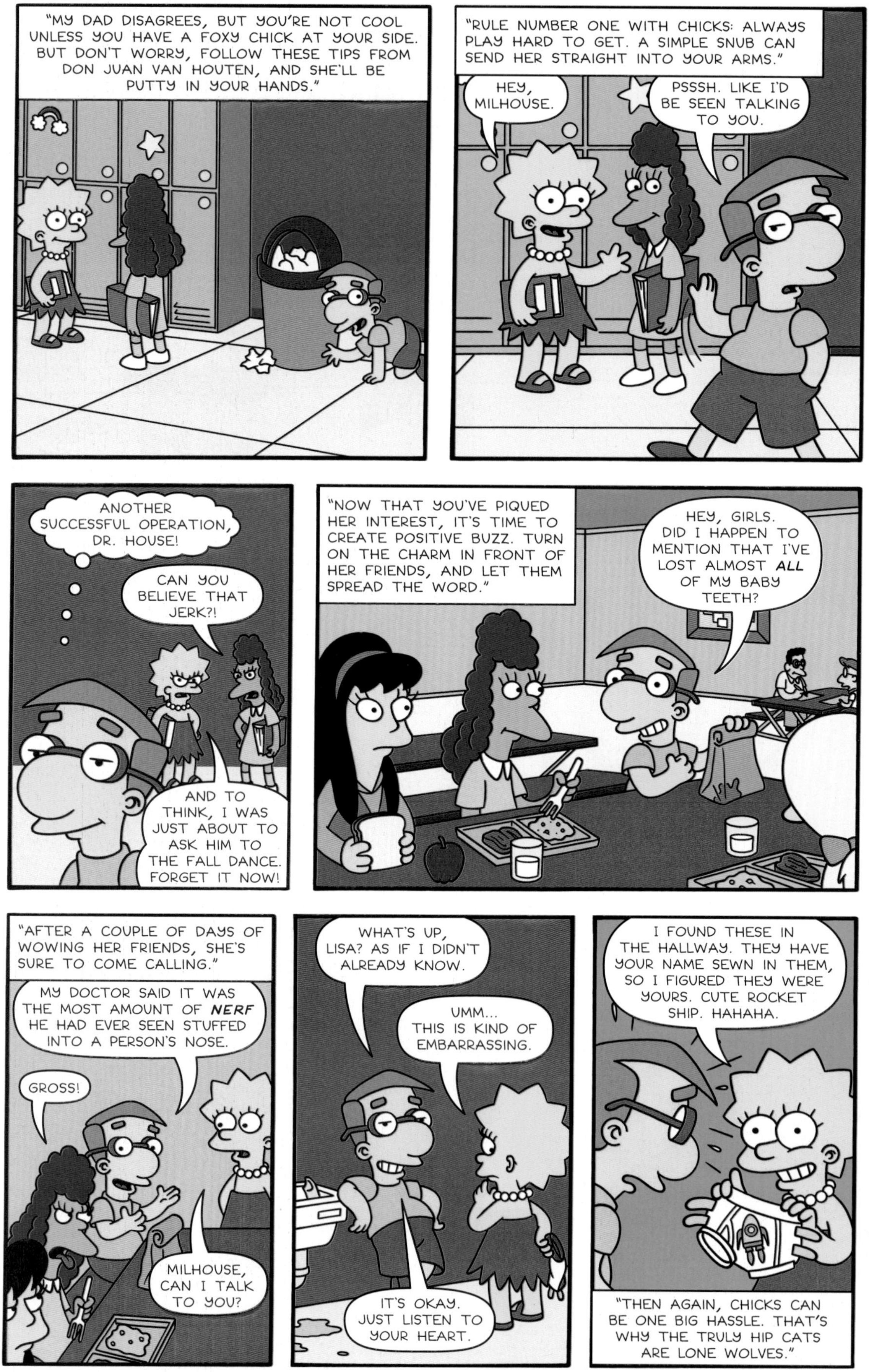
"MY DAD DISAGREES, BUT YOU'RE NOT COOL UNLESS YOU HAVE A FOXY CHICK AT YOUR SIDE. BUT DON'T WORRY, FOLLOW THESE TIPS FROM DON JUAN VAN HOUTEN, AND SHE'LL BE PUTTY IN YOUR HANDS."
"RULE NUMBER ONE WITH CHICKS: ALWAYS PLAY HARD TO GET. A SIMPLE SNUB CAN SEND HER STRAIGHT INTO YOUR ARMS."
HEY, MILHOUSE.
PSSSH. LIKE I'D BE SEEN TALKING TO YOU.
ANOTHER SUCCESSFUL OPERATION, DR. HOUSE!
CAN YOU BELIEVE THAT JERK?!
AND TO THINK, I WAS JUST ABOUT TO ASK HIM TO THE FALL DANCE. FORGET IT NOW!
"NOW THAT YOU'VE PIQUED HER INTEREST, IT'S TIME TO CREATE POSITIVE BUZZ. TURN ON THE CHARM IN FRONT OF HER FRIENDS, AND LET THEM SPREAD THE WORD."
HEY, GIRLS. DID I HAPPEN TO MENTION THAT I'VE LOST ALMOST ***ALL*** OF MY BABY TEETH?
"AFTER A COUPLE OF DAYS OF WOWING HER FRIENDS, SHE'S SURE TO COME CALLING."
MY DOCTOR SAID IT WAS THE MOST AMOUNT OF ***NERF*** HE HAD EVER SEEN STUFFED INTO A PERSON'S NOSE.
GROSS!
MILHOUSE, CAN I TALK TO YOU?
WHAT'S UP, LISA? AS IF I DIDN'T ALREADY KNOW.
UMM... THIS IS KIND OF EMBARRASSING.
IT'S OKAY. JUST LISTEN TO YOUR HEART.
I FOUND THESE IN THE HALLWAY. THEY HAVE YOUR NAME SEWN IN THEM, SO I FIGURED THEY WERE YOURS. CUTE ROCKET SHIP. HAHAHA.
"THEN AGAIN, CHICKS CAN BE ONE BIG HASSLE. THAT'S WHY THE TRULY HIP CATS ARE LONE WOLVES."

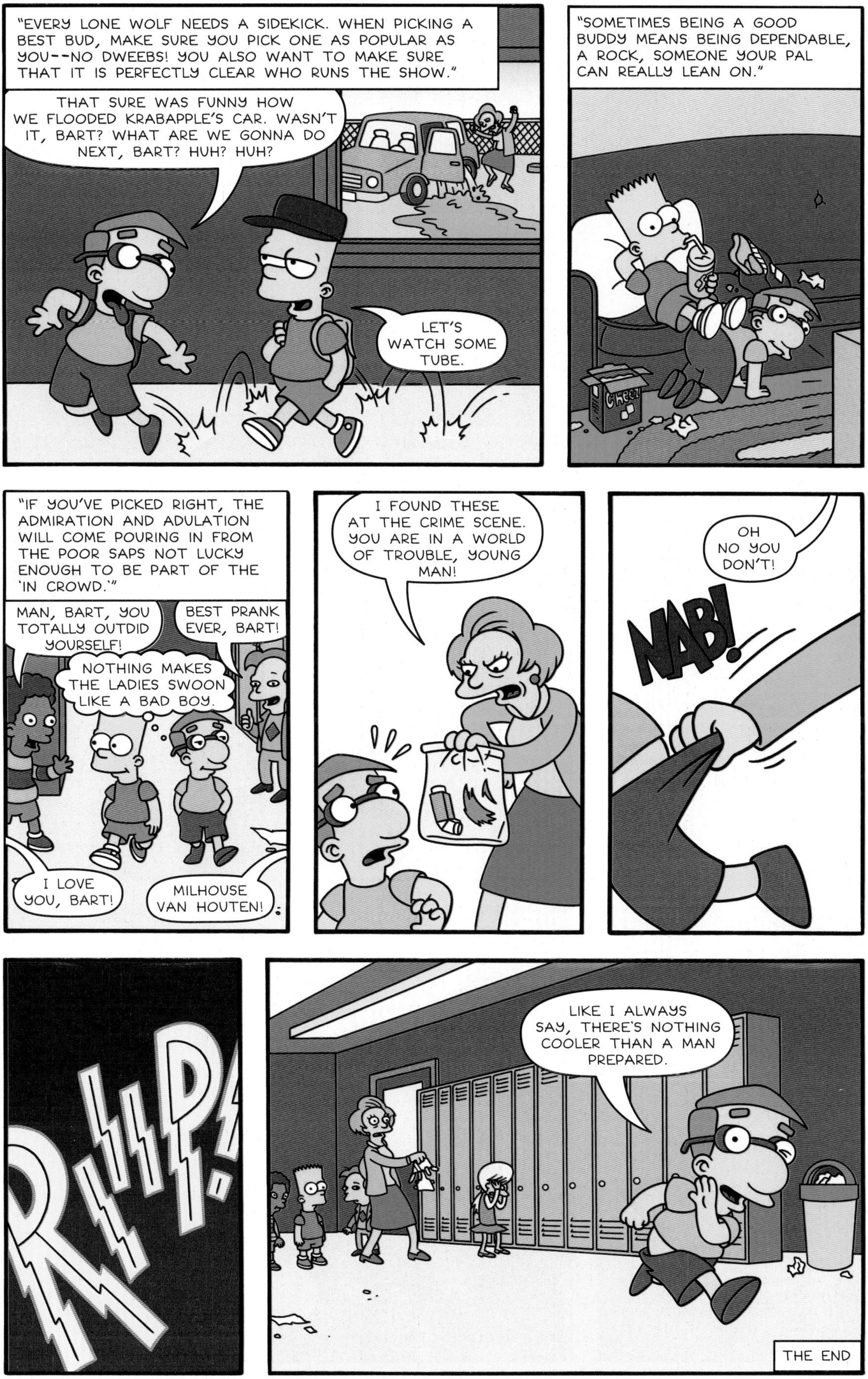
"EVERY LONE WOLF NEEDS A SIDEKICK. WHEN PICKING A BEST BUD, MAKE SURE YOU PICK ONE AS POPULAR AS YOU--NO DWEEBS! YOU ALSO WANT TO MAKE SURE THAT IT IS PERFECTLY CLEAR WHO RUNS THE SHOW."
THAT SURE WAS FUNNY HOW WE FLOODED KRABAPPLE'S CAR. WASN'T IT, BART? WHAT ARE WE GONNA DO NEXT, BART? HUH? HUH?
LET'S WATCH SOME TUBE.
"SOMETIMES BEING A GOOD BUDDY MEANS BEING DEPENDABLE, A ROCK, SOMEONE YOUR PAL CAN REALLY LEAN ON."
"IF YOU'VE PICKED RIGHT, THE ADMIRATION AND ADULATION WILL COME POURING IN FROM THE POOR SAPS NOT LUCKY ENOUGH TO BE PART OF THE 'IN CROWD.'"
MAN, BART, YOU TOTALLY OUTDID YOURSELF!
BEST PRANK EVER, BART!
NOTHING MAKES THE LADIES SWOON LIKE A BAD BOY.
I LOVE YOU, BART!
MILHOUSE VAN HOUTEN!
I FOUND THESE AT THE CRIME SCENE. YOU ARE IN A WORLD OF TROUBLE, YOUNG MAN!
OH NO YOU DON'T!
NAB!
RIIIP!
LIKE I ALWAYS SAY, THERE'S NOTHING COOLER THAN A MAN PREPARED.
THE END

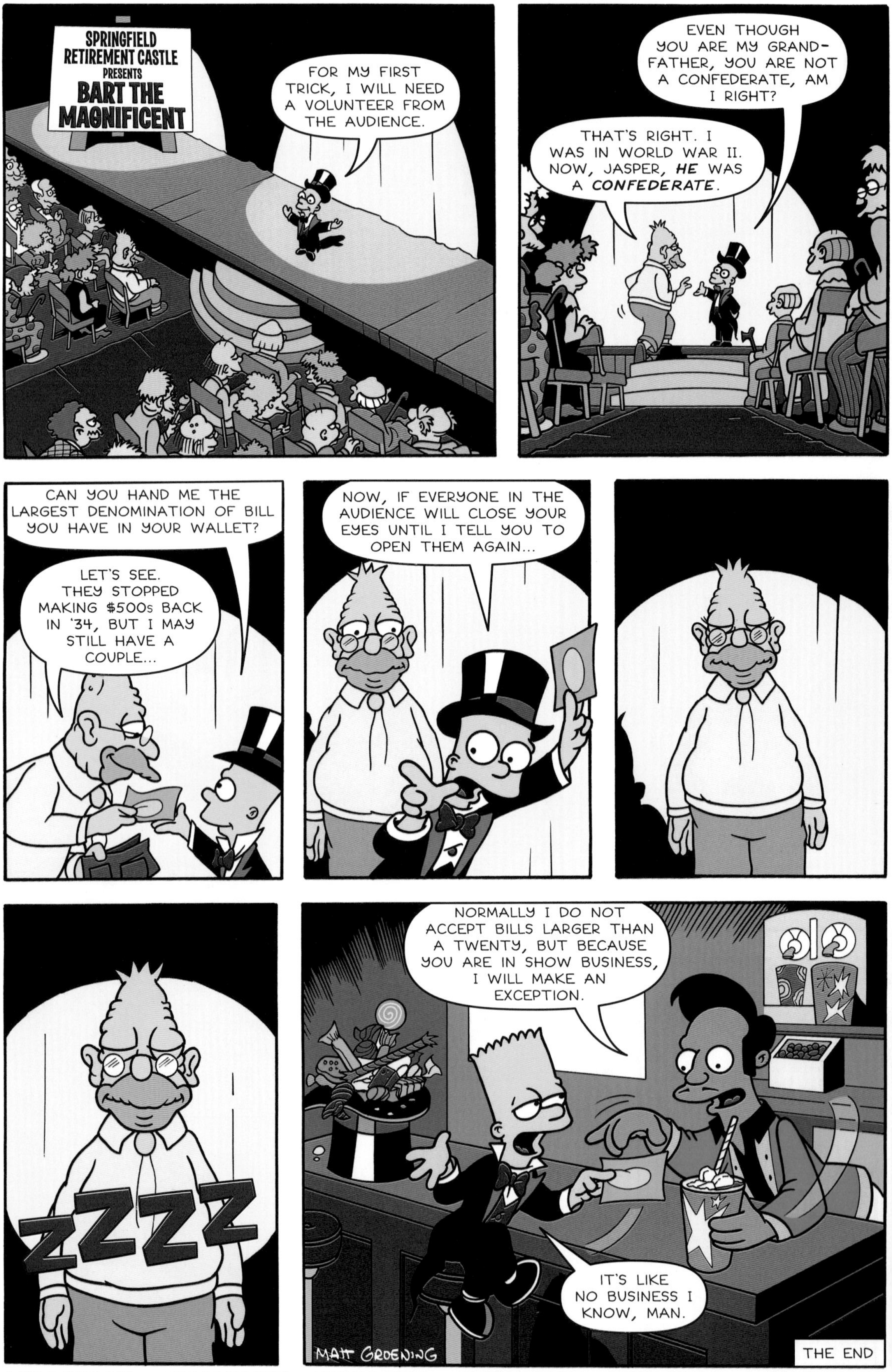
SPRINGFIELD RETIREMENT CASTLE PRESENTS BART THE MAGNIFICENT
FOR MY FIRST TRICK, I WILL NEED A VOLUNTEER FROM THE AUDIENCE.
EVEN THOUGH YOU ARE MY GRAND-FATHER, YOU ARE NOT A CONFEDERATE, AM I RIGHT?
THAT'S RIGHT. I WAS IN WORLD WAR II. NOW, JASPER, ***HE*** WAS A ***CONFEDERATE***.
CAN YOU HAND ME THE LARGEST DENOMINATION OF BILL YOU HAVE IN YOUR WALLET?
LET'S SEE. THEY STOPPED MAKING $500s BACK IN '34, BUT I MAY STILL HAVE A COUPLE...
NOW, IF EVERYONE IN THE AUDIENCE WILL CLOSE YOUR EYES UNTIL I TELL YOU TO OPEN THEM AGAIN...
zZZZ
NORMALLY I DO NOT ACCEPT BILLS LARGER THAN A TWENTY, BUT BECAUSE YOU ARE IN SHOW BUSINESS, I WILL MAKE AN EXCEPTION.
IT'S LIKE NO BUSINESS I KNOW, MAN.
MATT GROENING
THE END

PATRIC VERRONE SCRIPT
CARLOS VALENTI PENCILS
PHYLLIS NOVIN INKS
NATHAN HAMILL COLORS
KAREN BATES LETTERS
BILL MORRSION EDITOR

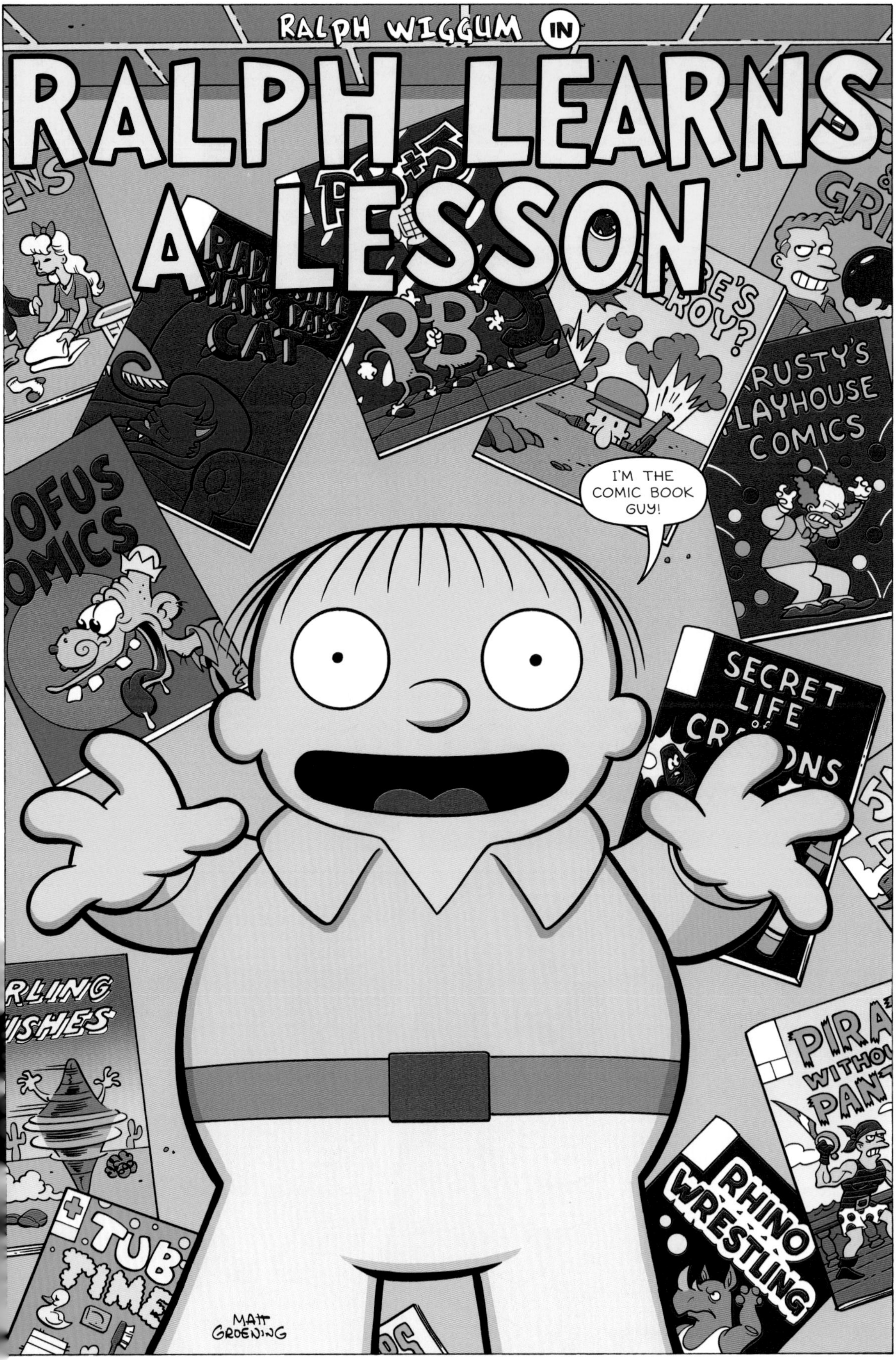
RALPH WIGGUM IN
RALPH LEARNS A LESSON
I'M THE COMIC BOOK GUY!
RHINO WRESTLING
MATT GROENING

JESSE LEON MCCANN
SCRIPT

JAMES LLOYD
PENCILS

ANDREW PEPOY
INKS

NATHAN HAMILL
COLORS

KAREN BATES
LETTERS

BILL MORRISON
EDITOR

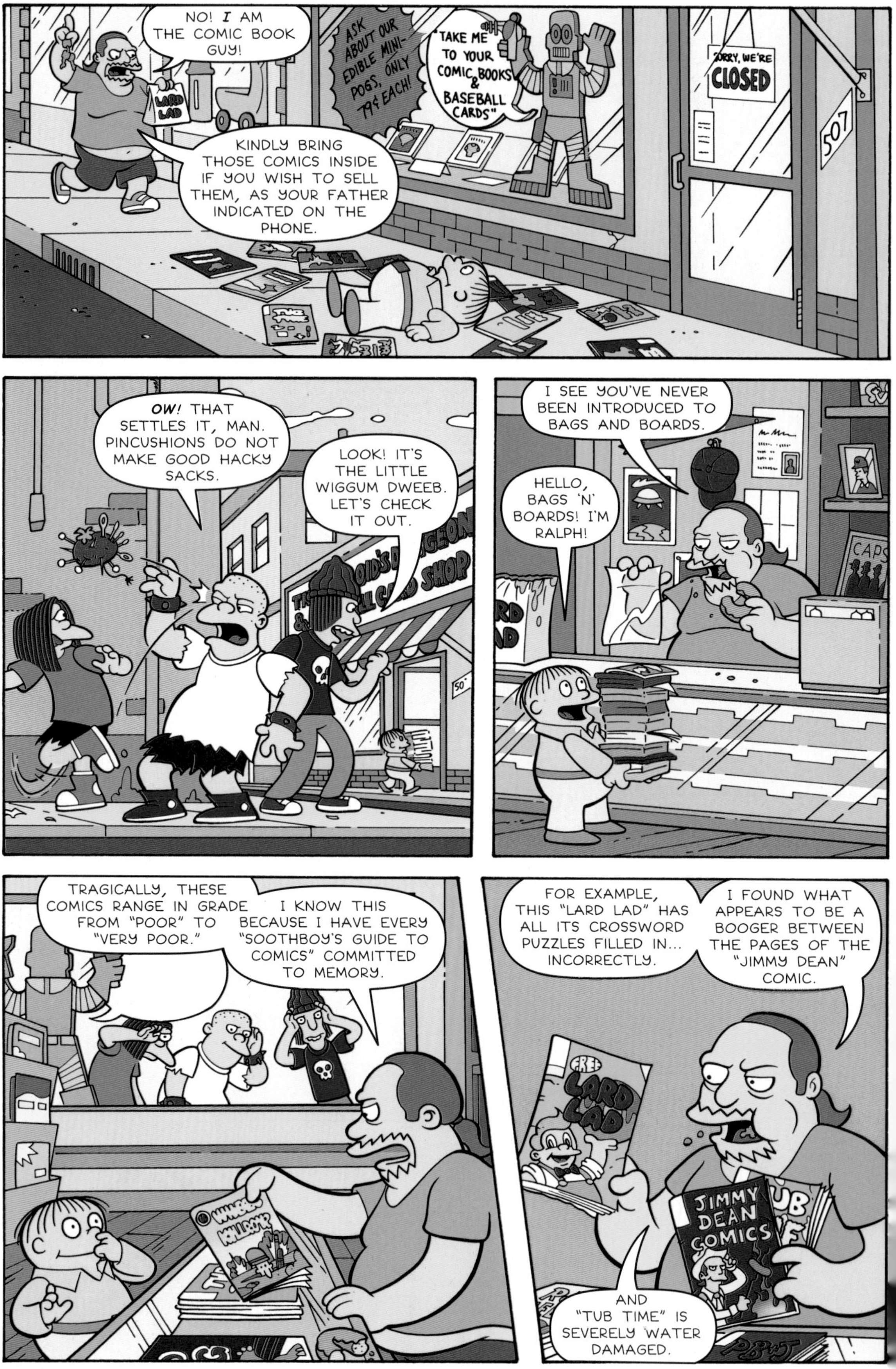
NO! *I* AM THE COMIC BOOK GUY!
ASK ABOUT OUR EDIBLE MINI-POGS, ONLY 79¢ EACH!
"TAKE ME TO YOUR COMIC BOOKS & BASEBALL CARDS"
SORRY, WE'RE CLOSED
507
LARD LAD
KINDLY BRING THOSE COMICS INSIDE IF YOU WISH TO SELL THEM, AS YOUR FATHER INDICATED ON THE PHONE.
OW! THAT SETTLES IT, MAN. PINCUSHIONS DO NOT MAKE GOOD HACKY SACKS.
LOOK! IT'S THE LITTLE WIGGUM DWEEB. LET'S CHECK IT OUT.
I SEE YOU'VE NEVER BEEN INTRODUCED TO BAGS AND BOARDS.
HELLO, BAGS 'N' BOARDS! I'M RALPH!
TRAGICALLY, THESE COMICS RANGE IN GRADE FROM "POOR" TO "VERY POOR."
I KNOW THIS BECAUSE I HAVE EVERY "SOOTHBOY'S GUIDE TO COMICS" COMMITTED TO MEMORY.
FOR EXAMPLE, THIS "LARD LAD" HAS ALL ITS CROSSWORD PUZZLES FILLED IN... INCORRECTLY.
I FOUND WHAT APPEARS TO BE A BOOGER BETWEEN THE PAGES OF THE "JIMMY DEAN" COMIC.
FREE LARD LAD
JIMMY DEAN COMICS
AND "TUB TIME" IS SEVERELY WATER DAMAGED.

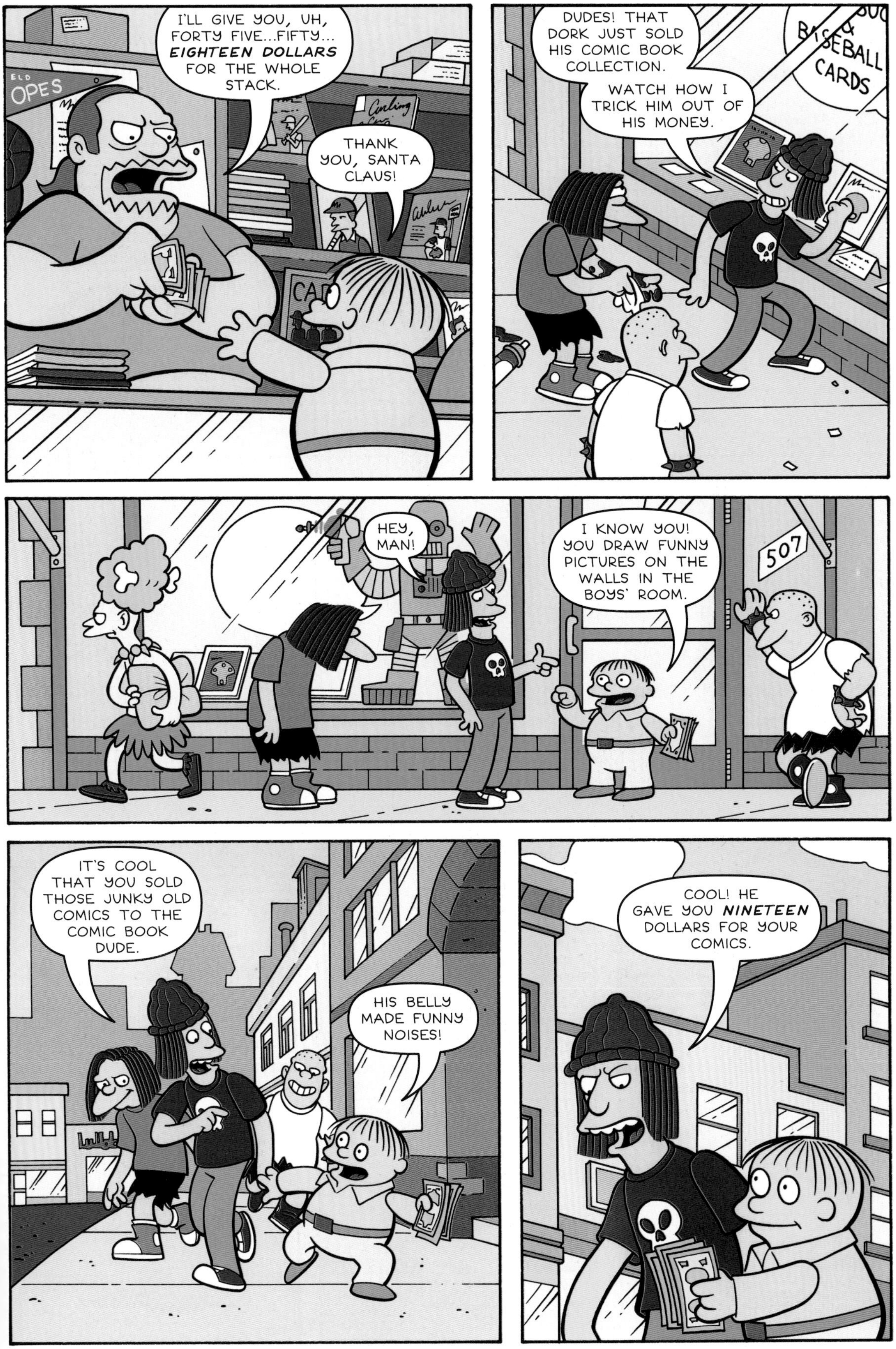
I'LL GIVE YOU, UH, FORTY FIVE...FIFTY... **EIGHTEEN DOLLARS** FOR THE WHOLE STACK.
THANK YOU, SANTA CLAUS!
DUDES! THAT DORK JUST SOLD HIS COMIC BOOK COLLECTION.
WATCH HOW I TRICK HIM OUT OF HIS MONEY.
HEY, MAN!
I KNOW YOU! YOU DRAW FUNNY PICTURES ON THE WALLS IN THE BOYS' ROOM.
507
IT'S COOL THAT YOU SOLD THOSE JUNKY OLD COMICS TO THE COMIC BOOK DUDE.
HIS BELLY MADE FUNNY NOISES!
COOL! HE GAVE YOU **NINETEEN** DOLLARS FOR YOUR COMICS.

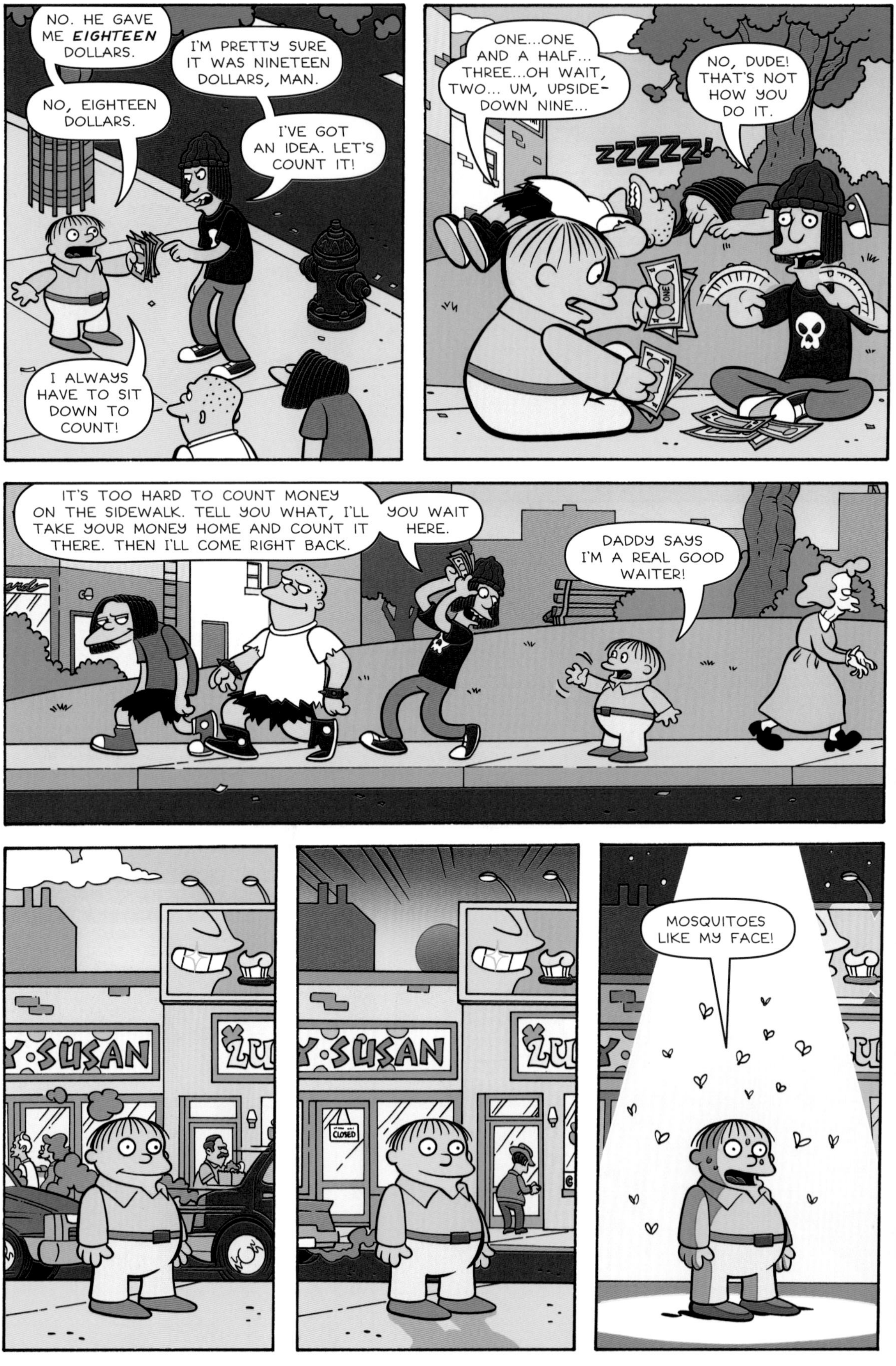
NO. HE GAVE ME EIGHTEEN DOLLARS.
I'M PRETTY SURE IT WAS NINETEEN DOLLARS, MAN.
NO, EIGHTEEN DOLLARS.
I'VE GOT AN IDEA. LET'S COUNT IT!
I ALWAYS HAVE TO SIT DOWN TO COUNT!
ONE...ONE AND A HALF... THREE...OH WAIT, TWO... UM, UPSIDE-DOWN NINE...
NO, DUDE! THAT'S NOT HOW YOU DO IT.
ZZZZZ!
ONE
IT'S TOO HARD TO COUNT MONEY ON THE SIDEWALK. TELL YOU WHAT, I'LL TAKE YOUR MONEY HOME AND COUNT IT THERE. THEN I'LL COME RIGHT BACK.
YOU WAIT HERE.
DADDY SAYS I'M A REAL GOOD WAITER!
SUSAN
CLOSED
MOSQUITOES LIKE MY FACE!

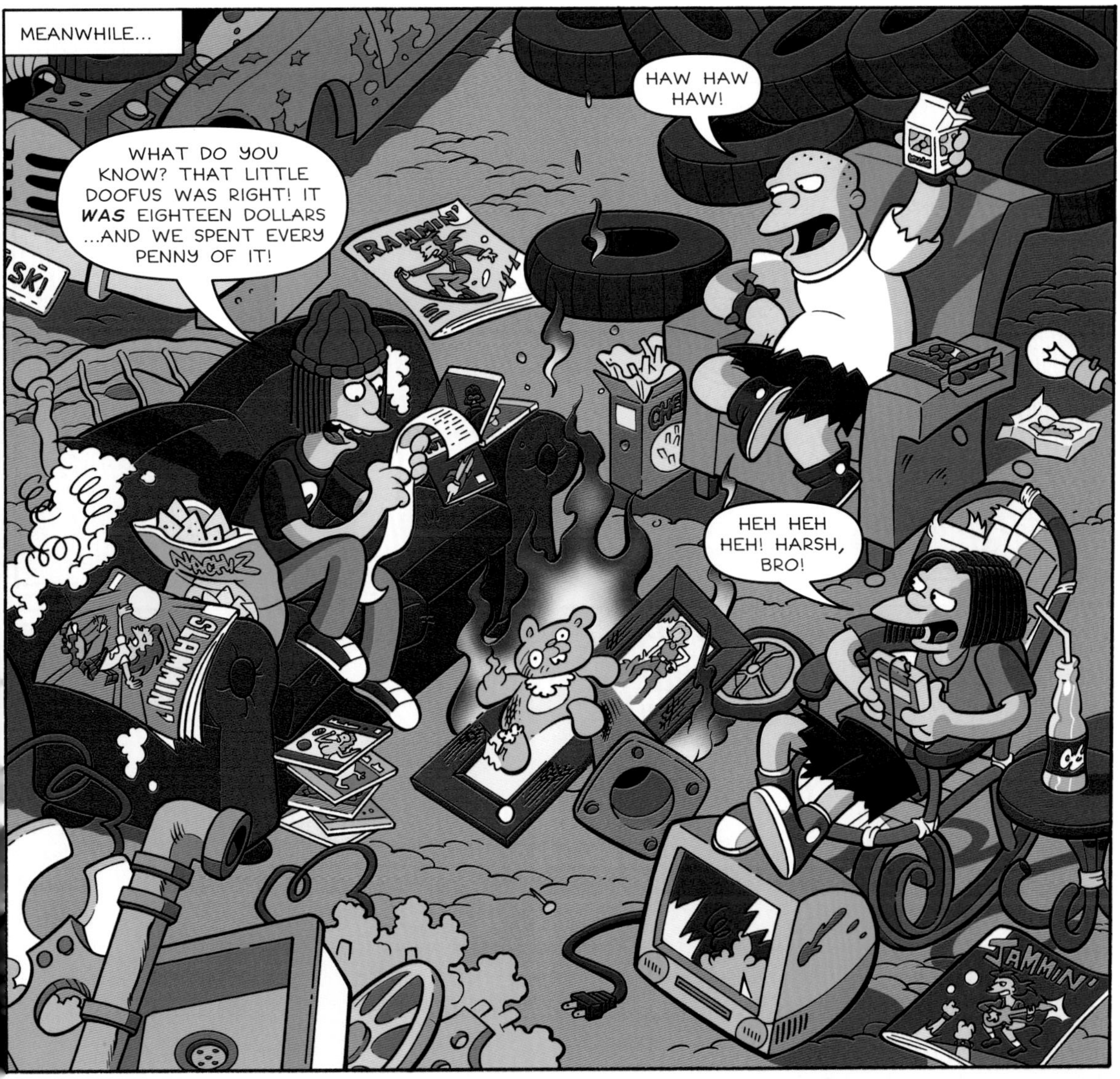
MEANWHILE...
WHAT DO YOU KNOW? THAT LITTLE DOOFUS WAS RIGHT! IT *WAS* EIGHTEEN DOLLARS ...AND WE SPENT EVERY PENNY OF IT!
HAW HAW HAW!
HEH HEH HEH! HARSH, BRO!
RAMMIN'
SLAMMIN'
JAMMIN'
NACHOZ

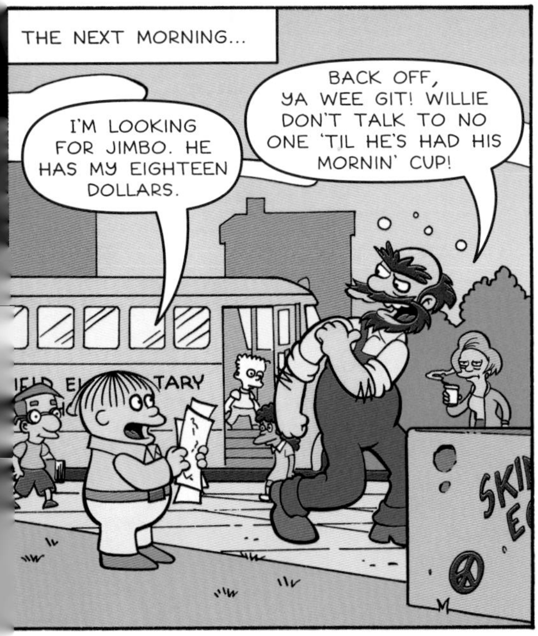
THE NEXT MORNING...
I'M LOOKING FOR JIMBO. HE HAS MY EIGHTEEN DOLLARS.
BACK OFF, YA WEE GIT! WILLIE DON'T TALK TO NO ONE 'TIL HE'S HAD HIS MORNIN' CUP!

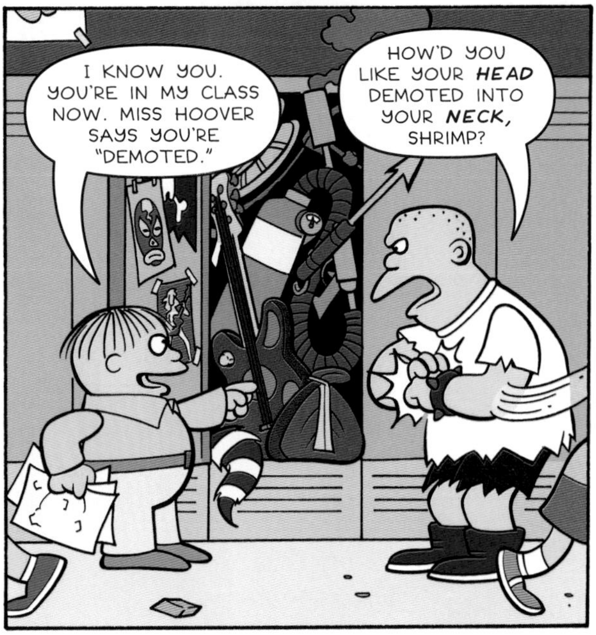
I KNOW YOU. YOU'RE IN MY CLASS NOW. MISS HOOVER SAYS YOU'RE "DEMOTED."
HOW'D YOU LIKE YOUR *HEAD* DEMOTED INTO YOUR *NECK*, SHRIMP?

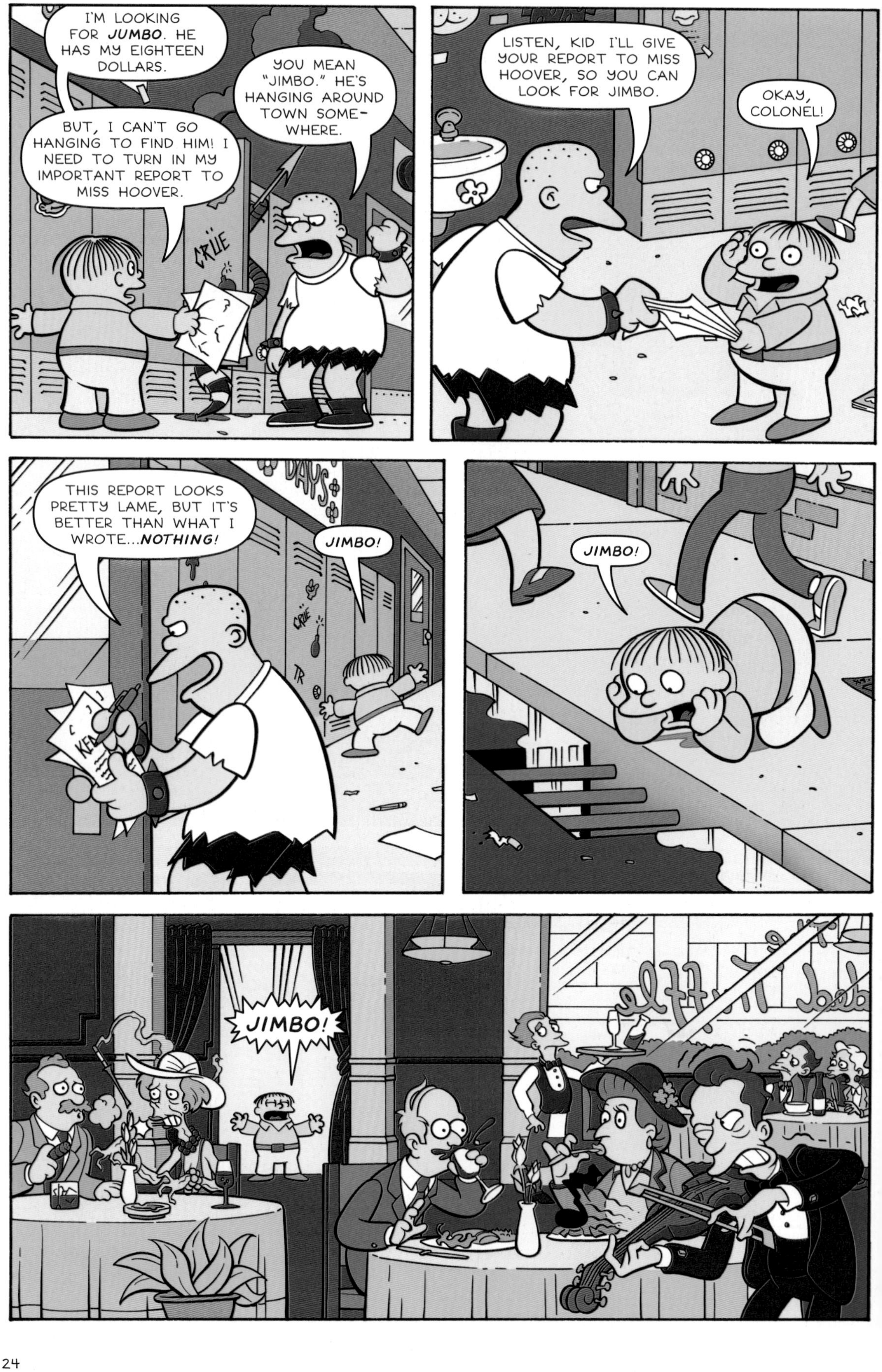
I'M LOOKING FOR **JUMBO**. HE HAS MY EIGHTEEN DOLLARS.
BUT, I CAN'T GO HANGING TO FIND HIM! I NEED TO TURN IN MY IMPORTANT REPORT TO MISS HOOVER.
YOU MEAN "JIMBO." HE'S HANGING AROUND TOWN SOME-WHERE.
CRÜE
LISTEN, KID I'LL GIVE YOUR REPORT TO MISS HOOVER, SO YOU CAN LOOK FOR JIMBO.
OKAY, COLONEL!
THIS REPORT LOOKS PRETTY LAME, BUT IT'S BETTER THAN WHAT I WROTE...***NOTHING!***
JIMBO!
JIMBO!
JIMBO!

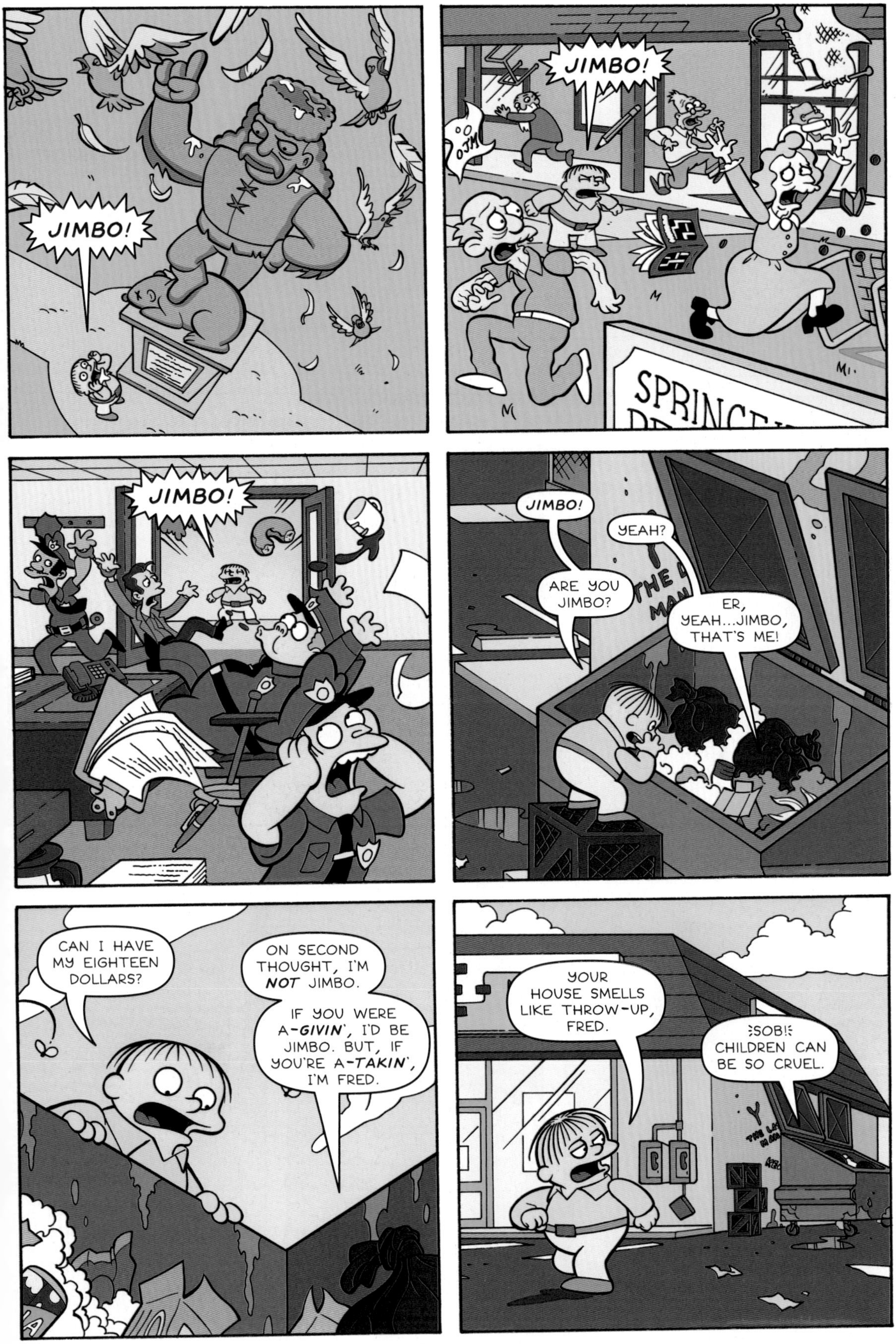
JIMBO!
JIMBO!
JIMBO!
JIMBO!
ARE YOU JIMBO?
YEAH?
ER, YEAH...JIMBO, THAT'S ME!
CAN I HAVE MY EIGHTEEN DOLLARS?
ON SECOND THOUGHT, I'M **NOT** JIMBO.
IF YOU WERE A-**GIVIN'**, I'D BE JIMBO. BUT, IF YOU'RE A-**TAKIN'**, I'M FRED.
YOUR HOUSE SMELLS LIKE THROW-UP, FRED.
¡SOB!
CHILDREN CAN BE SO CRUEL.

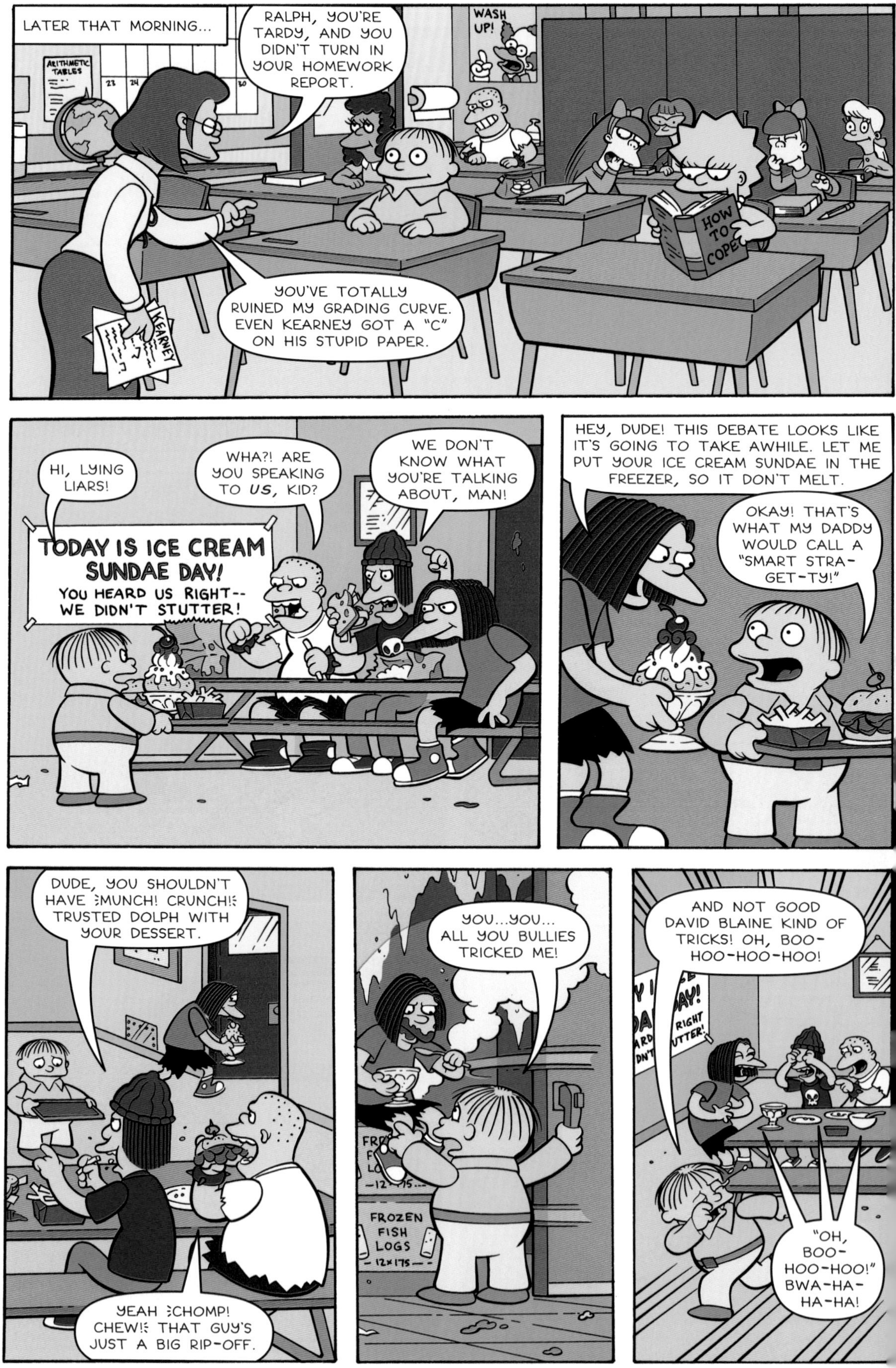
LATER THAT MORNING...
RALPH, YOU'RE TARDY, AND YOU DIDN'T TURN IN YOUR HOMEWORK REPORT.
WASH UP!
ARITHMETIC TABLES
HOW TO COPE
KEARNEY
YOU'VE TOTALLY RUINED MY GRADING CURVE. EVEN KEARNEY GOT A "C" ON HIS STUPID PAPER.
HI, LYING LIARS!
TODAY IS ICE CREAM SUNDAE DAY! YOU HEARD US RIGHT-- WE DIDN'T STUTTER!
WHA?! ARE YOU SPEAKING TO *US*, KID?
WE DON'T KNOW WHAT YOU'RE TALKING ABOUT, MAN!
HEY, DUDE! THIS DEBATE LOOKS LIKE IT'S GOING TO TAKE AWHILE. LET ME PUT YOUR ICE CREAM SUNDAE IN THE FREEZER, SO IT DON'T MELT.
OKAY! THAT'S WHAT MY DADDY WOULD CALL A "SMART STRA-GET-TY!"
DUDE, YOU SHOULDN'T HAVE :MUNCH! CRUNCH!: TRUSTED DOLPH WITH YOUR DESSERT.
YEAH :CHOMP! CHEW!: THAT GUY'S JUST A BIG RIP-OFF.
YOU...YOU... ALL YOU BULLIES TRICKED ME!
FROZEN FISH LOGS 12×175
AND NOT GOOD DAVID BLAINE KIND OF TRICKS! OH, BOO-HOO-HOO-HOO!
"OH, BOO-HOO-HOO!" BWA-HA-HA-HA!

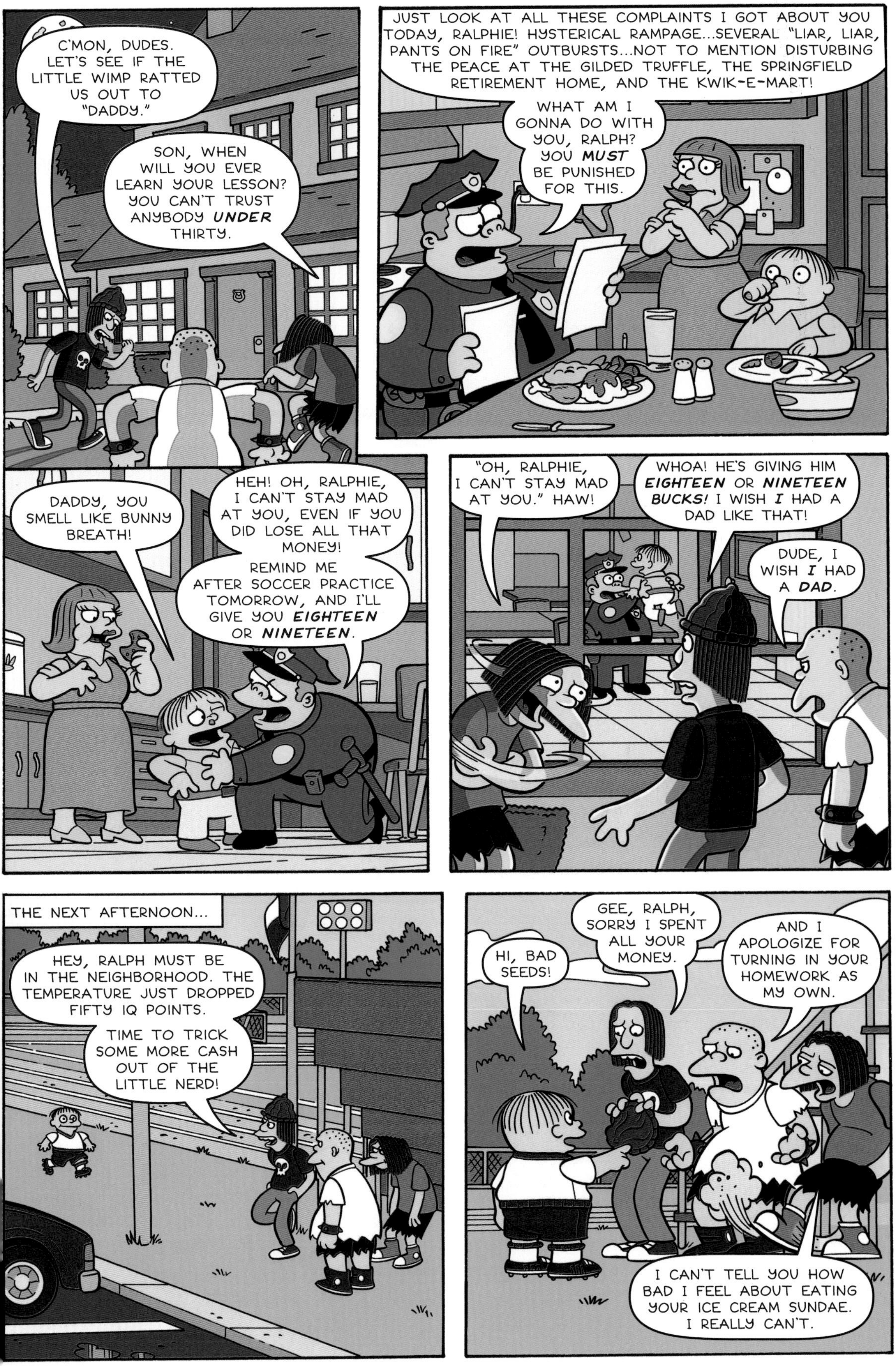
C'MON, DUDES. LET'S SEE IF THE LITTLE WIMP RATTED US OUT TO "DADDY."
SON, WHEN WILL YOU EVER LEARN YOUR LESSON? YOU CAN'T TRUST ANYBODY UNDER THIRTY.
JUST LOOK AT ALL THESE COMPLAINTS I GOT ABOUT YOU TODAY, RALPHIE! HYSTERICAL RAMPAGE...SEVERAL "LIAR, LIAR, PANTS ON FIRE" OUTBURSTS...NOT TO MENTION DISTURBING THE PEACE AT THE GILDED TRUFFLE, THE SPRINGFIELD RETIREMENT HOME, AND THE KWIK-E-MART!
WHAT AM I GONNA DO WITH YOU, RALPH? YOU MUST BE PUNISHED FOR THIS.
DADDY, YOU SMELL LIKE BUNNY BREATH!
HEH! OH, RALPHIE, I CAN'T STAY MAD AT YOU, EVEN IF YOU DID LOSE ALL THAT MONEY!
REMIND ME AFTER SOCCER PRACTICE TOMORROW, AND I'LL GIVE YOU EIGHTEEN OR NINETEEN.
"OH, RALPHIE, I CAN'T STAY MAD AT YOU." HAW!
WHOA! HE'S GIVING HIM EIGHTEEN OR NINETEEN BUCKS! I WISH I HAD A DAD LIKE THAT!
DUDE, I WISH I HAD A DAD.
THE NEXT AFTERNOON...
HEY, RALPH MUST BE IN THE NEIGHBORHOOD. THE TEMPERATURE JUST DROPPED FIFTY IQ POINTS.
TIME TO TRICK SOME MORE CASH OUT OF THE LITTLE NERD!
HI, BAD SEEDS!
GEE, RALPH, SORRY I SPENT ALL YOUR MONEY.
AND I APOLOGIZE FOR TURNING IN YOUR HOMEWORK AS MY OWN.
I CAN'T TELL YOU HOW BAD I FEEL ABOUT EATING YOUR ICE CREAM SUNDAE. I REALLY CAN'T.

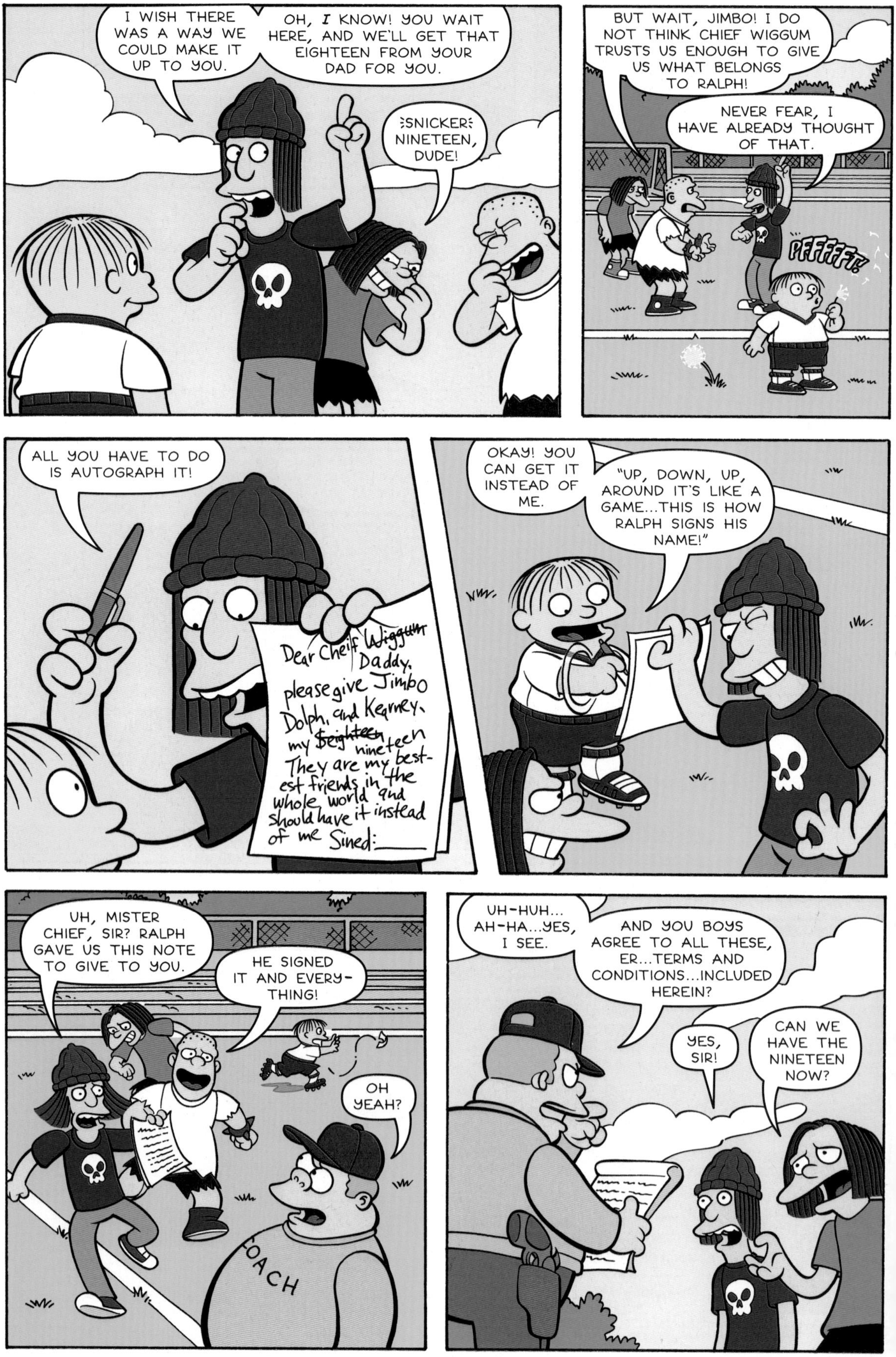
I WISH THERE WAS A WAY WE COULD MAKE IT UP TO YOU.
OH, I KNOW! YOU WAIT HERE, AND WE'LL GET THAT EIGHTEEN FROM YOUR DAD FOR YOU.
SNICKER NINETEEN, DUDE!
BUT WAIT, JIMBO! I DO NOT THINK CHIEF WIGGUM TRUSTS US ENOUGH TO GIVE US WHAT BELONGS TO RALPH!
NEVER FEAR, I HAVE ALREADY THOUGHT OF THAT.
PFFFFFT!
ALL YOU HAVE TO DO IS AUTOGRAPH IT!
Dear Cheif Wiggum Daddy, please give Jimbo Dolph, and Kearney, my eighteen nineteen They are my best-est friends in the whole world and should have it instead of me Sined:____
OKAY! YOU CAN GET IT INSTEAD OF ME.
"UP, DOWN, UP, AROUND IT'S LIKE A GAME...THIS IS HOW RALPH SIGNS HIS NAME!"
UH, MISTER CHIEF, SIR? RALPH GAVE US THIS NOTE TO GIVE TO YOU.
HE SIGNED IT AND EVERY-THING!
OH YEAH?
COACH
UH-HUH... AH-HA...YES, I SEE.
AND YOU BOYS AGREE TO ALL THESE, ER...TERMS AND CONDITIONS...INCLUDED HEREIN?
YES, SIR!
CAN WE HAVE THE NINETEEN NOW?

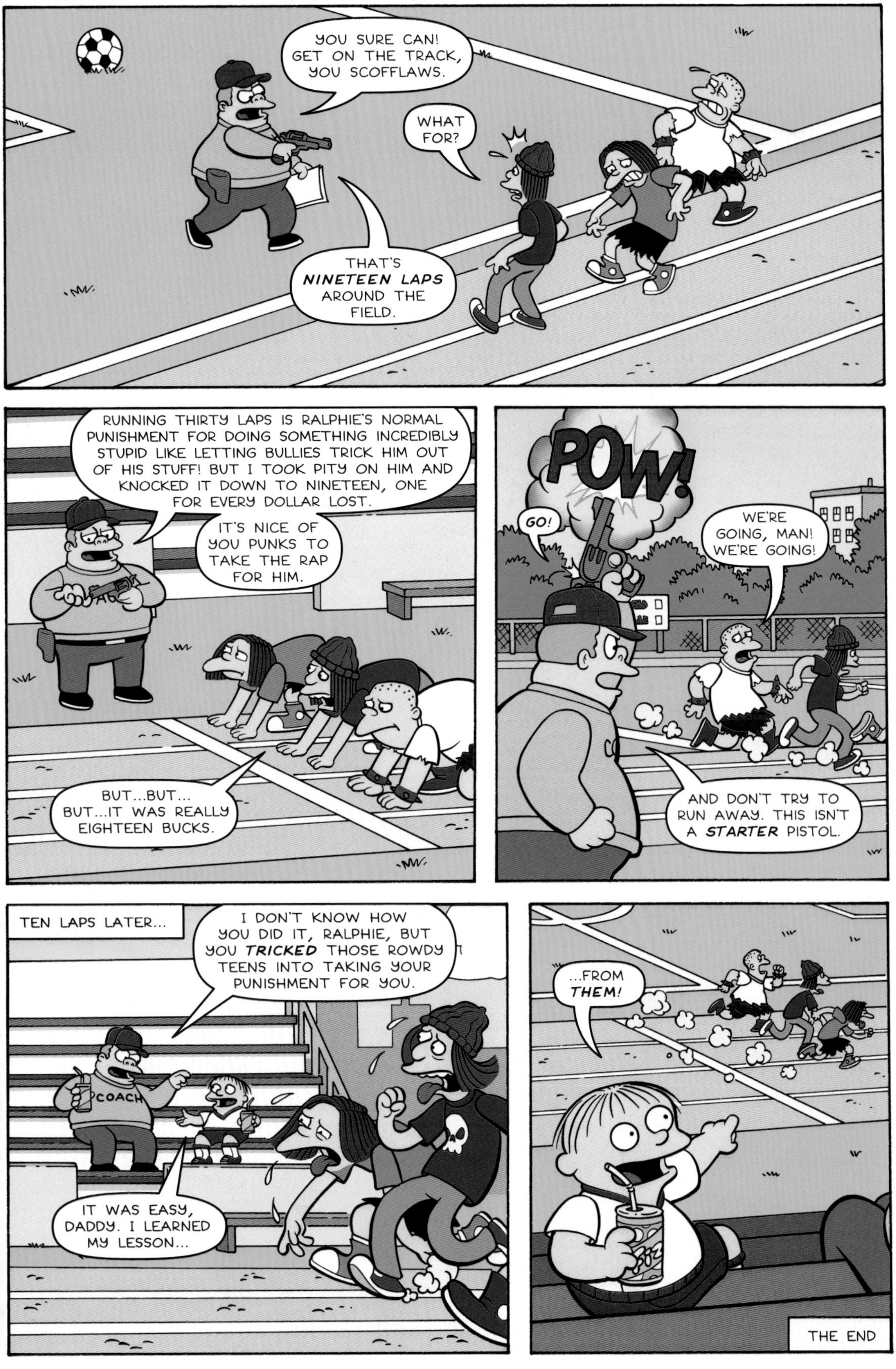

YOU SURE CAN! GET ON THE TRACK, YOU SCOFFLAWS.
WHAT FOR?
THAT'S NINETEEN LAPS AROUND THE FIELD.
RUNNING THIRTY LAPS IS RALPHIE'S NORMAL PUNISHMENT FOR DOING SOMETHING INCREDIBLY STUPID LIKE LETTING BULLIES TRICK HIM OUT OF HIS STUFF! BUT I TOOK PITY ON HIM AND KNOCKED IT DOWN TO NINETEEN, ONE FOR EVERY DOLLAR LOST.
IT'S NICE OF YOU PUNKS TO TAKE THE RAP FOR HIM.
BUT...BUT... BUT...IT WAS REALLY EIGHTEEN BUCKS.
POW!
GO!
WE'RE GOING, MAN! WE'RE GOING!
AND DON'T TRY TO RUN AWAY. THIS ISN'T A STARTER PISTOL.
TEN LAPS LATER...
I DON'T KNOW HOW YOU DID IT, RALPHIE, BUT YOU TRICKED THOSE ROWDY TEENS INTO TAKING YOUR PUNISHMENT FOR YOU.
COACH
IT WAS EASY, DADDY. I LEARNED MY LESSON...
...FROM THEM!
THE END

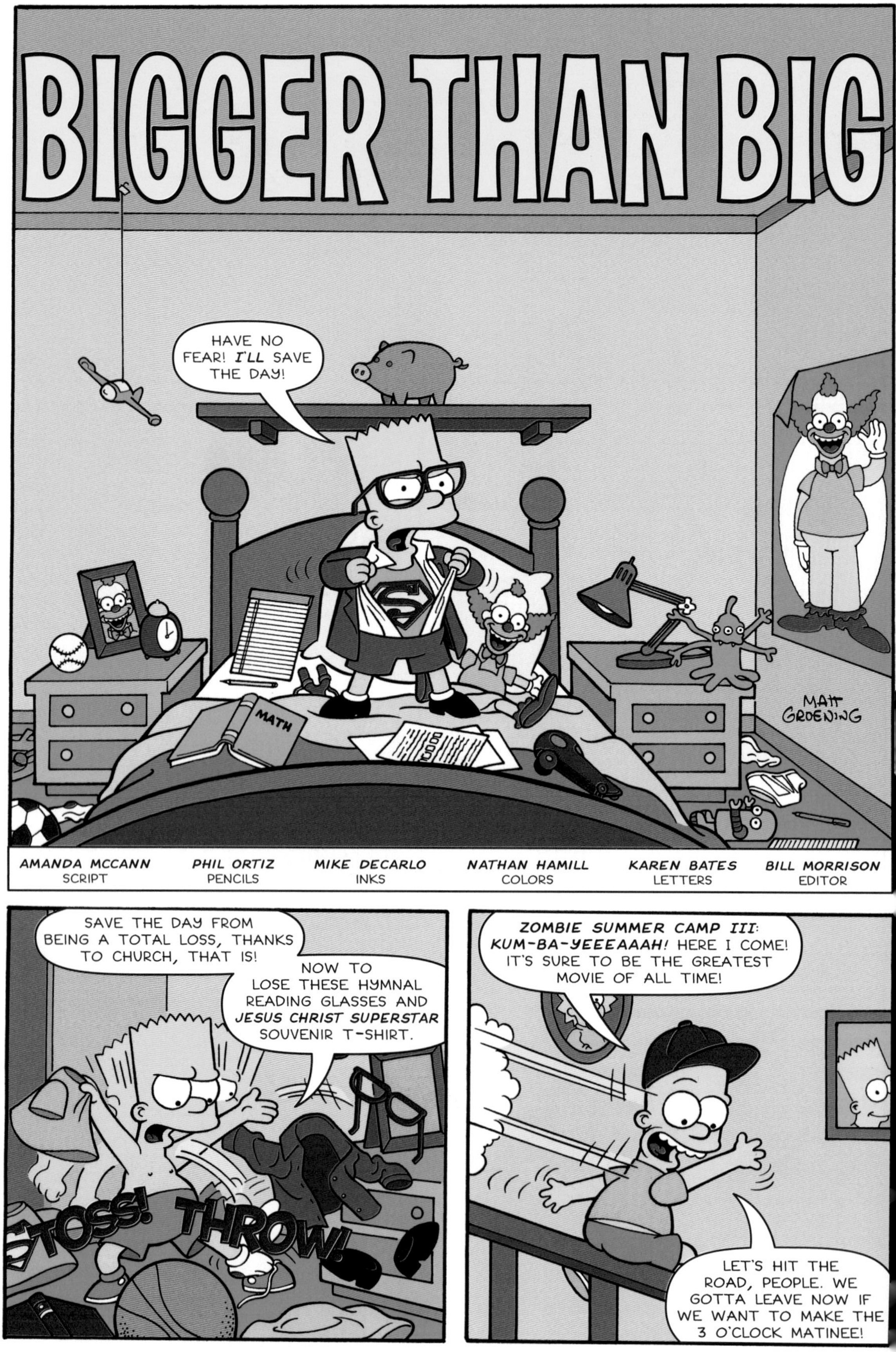
BIGGER THAN BIG
HAVE NO FEAR! I'LL SAVE THE DAY!
MATH
MATT GROENING
AMANDA MCCANN SCRIPT
PHIL ORTIZ PENCILS
MIKE DECARLO INKS
NATHAN HAMILL COLORS
KAREN BATES LETTERS
BILL MORRISON EDITOR
SAVE THE DAY FROM BEING A TOTAL LOSS, THANKS TO CHURCH, THAT IS!
NOW TO LOSE THESE HYMNAL READING GLASSES AND JESUS CHRIST SUPERSTAR SOUVENIR T-SHIRT.
TOSS! THROW!
ZOMBIE SUMMER CAMP III: KUM-BA-YEEEAAAH! HERE I COME! IT'S SURE TO BE THE GREATEST MOVIE OF ALL TIME!
LET'S HIT THE ROAD, PEOPLE. WE GOTTA LEAVE NOW IF WE WANT TO MAKE THE 3 O'CLOCK MATINEE!

MOM, ARE YOU GONNA GO IN *THAT*? 'CAUSE THAT'S FINE. LET ME BE THE FIRST TO SAY YOU LOOK SPLENDID, BUT WE SHOULD REALLY *GO*! CHOP, CHOP!

NOT NOW, BART! I HAVE TO HELP LISA WITH HER SCHOOL PROJECT, AND IT'S DUE TOMORROW!

WE'RE MAKING A REPLICA OF THE ASSASSINATION OF JULIUS CAESAR OUT OF DIFFERENT KINDS OF FOODS.

AAAAH!

I ALREADY FINISHED THIS PROJECT LAST WEEK, BUT SOMEBODY *ATE* THE FIRST ONE.

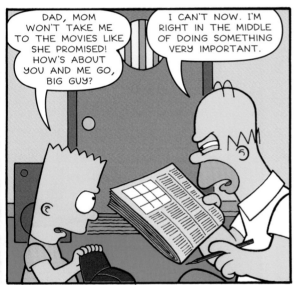

DAD, MOM WON'T TAKE ME TO THE MOVIES LIKE SHE PROMISED! HOW'S ABOUT YOU AND ME GO, BIG GUY?

I CAN'T NOW. I'M RIGHT IN THE MIDDLE OF DOING SOMETHING VERY IMPORTANT.

PLEASE! IT WOULDN'T BE AS FUN WITHOUT YOU...SINCE IT'S RATED "R" AND I'M NOT OLD ENOUGH TO GET IN ALONE.

BART! I CAN'T CONCENTRATE WITH YOU HOVERING. WHY DON'T YOU GO TO THE MOVIES OR SOMETHING?

LATER, AT THE AZTEC CINEMA...

ZOMBIE SUMMER CAMP III
STARRING DANNY (THE TANK) RICKER AND 'ROLLER BABE' KATIE JOHNSON

ZOMBIE SUMMER CAMP III

WHOA! AWESOME!

NOW, ALL I NEED TO DO IS FOOL THE DOPEY BOX OFFICE DORK, AND I'M IN!

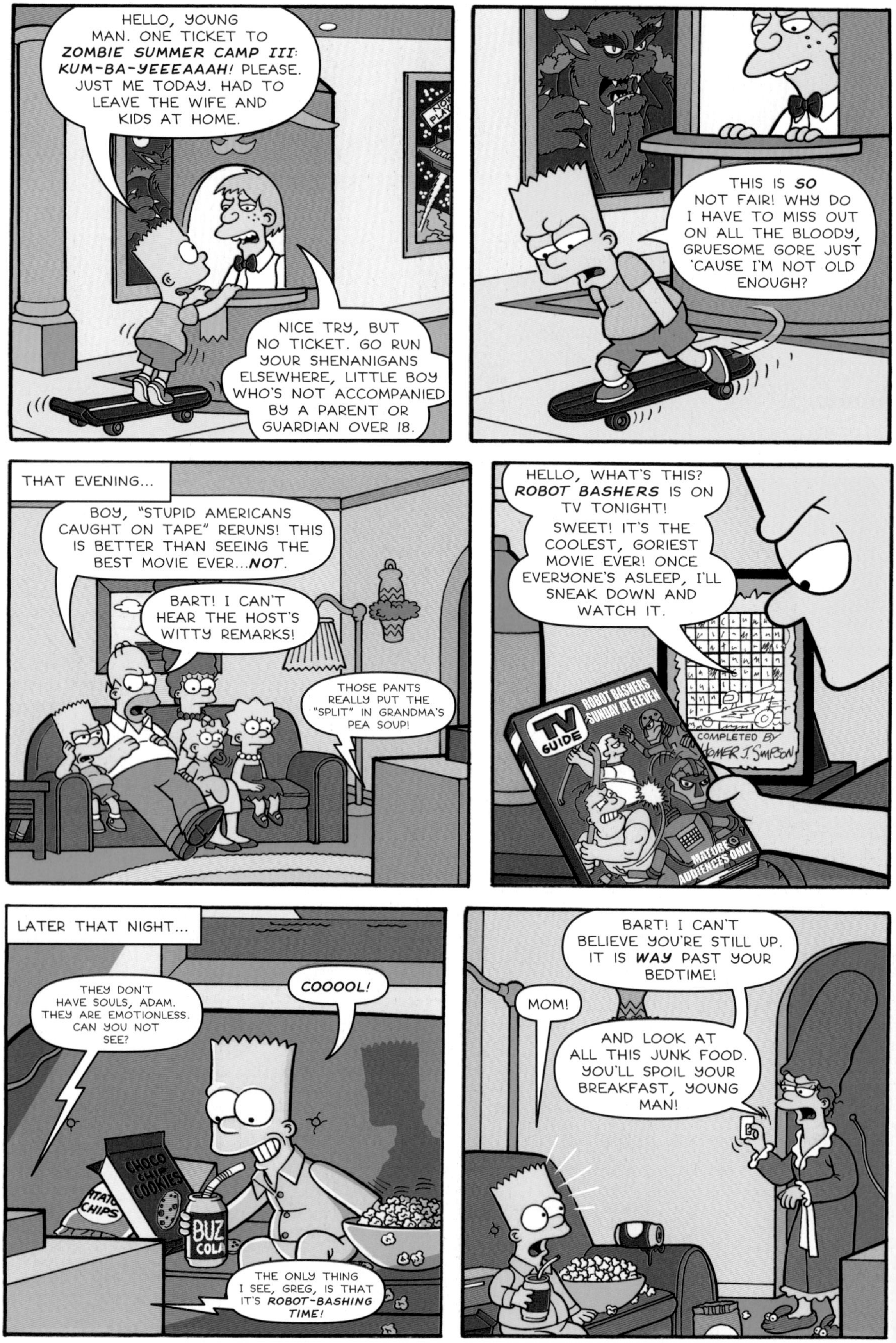
HELLO, YOUNG MAN. ONE TICKET TO *ZOMBIE SUMMER CAMP III: KUM-BA-YEEEAAAH!* PLEASE. JUST ME TODAY. HAD TO LEAVE THE WIFE AND KIDS AT HOME.
NICE TRY, BUT NO TICKET. GO RUN YOUR SHENANIGANS ELSEWHERE, LITTLE BOY WHO'S NOT ACCOMPANIED BY A PARENT OR GUARDIAN OVER 18.
THIS IS *SO* NOT FAIR! WHY DO I HAVE TO MISS OUT ON ALL THE BLOODY, GRUESOME GORE JUST 'CAUSE I'M NOT OLD ENOUGH?
THAT EVENING...
BOY, "STUPID AMERICANS CAUGHT ON TAPE" RERUNS! THIS IS BETTER THAN SEEING THE BEST MOVIE EVER...*NOT*.
BART! I CAN'T HEAR THE HOST'S WITTY REMARKS!
THOSE PANTS REALLY PUT THE "SPLIT" IN GRANDMA'S PEA SOUP!
HELLO, WHAT'S THIS? *ROBOT BASHERS* IS ON TV TONIGHT!
SWEET! IT'S THE COOLEST, GORIEST MOVIE EVER! ONCE EVERYONE'S ASLEEP, I'LL SNEAK DOWN AND WATCH IT.
TV GUIDE
ROBOT BASHERS SUNDAY AT ELEVEN
MATURE AUDIENCES ONLY
COMPLETED BY HOMER J. SIMPSON
LATER THAT NIGHT...
THEY DON'T HAVE SOULS, ADAM. THEY ARE EMOTIONLESS. CAN YOU NOT SEE?
COOOOL!
CHOCO CHIP COOKIES
CHIPS
BUZZ COLA
THE ONLY THING I SEE, GREG, IS THAT IT'S *ROBOT-BASHING TIME!*
BART! I CAN'T BELIEVE YOU'RE STILL UP. IT IS *WAY* PAST YOUR BEDTIME!
MOM!
AND LOOK AT ALL THIS JUNK FOOD. YOU'LL SPOIL YOUR BREAKFAST, YOUNG MAN!

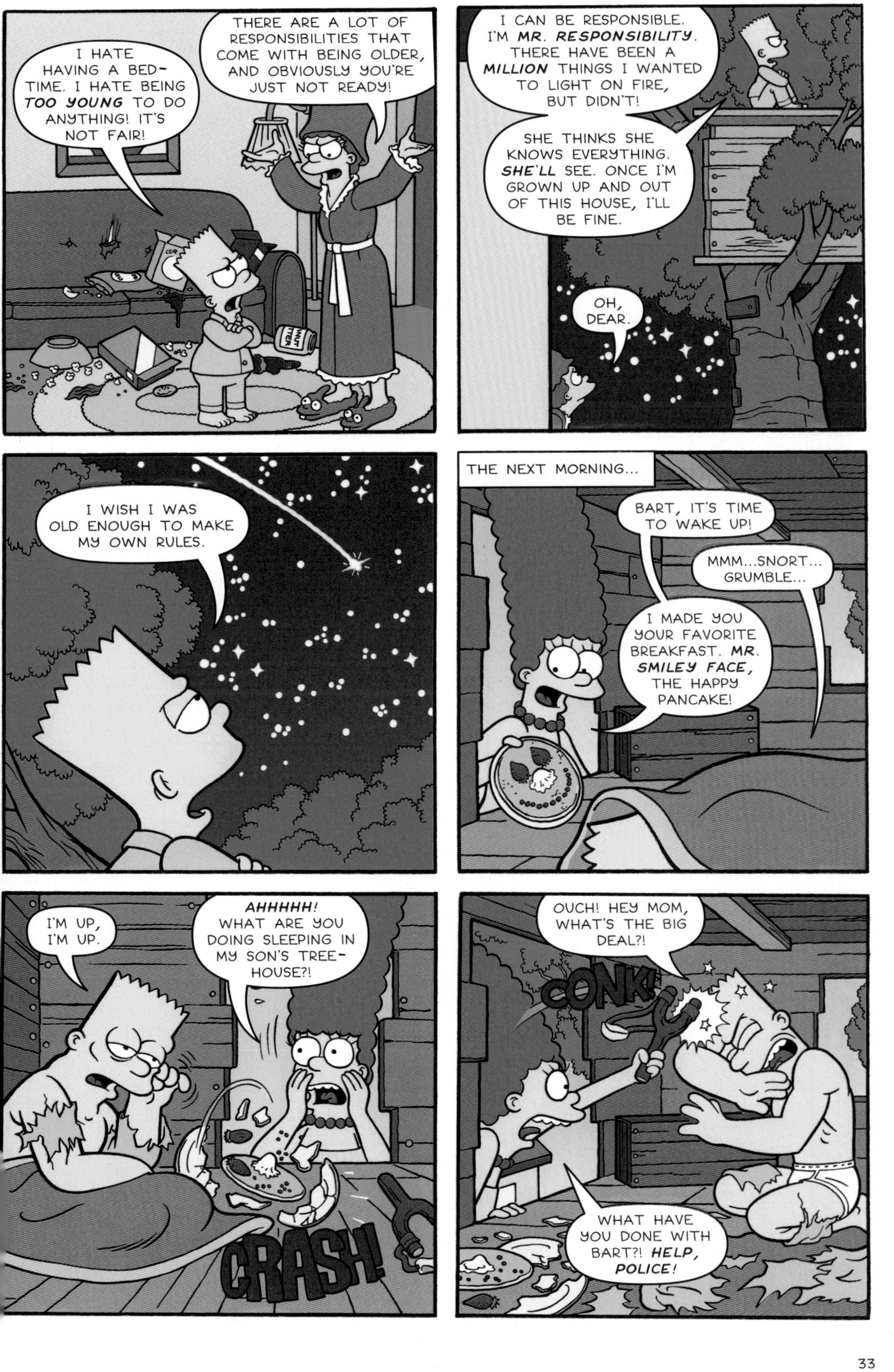
I HATE HAVING A BED-TIME. I HATE BEING **TOO YOUNG** TO DO ANYTHING! IT'S NOT FAIR!
THERE ARE A LOT OF RESPONSIBILITIES THAT COME WITH BEING OLDER, AND OBVIOUSLY YOU'RE JUST NOT READY!
I CAN BE RESPONSIBLE. I'M **MR. RESPONSIBILITY**. THERE HAVE BEEN A **MILLION** THINGS I WANTED TO LIGHT ON FIRE, BUT DIDN'T!
SHE THINKS SHE KNOWS EVERYTHING. **SHE'LL** SEE. ONCE I'M GROWN UP AND OUT OF THIS HOUSE, I'LL BE FINE.
OH, DEAR.
I WISH I WAS OLD ENOUGH TO MAKE MY OWN RULES.
THE NEXT MORNING...
BART, IT'S TIME TO WAKE UP!
MMM...SNORT... GRUMBLE...
I MADE YOU YOUR FAVORITE BREAKFAST. **MR. SMILEY FACE,** THE HAPPY PANCAKE!
I'M UP, I'M UP.
AHHHHH! WHAT ARE YOU DOING SLEEPING IN MY SON'S TREE-HOUSE?!
CRASH!
OUCH! HEY MOM, WHAT'S THE BIG DEAL?!
CONK!
WHAT HAVE YOU DONE WITH BART?! **HELP, POLICE!**

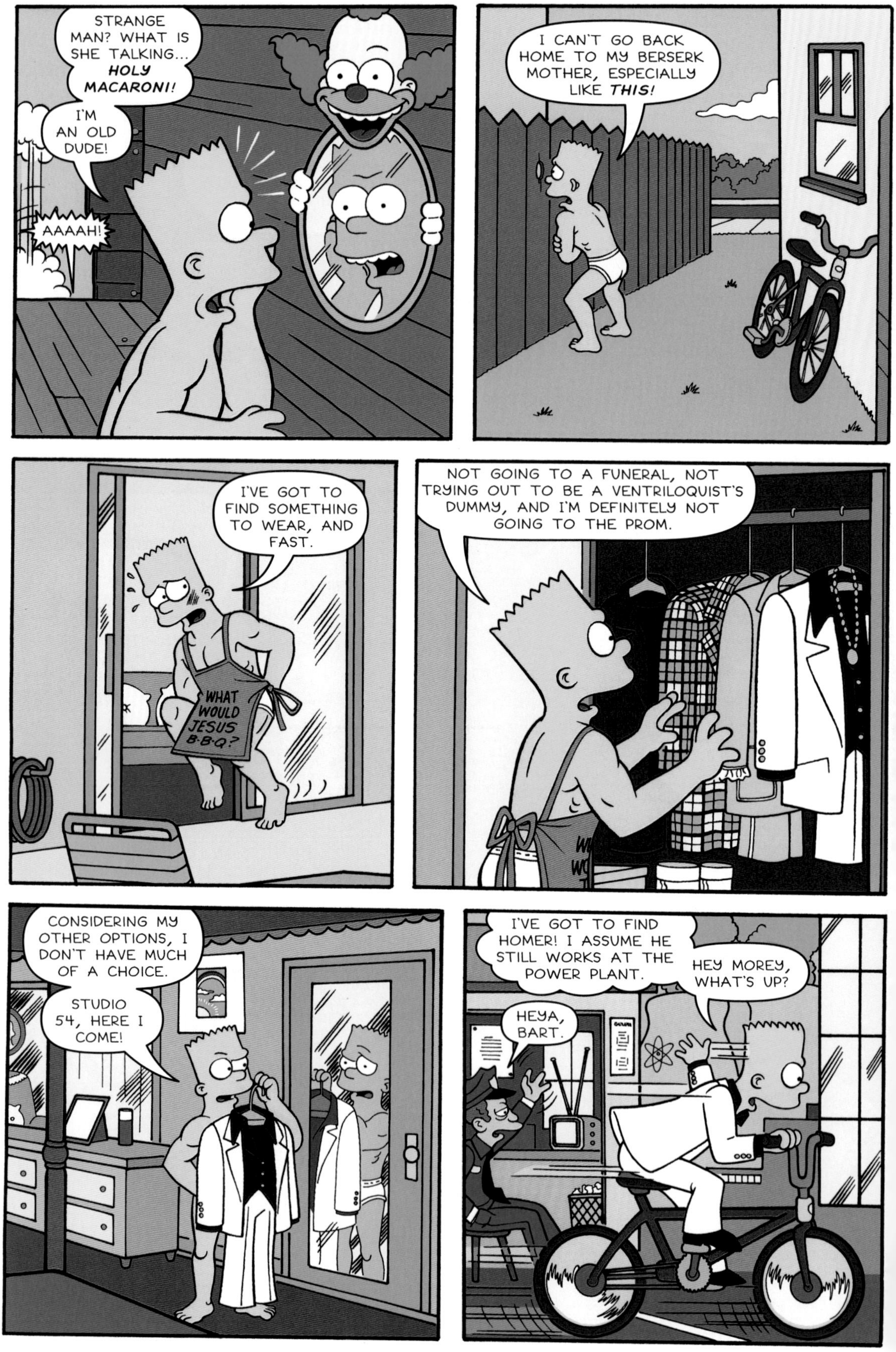
STRANGE MAN? WHAT IS SHE TALKING... HOLY MACARONI!
I'M AN OLD DUDE!
AAAAH!
I CAN'T GO BACK HOME TO MY BERSERK MOTHER, ESPECIALLY LIKE THIS!
I'VE GOT TO FIND SOMETHING TO WEAR, AND FAST.
WHAT WOULD JESUS B-B-Q?
NOT GOING TO A FUNERAL, NOT TRYING OUT TO BE A VENTRILOQUIST'S DUMMY, AND I'M DEFINITELY NOT GOING TO THE PROM.
CONSIDERING MY OTHER OPTIONS, I DON'T HAVE MUCH OF A CHOICE.
STUDIO 54, HERE I COME!
I'VE GOT TO FIND HOMER! I ASSUME HE STILL WORKS AT THE POWER PLANT.
HEY MOREY, WHAT'S UP?
HEYA, BART.

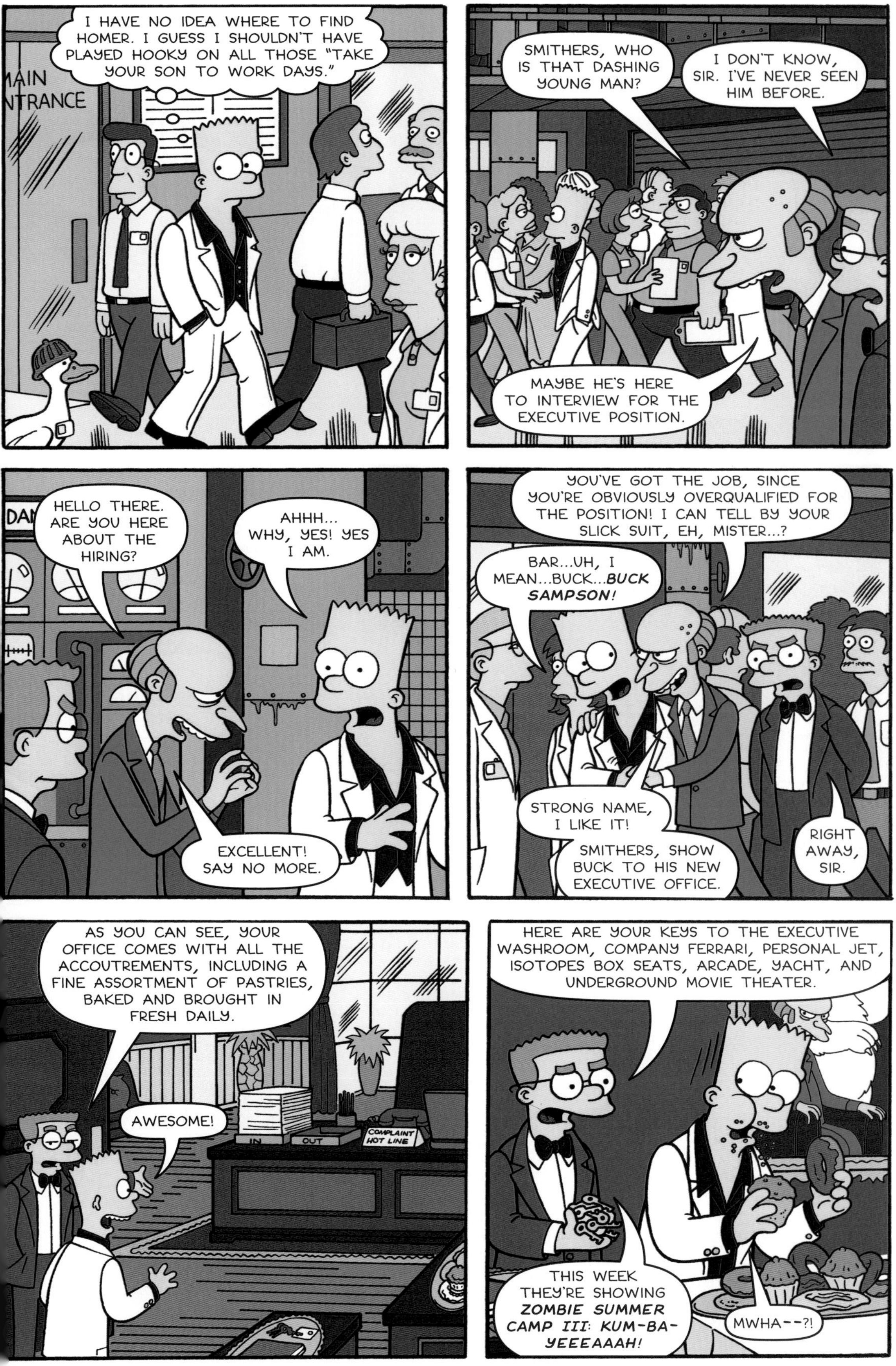

MAIN ENTRANCE
I HAVE NO IDEA WHERE TO FIND HOMER. I GUESS I SHOULDN'T HAVE PLAYED HOOKY ON ALL THOSE "TAKE YOUR SON TO WORK DAYS."
SMITHERS, WHO IS THAT DASHING YOUNG MAN?
I DON'T KNOW, SIR. I'VE NEVER SEEN HIM BEFORE.
MAYBE HE'S HERE TO INTERVIEW FOR THE EXECUTIVE POSITION.
HELLO THERE. ARE YOU HERE ABOUT THE HIRING?
AHHH... WHY, YES! YES I AM.
EXCELLENT! SAY NO MORE.
YOU'VE GOT THE JOB, SINCE YOU'RE OBVIOUSLY OVERQUALIFIED FOR THE POSITION! I CAN TELL BY YOUR SLICK SUIT, EH, MISTER...?
BAR...UH, I MEAN...BUCK...***BUCK SAMPSON!***
STRONG NAME, I LIKE IT!
SMITHERS, SHOW BUCK TO HIS NEW EXECUTIVE OFFICE.
RIGHT AWAY, SIR.
AS YOU CAN SEE, YOUR OFFICE COMES WITH ALL THE ACCOUTREMENTS, INCLUDING A FINE ASSORTMENT OF PASTRIES, BAKED AND BROUGHT IN FRESH DAILY.
AWESOME!
IN
OUT
COMPLAINT HOT LINE
HERE ARE YOUR KEYS TO THE EXECUTIVE WASHROOM, COMPANY FERRARI, PERSONAL JET, ISOTOPES BOX SEATS, ARCADE, YACHT, AND UNDERGROUND MOVIE THEATER.
THIS WEEK THEY'RE SHOWING ***ZOMBIE SUMMER CAMP III: KUM-BA-YEEEAAAH!***
MWHA--?!

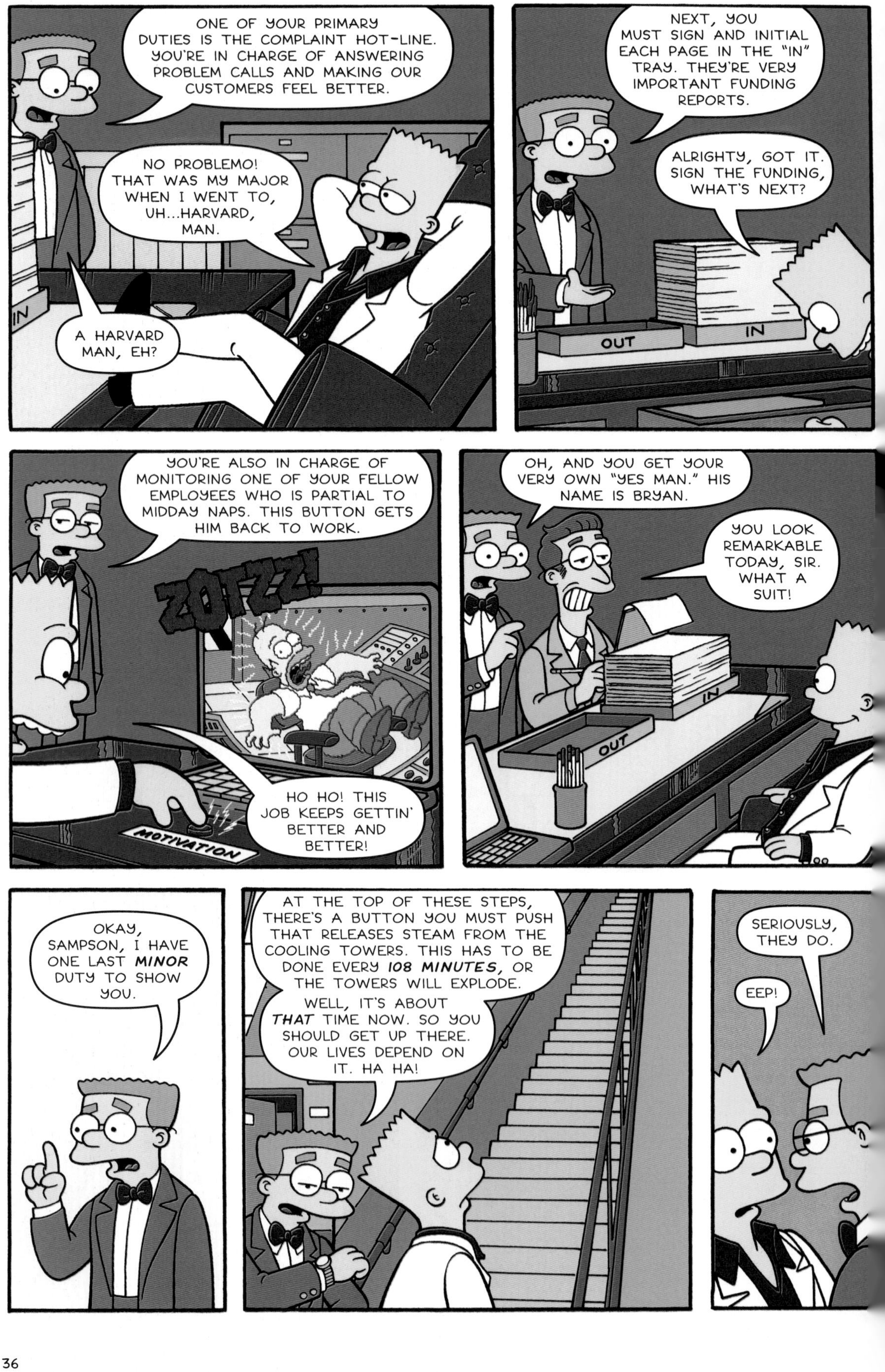
ONE OF YOUR PRIMARY DUTIES IS THE COMPLAINT HOT-LINE. YOU'RE IN CHARGE OF ANSWERING PROBLEM CALLS AND MAKING OUR CUSTOMERS FEEL BETTER.
NO PROBLEMO! THAT WAS MY MAJOR WHEN I WENT TO, UH...HARVARD, MAN.
A HARVARD MAN, EH?
IN
NEXT, YOU MUST SIGN AND INITIAL EACH PAGE IN THE "IN" TRAY. THEY'RE VERY IMPORTANT FUNDING REPORTS.
ALRIGHTY, GOT IT. SIGN THE FUNDING, WHAT'S NEXT?
OUT
IN
YOU'RE ALSO IN CHARGE OF MONITORING ONE OF YOUR FELLOW EMPLOYEES WHO IS PARTIAL TO MIDDAY NAPS. THIS BUTTON GETS HIM BACK TO WORK.
ZOTZZ!
MOTIVATION
HO HO! THIS JOB KEEPS GETTIN' BETTER AND BETTER!
OH, AND YOU GET YOUR VERY OWN "YES MAN." HIS NAME IS BRYAN.
YOU LOOK REMARKABLE TODAY, SIR. WHAT A SUIT!
IN
OUT
OKAY, SAMPSON, I HAVE ONE LAST MINOR DUTY TO SHOW YOU.
AT THE TOP OF THESE STEPS, THERE'S A BUTTON YOU MUST PUSH THAT RELEASES STEAM FROM THE COOLING TOWERS. THIS HAS TO BE DONE EVERY 108 MINUTES, OR THE TOWERS WILL EXPLODE.
WELL, IT'S ABOUT THAT TIME NOW. SO YOU SHOULD GET UP THERE. OUR LIVES DEPEND ON IT. HA HA!
SERIOUSLY, THEY DO.
EEP!

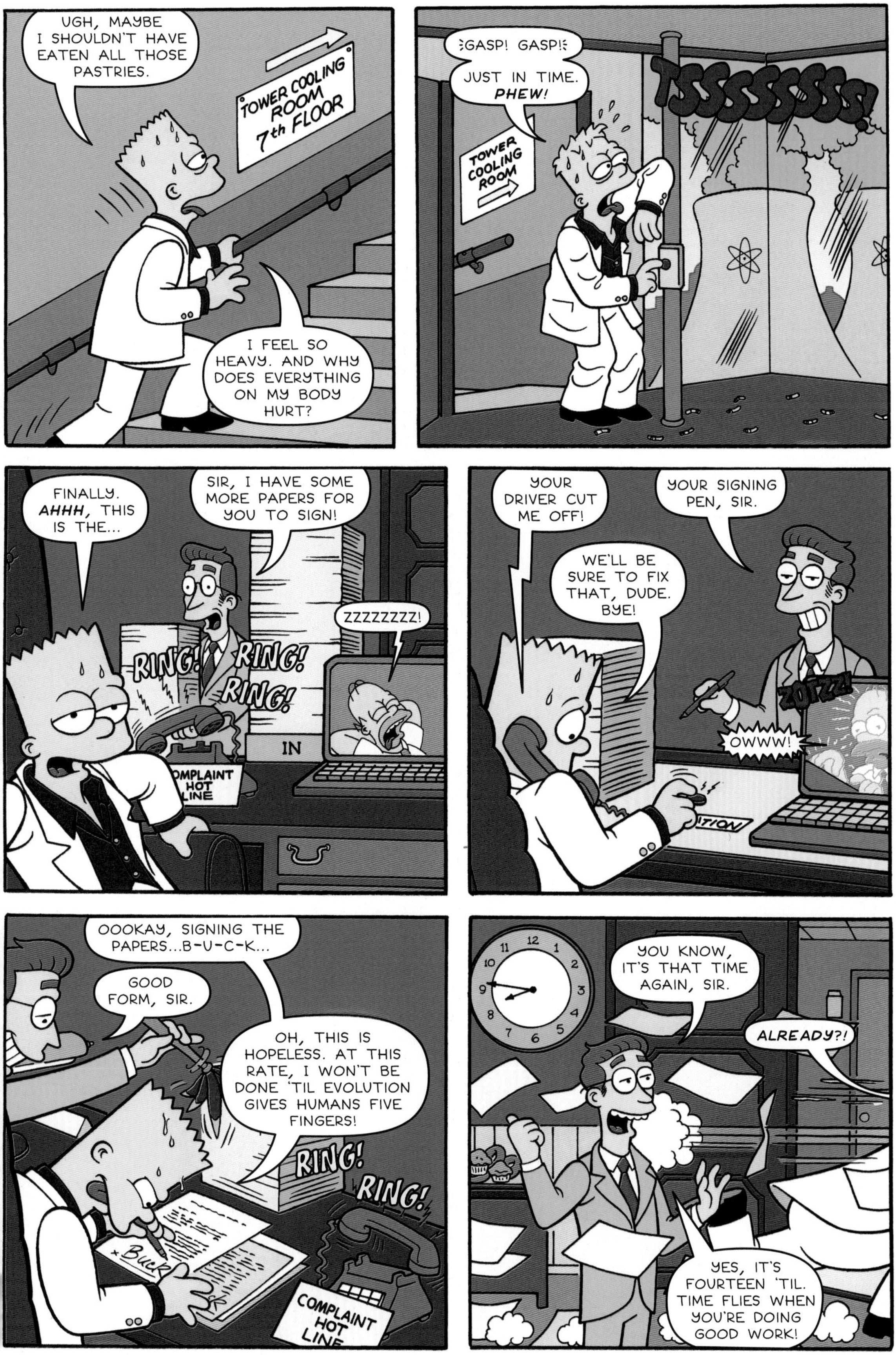
UGH, MAYBE I SHOULDN'T HAVE EATEN ALL THOSE PASTRIES.
TOWER COOLING ROOM 7th FLOOR
I FEEL SO HEAVY. AND WHY DOES EVERYTHING ON MY BODY HURT?
GASP! GASP!
JUST IN TIME. PHEW!
TOWER COOLING ROOM
TSSSSSSSS!
FINALLY. AHHH, THIS IS THE...
SIR, I HAVE SOME MORE PAPERS FOR YOU TO SIGN!
RING! RING! RING!
ZZZZZZZZ!
IN
COMPLAINT HOT LINE
YOUR DRIVER CUT ME OFF!
YOUR SIGNING PEN, SIR.
WE'LL BE SURE TO FIX THAT, DUDE. BYE!
ZOTZZ!
OWWW!
OOOKAY, SIGNING THE PAPERS...B-U-C-K...
GOOD FORM, SIR.
OH, THIS IS HOPELESS. AT THIS RATE, I WON'T BE DONE 'TIL EVOLUTION GIVES HUMANS FIVE FINGERS!
BUCK
RING! RING!
COMPLAINT HOT LINE
YOU KNOW, IT'S THAT TIME AGAIN, SIR.
ALREADY?!
YES, IT'S FOURTEEN 'TIL. TIME FLIES WHEN YOU'RE DOING GOOD WORK!

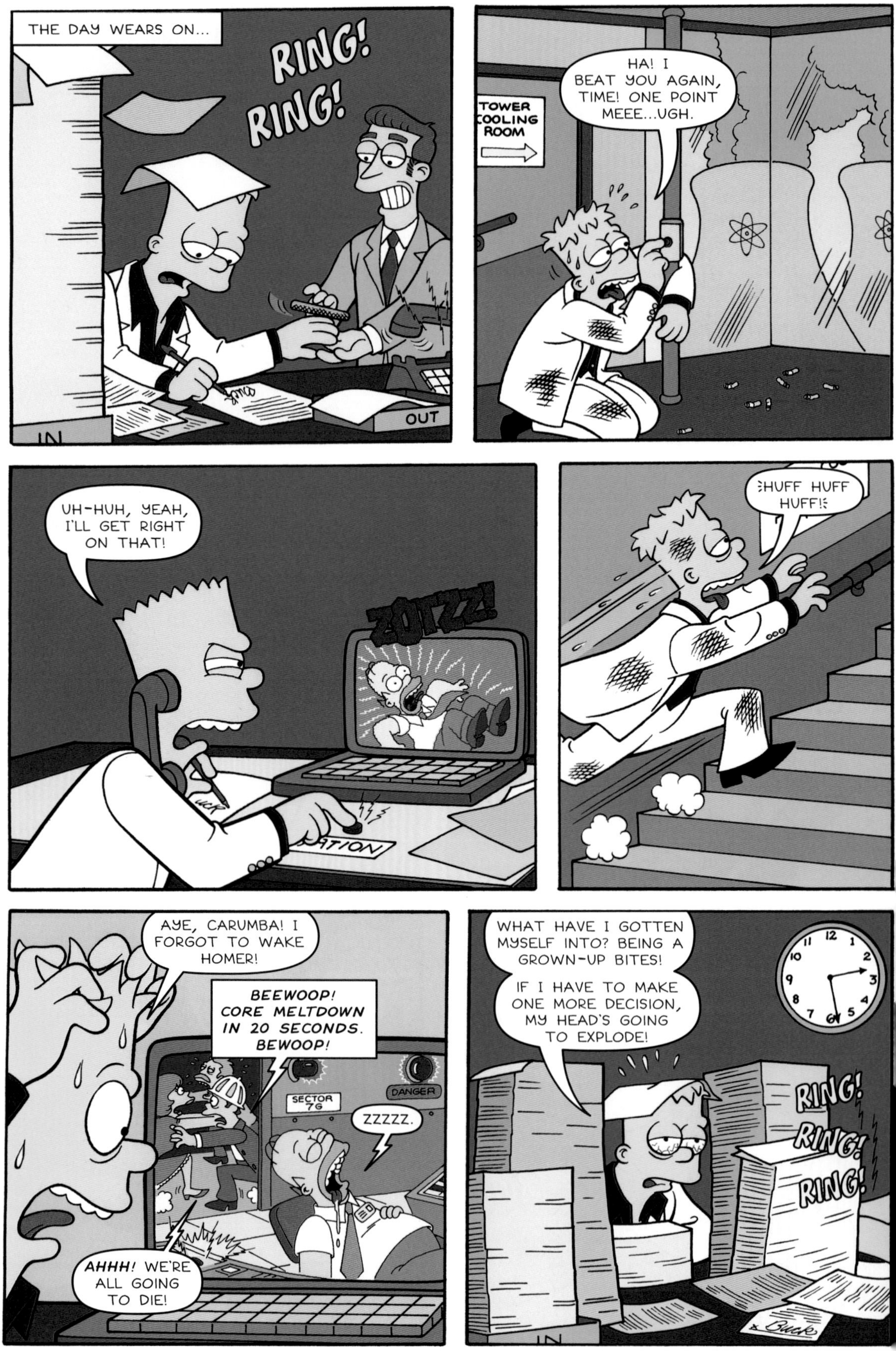
THE DAY WEARS ON...
RING! RING!
IN
OUT
HA! I BEAT YOU AGAIN, TIME! ONE POINT MEEE...UGH.
TOWER COOLING ROOM
UH-HUH, YEAH, I'LL GET RIGHT ON THAT!
ZOTZZ!
HUFF HUFF HUFF!
AYE, CARUMBA! I FORGOT TO WAKE HOMER!
BEEWOOP! CORE MELTDOWN IN 20 SECONDS. BEWOOP!
SECTOR 7G
DANGER
ZZZZZ.
AHHH! WE'RE ALL GOING TO DIE!
WHAT HAVE I GOTTEN MYSELF INTO? BEING A GROWN-UP BITES!
IF I HAVE TO MAKE ONE MORE DECISION, MY HEAD'S GOING TO EXPLODE!
RING! RING! RING!
IN

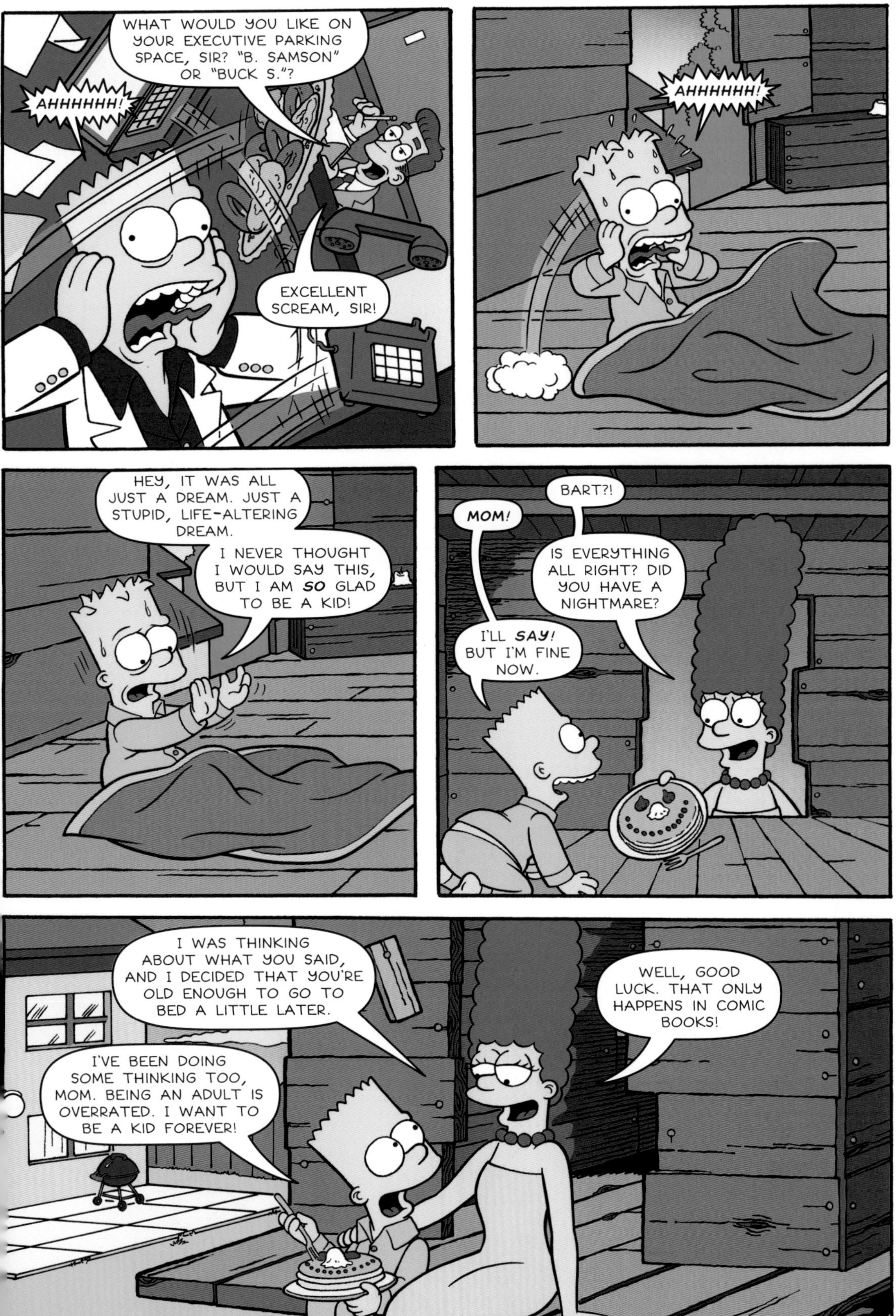
WHAT WOULD YOU LIKE ON YOUR EXECUTIVE PARKING SPACE, SIR? "B. SAMSON" OR "BUCK S."?
AHHHHHH!
EXCELLENT SCREAM, SIR!
AHHHHHH!
HEY, IT WAS ALL JUST A DREAM. JUST A STUPID, LIFE-ALTERING DREAM.
I NEVER THOUGHT I WOULD SAY THIS, BUT I AM *SO* GLAD TO BE A KID!
BART?!
MOM!
IS EVERYTHING ALL RIGHT? DID YOU HAVE A NIGHTMARE?
I'LL *SAY!* BUT I'M FINE NOW.
I WAS THINKING ABOUT WHAT YOU SAID, AND I DECIDED THAT YOU'RE OLD ENOUGH TO GO TO BED A LITTLE LATER.
I'VE BEEN DOING SOME THINKING TOO, MOM. BEING AN ADULT IS OVERRATED. I WANT TO BE A KID FOREVER!
WELL, GOOD LUCK. THAT ONLY HAPPENS IN COMIC BOOKS!
THE END

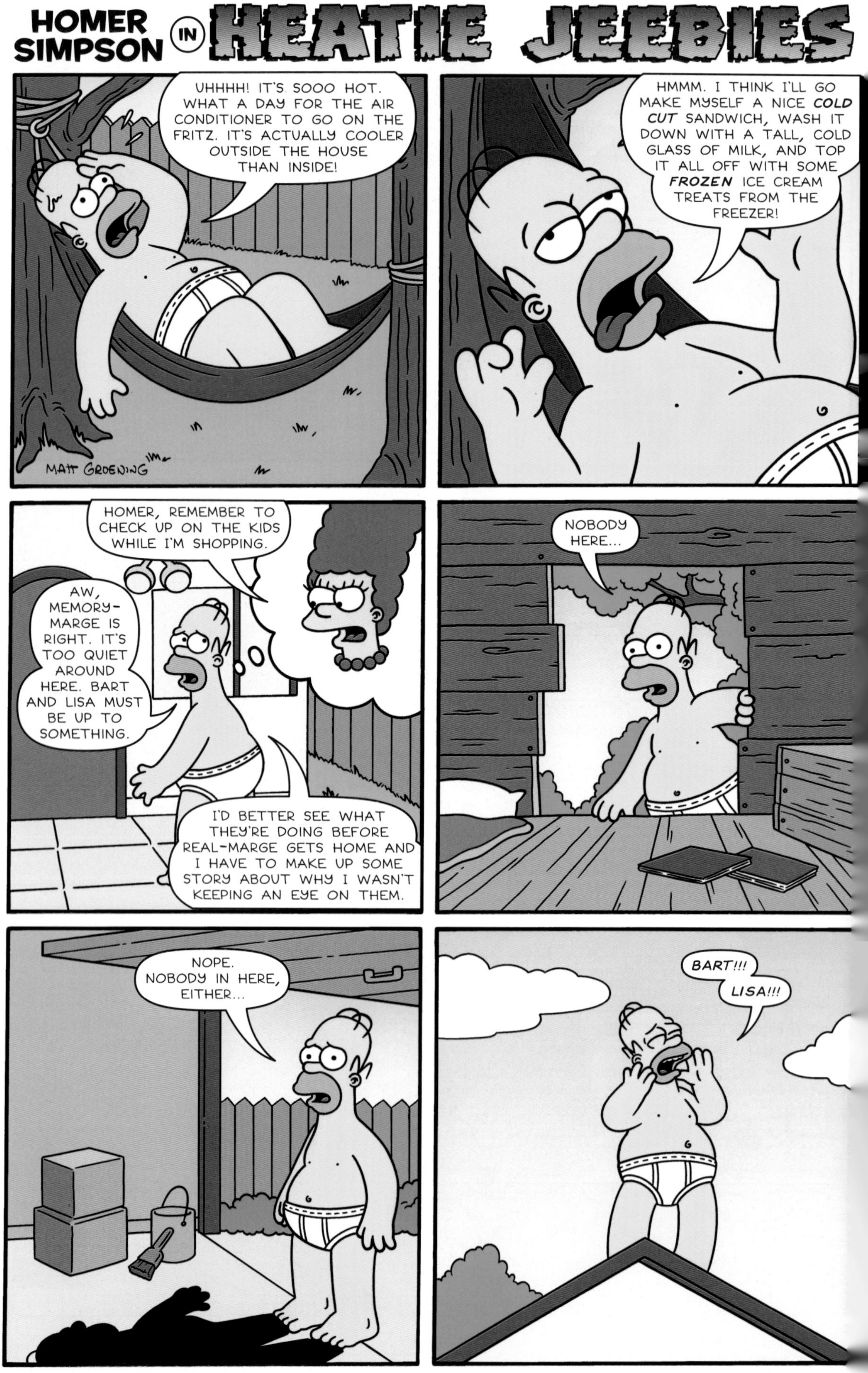
HOMER SIMPSON IN HEATIE JEEBIES
UHHHH! IT'S SOOO HOT. WHAT A DAY FOR THE AIR CONDITIONER TO GO ON THE FRITZ. IT'S ACTUALLY COOLER OUTSIDE THE HOUSE THAN INSIDE!
MATT GROENING
HMMM. I THINK I'LL GO MAKE MYSELF A NICE COLD CUT SANDWICH, WASH IT DOWN WITH A TALL, COLD GLASS OF MILK, AND TOP IT ALL OFF WITH SOME FROZEN ICE CREAM TREATS FROM THE FREEZER!
HOMER, REMEMBER TO CHECK UP ON THE KIDS WHILE I'M SHOPPING.
AW, MEMORY-MARGE IS RIGHT. IT'S TOO QUIET AROUND HERE. BART AND LISA MUST BE UP TO SOMETHING.
I'D BETTER SEE WHAT THEY'RE DOING BEFORE REAL-MARGE GETS HOME AND I HAVE TO MAKE UP SOME STORY ABOUT WHY I WASN'T KEEPING AN EYE ON THEM.
NOBODY HERE...
NOPE. NOBODY IN HERE, EITHER...
BART!!!
LISA!!!

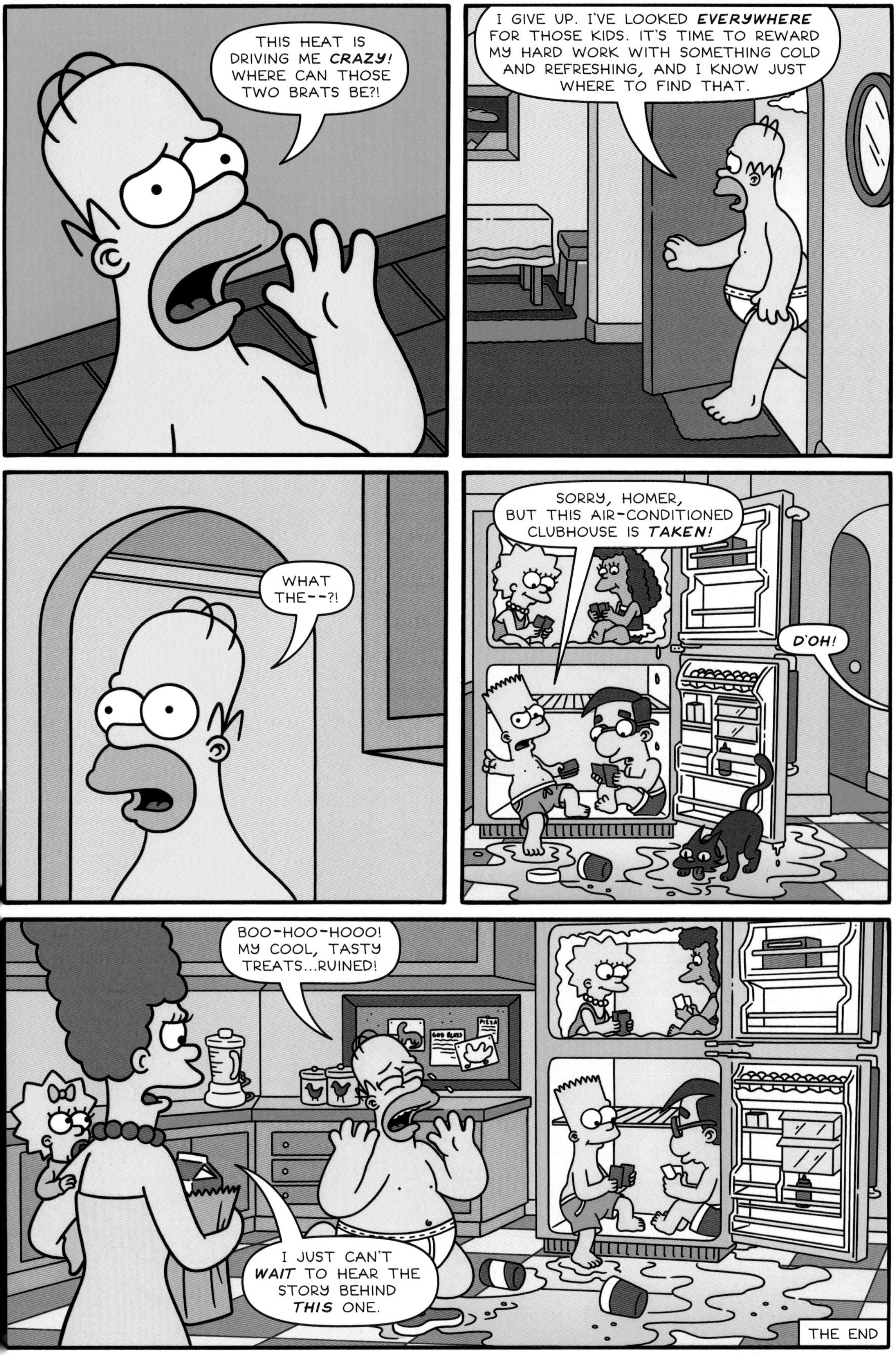
THIS HEAT IS DRIVING ME CRAZY! WHERE CAN THOSE TWO BRATS BE?!
I GIVE UP. I'VE LOOKED EVERYWHERE FOR THOSE KIDS. IT'S TIME TO REWARD MY HARD WORK WITH SOMETHING COLD AND REFRESHING, AND I KNOW JUST WHERE TO FIND THAT.
WHAT THE--?!
SORRY, HOMER, BUT THIS AIR-CONDITIONED CLUBHOUSE IS TAKEN!
D'OH!
BOO-HOO-HOOO! MY COOL, TASTY TREATS...RUINED!
I JUST CAN'T WAIT TO HEAR THE STORY BEHIND THIS ONE.
THE END

CHRIS YAMBAR SCRIPT · KIM NARSETE PENCILS · MIKE ROTE INKS · ART VILLANUEVA COLORS · KAREN BATES LETTERS · BILL MORRISON EDITOR

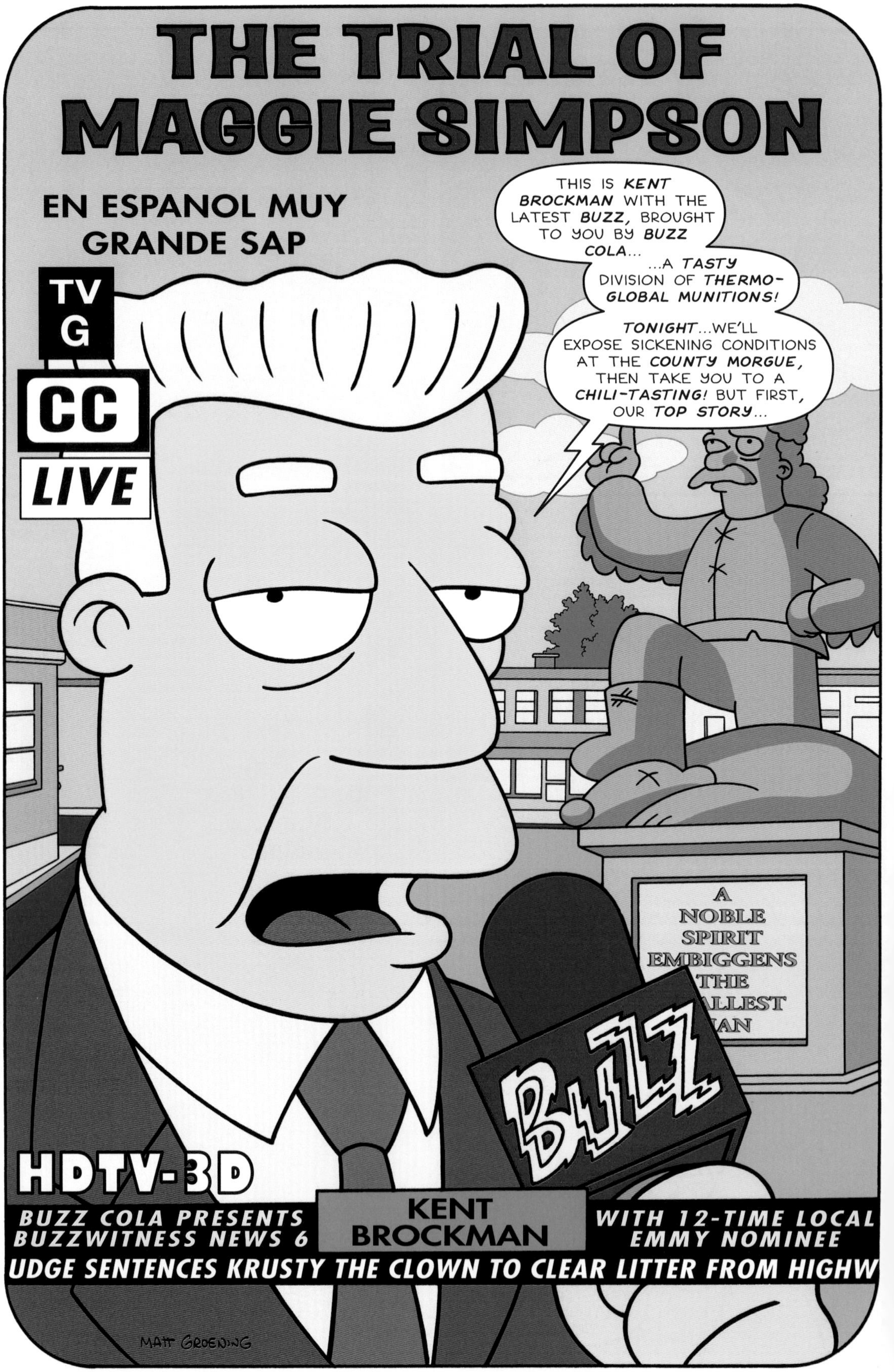
THE TRIAL OF MAGGIE SIMPSON
EN ESPANOL MUY GRANDE SAP
TV G
CC
LIVE
THIS IS KENT BROCKMAN WITH THE LATEST BUZZ, BROUGHT TO YOU BY BUZZ COLA...
...A TASTY DIVISION OF THERMO-GLOBAL MUNITIONS!
TONIGHT...WE'LL EXPOSE SICKENING CONDITIONS AT THE COUNTY MORGUE, THEN TAKE YOU TO A CHILI-TASTING! BUT FIRST, OUR TOP STORY...
A NOBLE SPIRIT EMBIGGENS THE
BUZZ
HDTV-3D
BUZZ COLA PRESENTS BUZZWITNESS NEWS 6
KENT BROCKMAN
WITH 12-TIME LOCAL EMMY NOMINEE
UDGE SENTENCES KRUSTY THE CLOWN TO CLEAR LITTER FROM HIGHW
MATT GROENING

TOM PEYER SCRIPT · *JOHN COSTANZA* PENCILS · *PHYLLIS NOVIN* INKS · *NATHAN HAMILL* COLORS · *KAREN BATES* LETTERS · *BILL MORRISON* EDITOR

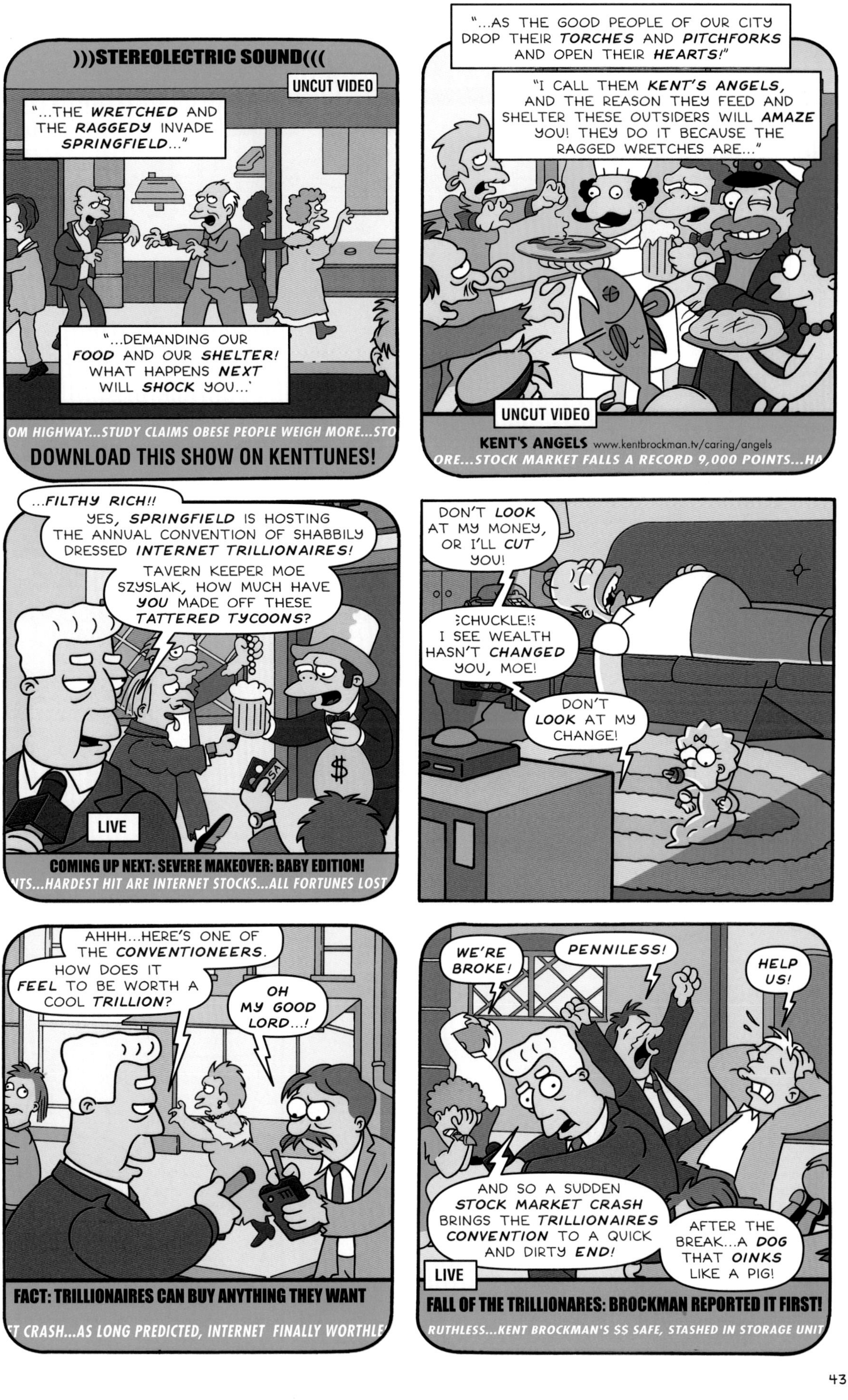
)))STEREOLECTRIC SOUND(((
UNCUT VIDEO
"...THE WRETCHED AND THE RAGGEDY INVADE SPRINGFIELD..."
"...DEMANDING OUR FOOD AND OUR SHELTER! WHAT HAPPENS NEXT WILL SHOCK YOU...'
OM HIGHWAY...STUDY CLAIMS OBESE PEOPLE WEIGH MORE...STO
DOWNLOAD THIS SHOW ON KENTTUNES!
"...AS THE GOOD PEOPLE OF OUR CITY DROP THEIR TORCHES AND PITCHFORKS AND OPEN THEIR HEARTS!"
"I CALL THEM KENT'S ANGELS, AND THE REASON THEY FEED AND SHELTER THESE OUTSIDERS WILL AMAZE YOU! THEY DO IT BECAUSE THE RAGGED WRETCHES ARE..."
UNCUT VIDEO
KENT'S ANGELS www.kentbrockman.tv/caring/angels
ORE...STOCK MARKET FALLS A RECORD 9,000 POINTS...HA
...FILTHY RICH!! YES, SPRINGFIELD IS HOSTING THE ANNUAL CONVENTION OF SHABBILY DRESSED INTERNET TRILLIONAIRES!
TAVERN KEEPER MOE SZYSLAK, HOW MUCH HAVE YOU MADE OFF THESE TATTERED TYCOONS?
LIVE
COMING UP NEXT: SEVERE MAKEOVER: BABY EDITION!
NTS...HARDEST HIT ARE INTERNET STOCKS...ALL FORTUNES LOST
DON'T LOOK AT MY MONEY, OR I'LL CUT YOU!
CHUCKLE! I SEE WEALTH HASN'T CHANGED YOU, MOE!
DON'T LOOK AT MY CHANGE!
AHHH...HERE'S ONE OF THE CONVENTIONEERS.
HOW DOES IT FEEL TO BE WORTH A COOL TRILLION?
OH MY GOOD LORD...!
FACT: TRILLIONAIRES CAN BUY ANYTHING THEY WANT
T CRASH...AS LONG PREDICTED, INTERNET FINALLY WORTHLE
WE'RE BROKE!
PENNILESS!
HELP US!
AND SO A SUDDEN STOCK MARKET CRASH BRINGS THE TRILLIONAIRES CONVENTION TO A QUICK AND DIRTY END!
AFTER THE BREAK...A DOG THAT OINKS LIKE A PIG!
LIVE
FALL OF THE TRILLIONARES: BROCKMAN REPORTED IT FIRST!
RUTHLESS...KENT BROCKMAN'S $$ SAFE, STASHED IN STORAGE UNIT

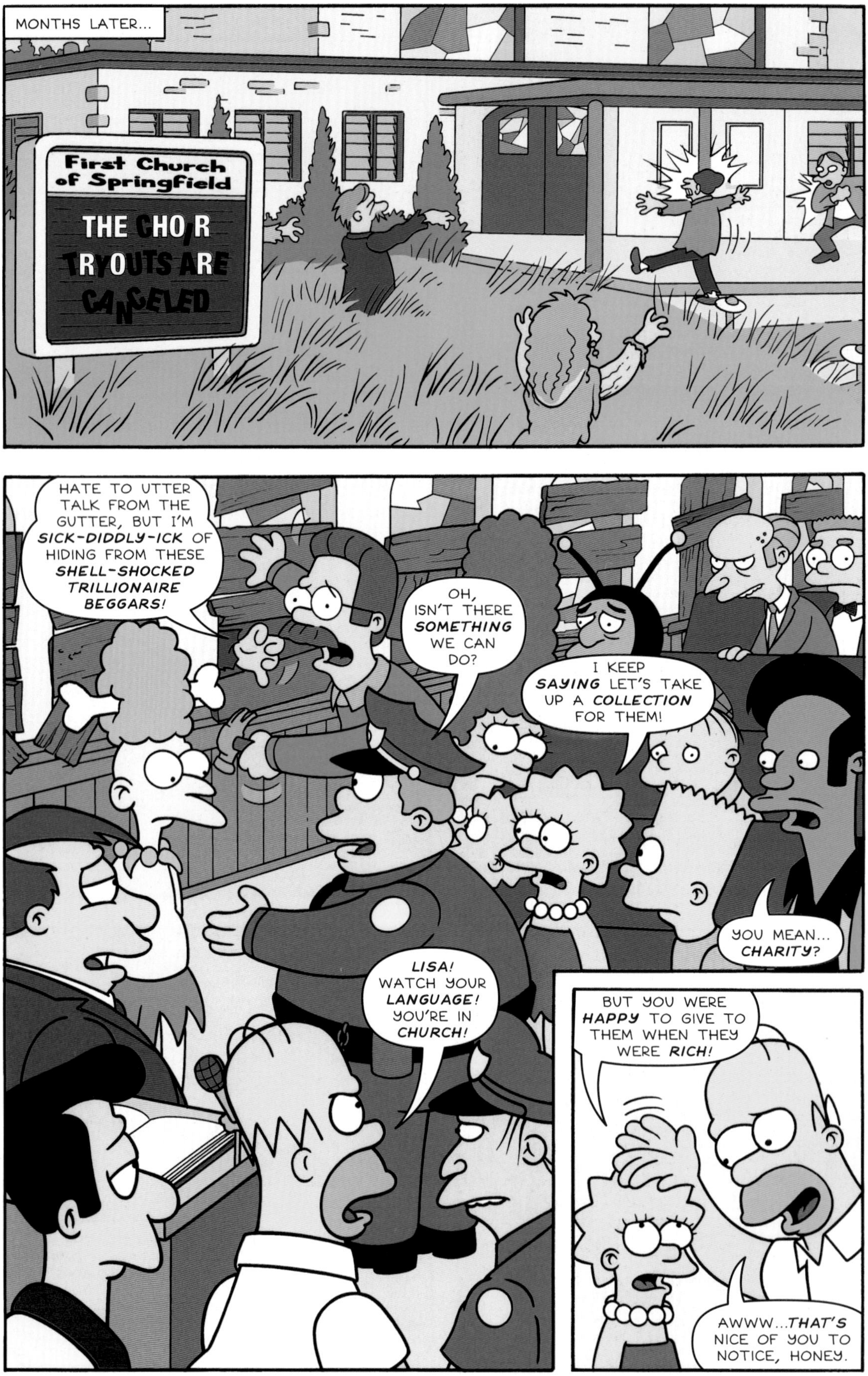

MONTHS LATER...
First Church of Springfield
THE CHOIR TRYOUTS ARE CANCELED
HATE TO UTTER TALK FROM THE GUTTER, BUT I'M *SICK-DIDDLY-ICK* OF HIDING FROM THESE *SHELL-SHOCKED TRILLIONAIRE BEGGARS!*
OH, ISN'T THERE *SOMETHING* WE CAN DO?
I KEEP *SAYING* LET'S TAKE UP A *COLLECTION* FOR THEM!
YOU MEAN... *CHARITY*?
LISA! WATCH YOUR *LANGUAGE!* YOU'RE IN *CHURCH!*
BUT YOU WERE *HAPPY* TO GIVE TO THEM WHEN THEY WERE *RICH!*
AWWW...*THAT'S* NICE OF YOU TO NOTICE, HONEY.

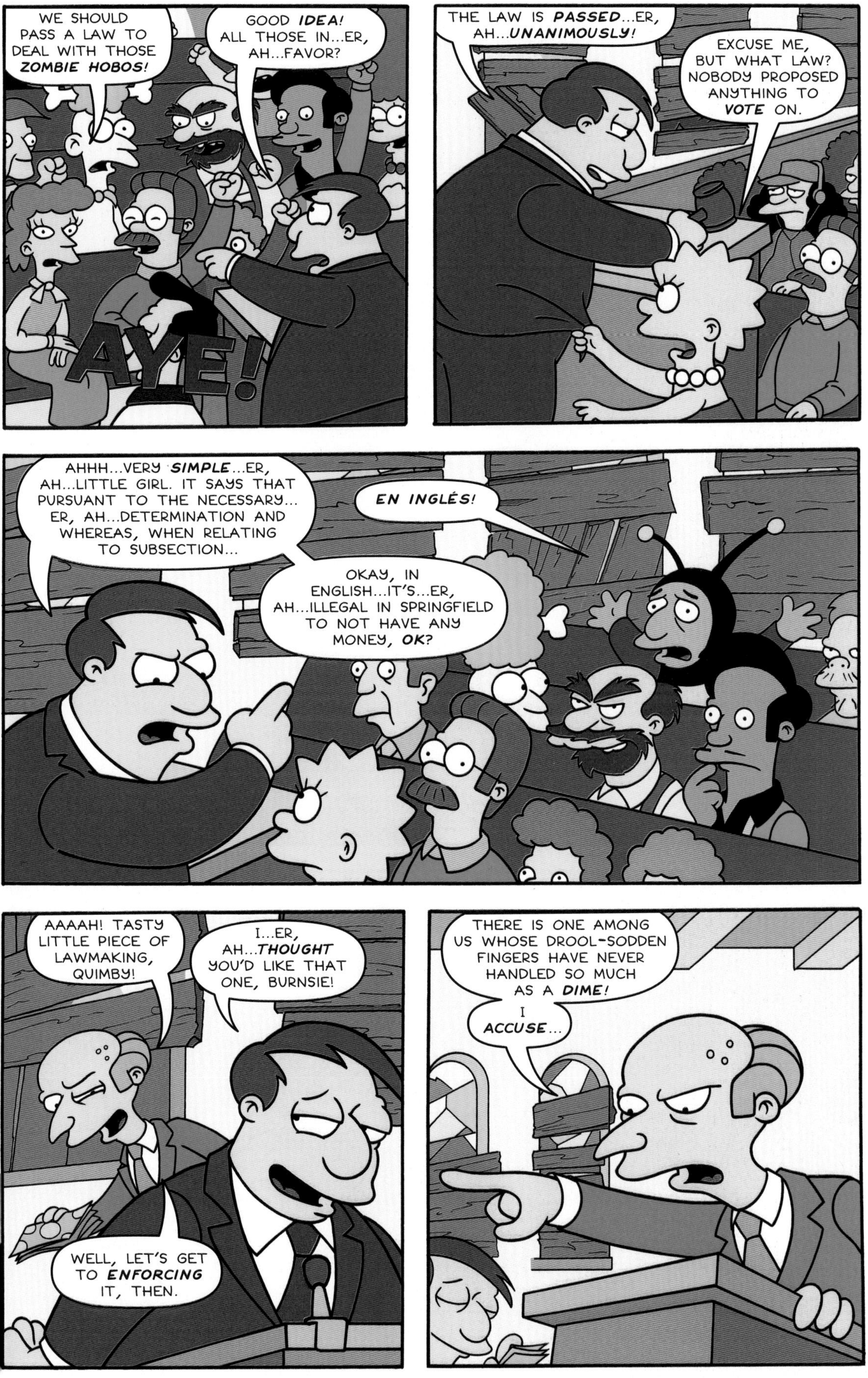
WE SHOULD PASS A LAW TO DEAL WITH THOSE ZOMBIE HOBOS!
GOOD IDEA! ALL THOSE IN...ER, AH...FAVOR?
AYE!
THE LAW IS PASSED...ER, AH...UNANIMOUSLY!
EXCUSE ME, BUT WHAT LAW? NOBODY PROPOSED ANYTHING TO VOTE ON.
AHHH...VERY SIMPLE...ER, AH...LITTLE GIRL. IT SAYS THAT PURSUANT TO THE NECESSARY... ER, AH...DETERMINATION AND WHEREAS, WHEN RELATING TO SUBSECTION...
EN INGLÉS!
OKAY, IN ENGLISH...IT'S...ER, AH...ILLEGAL IN SPRINGFIELD TO NOT HAVE ANY MONEY, OK?
AAAAH! TASTY LITTLE PIECE OF LAWMAKING, QUIMBY!
I...ER, AH...THOUGHT YOU'D LIKE THAT ONE, BURNSIE!
WELL, LET'S GET TO ENFORCING IT, THEN.
THERE IS ONE AMONG US WHOSE DROOL-SODDEN FINGERS HAVE NEVER HANDLED SO MUCH AS A DIME!
I ACCUSE...

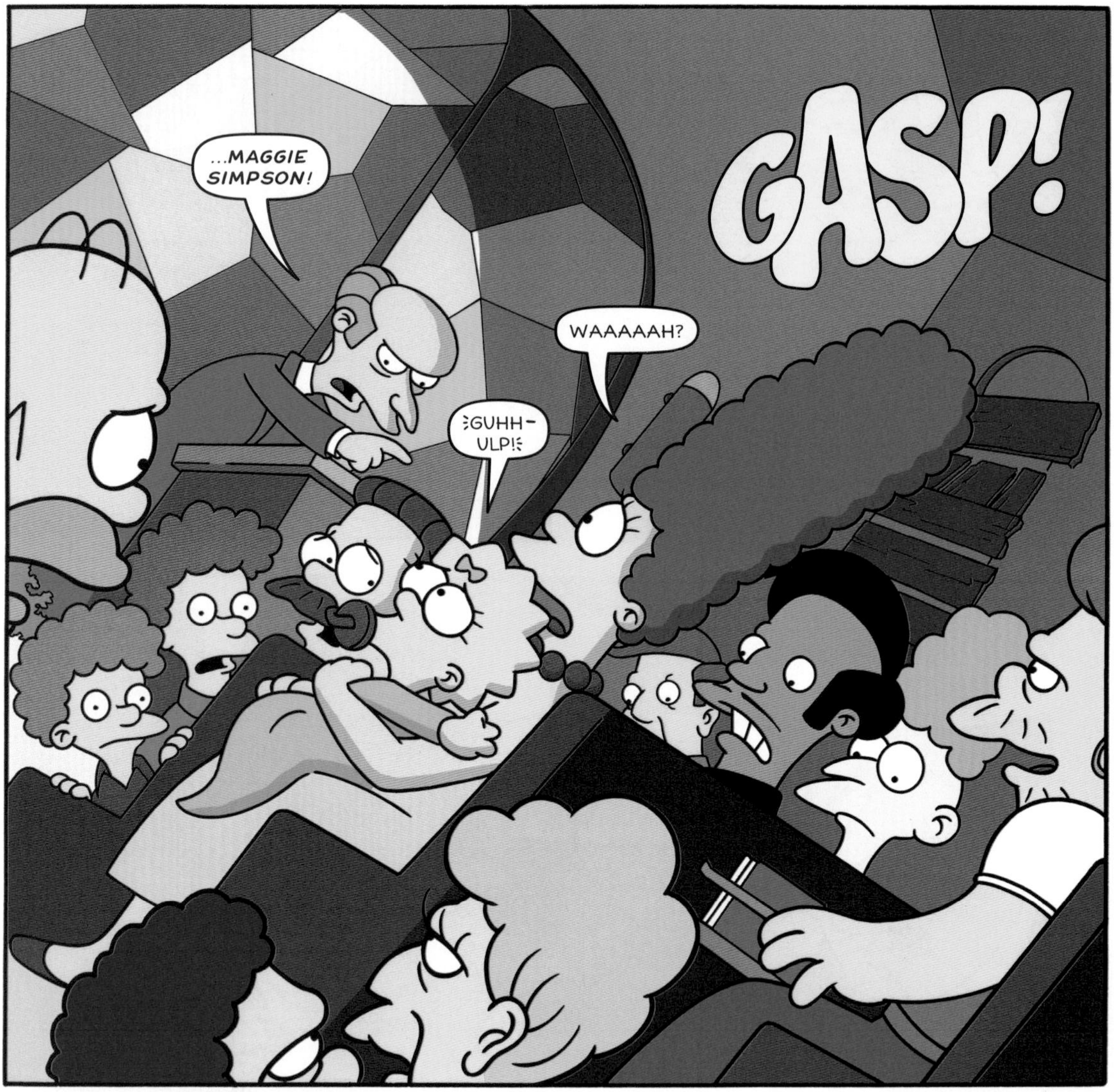
...MAGGIE SIMPSON!
GASP!
WAAAAAH?
GUHH-ULP!

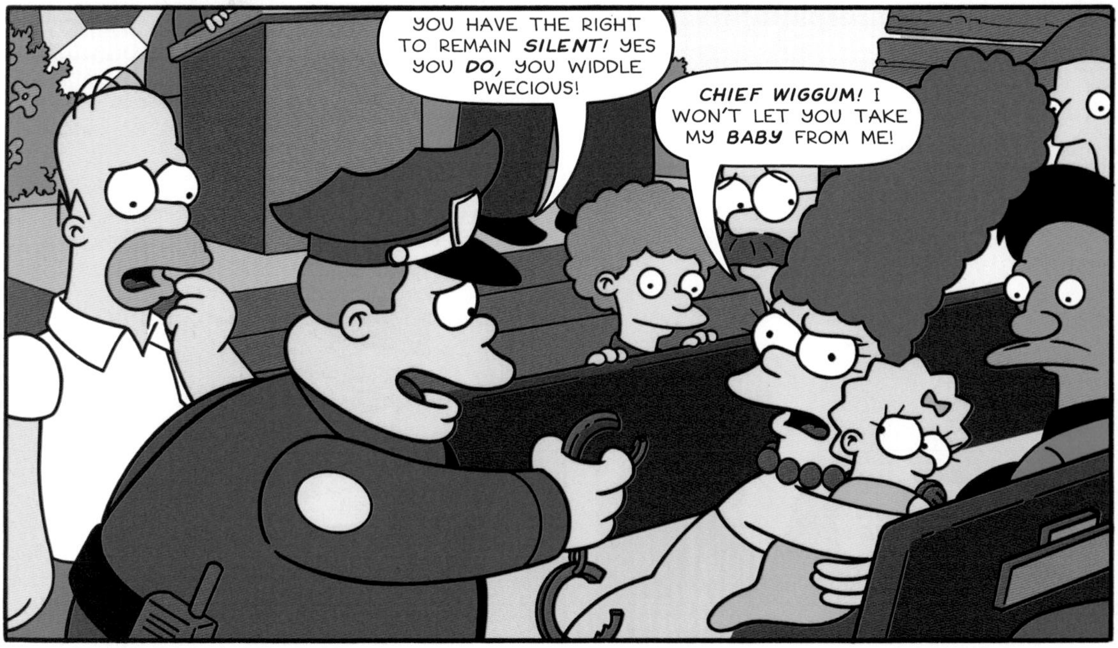
YOU HAVE THE RIGHT TO REMAIN SILENT! YES YOU DO, YOU WIDDLE PWECIOUS!
CHIEF WIGGUM! I WON'T LET YOU TAKE MY BABY FROM ME!

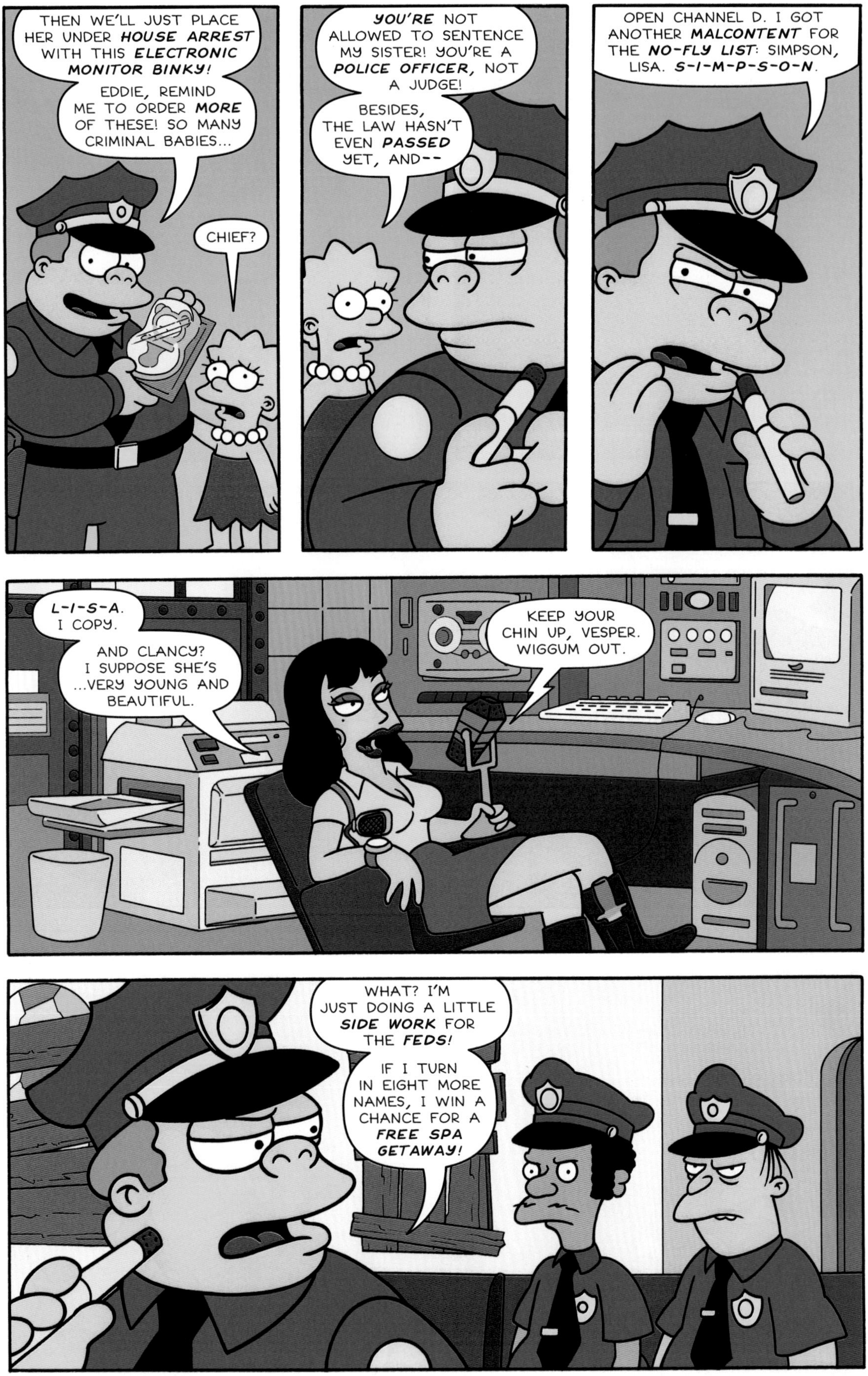
THEN WE'LL JUST PLACE HER UNDER HOUSE ARREST WITH THIS ELECTRONIC MONITOR BINKY!
EDDIE, REMIND ME TO ORDER MORE OF THESE! SO MANY CRIMINAL BABIES...
CHIEF?
YOU'RE NOT ALLOWED TO SENTENCE MY SISTER! YOU'RE A POLICE OFFICER, NOT A JUDGE!
BESIDES, THE LAW HASN'T EVEN PASSED YET, AND--
OPEN CHANNEL D. I GOT ANOTHER MALCONTENT FOR THE NO-FLY LIST: SIMPSON, LISA. S-I-M-P-S-O-N.
L-I-S-A. I COPY.
AND CLANCY? I SUPPOSE SHE'S ...VERY YOUNG AND BEAUTIFUL.
KEEP YOUR CHIN UP, VESPER. WIGGUM OUT.
WHAT? I'M JUST DOING A LITTLE SIDE WORK FOR THE FEDS!
IF I TURN IN EIGHT MORE NAMES, I WIN A CHANCE FOR A FREE SPA GETAWAY!

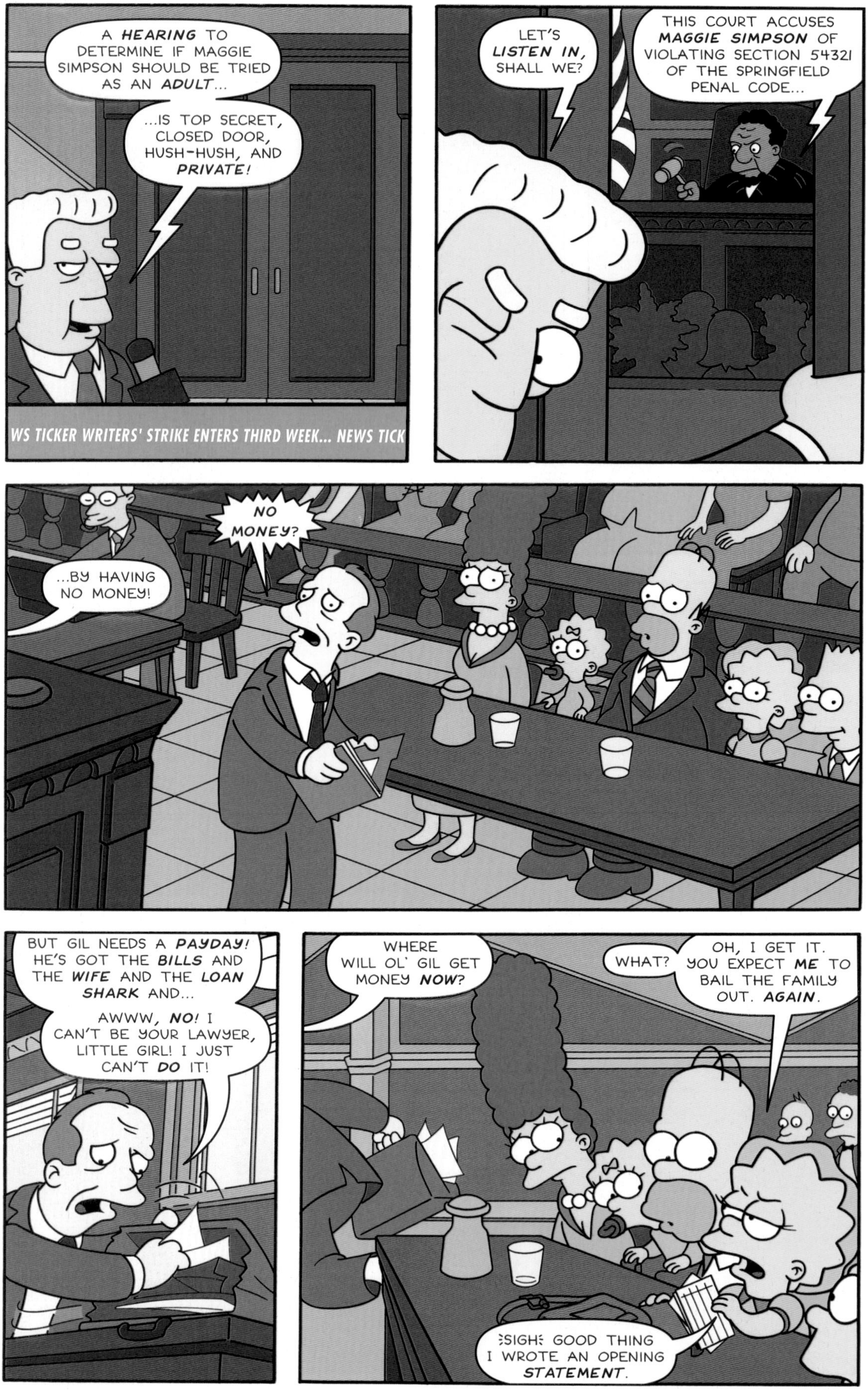
A HEARING TO DETERMINE IF MAGGIE SIMPSON SHOULD BE TRIED AS AN ADULT...
...IS TOP SECRET, CLOSED DOOR, HUSH-HUSH, AND PRIVATE!
WS TICKER WRITERS' STRIKE ENTERS THIRD WEEK... NEWS TICK
LET'S LISTEN IN, SHALL WE?
THIS COURT ACCUSES MAGGIE SIMPSON OF VIOLATING SECTION 54321 OF THE SPRINGFIELD PENAL CODE...
...BY HAVING NO MONEY!
NO MONEY?
BUT GIL NEEDS A PAYDAY! HE'S GOT THE BILLS AND THE WIFE AND THE LOAN SHARK AND...
AWWW, NO! I CAN'T BE YOUR LAWYER, LITTLE GIRL! I JUST CAN'T DO IT!
WHERE WILL OL' GIL GET MONEY NOW?
WHAT?
OH, I GET IT. YOU EXPECT ME TO BAIL THE FAMILY OUT. AGAIN.
SIGH GOOD THING I WROTE AN OPENING STATEMENT.

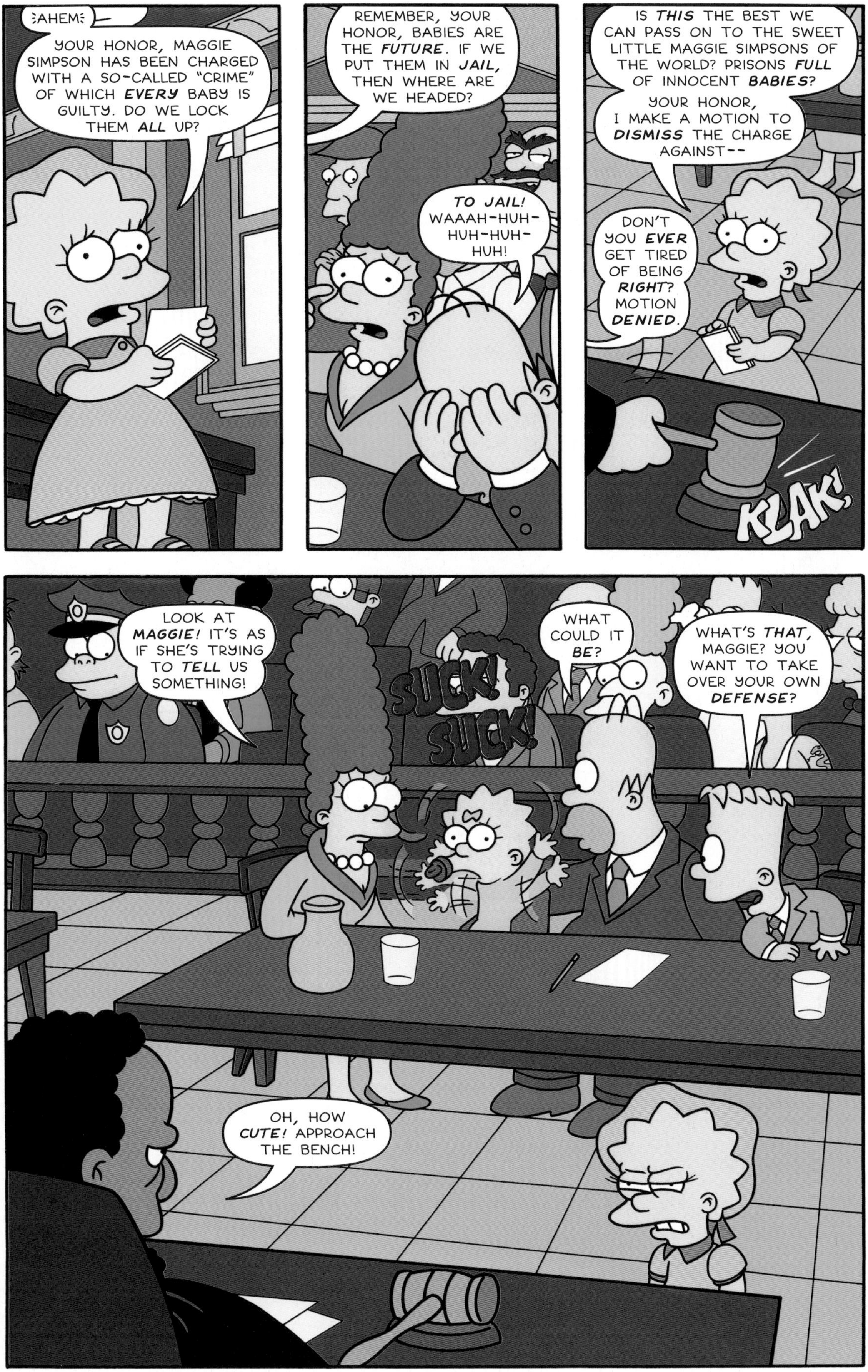
AHEM
YOUR HONOR, MAGGIE SIMPSON HAS BEEN CHARGED WITH A SO-CALLED "CRIME" OF WHICH EVERY BABY IS GUILTY. DO WE LOCK THEM ALL UP?
REMEMBER, YOUR HONOR, BABIES ARE THE FUTURE. IF WE PUT THEM IN JAIL, THEN WHERE ARE WE HEADED?
TO JAIL! WAAAH-HUH-HUH-HUH-HUH!
IS THIS THE BEST WE CAN PASS ON TO THE SWEET LITTLE MAGGIE SIMPSONS OF THE WORLD? PRISONS FULL OF INNOCENT BABIES?
YOUR HONOR, I MAKE A MOTION TO DISMISS THE CHARGE AGAINST--
DON'T YOU EVER GET TIRED OF BEING RIGHT? MOTION DENIED.
KLAK!
LOOK AT MAGGIE! IT'S AS IF SHE'S TRYING TO TELL US SOMETHING!
SUCK! SUCK!
WHAT COULD IT BE?
WHAT'S THAT, MAGGIE? YOU WANT TO TAKE OVER YOUR OWN DEFENSE?
OH, HOW CUTE! APPROACH THE BENCH!

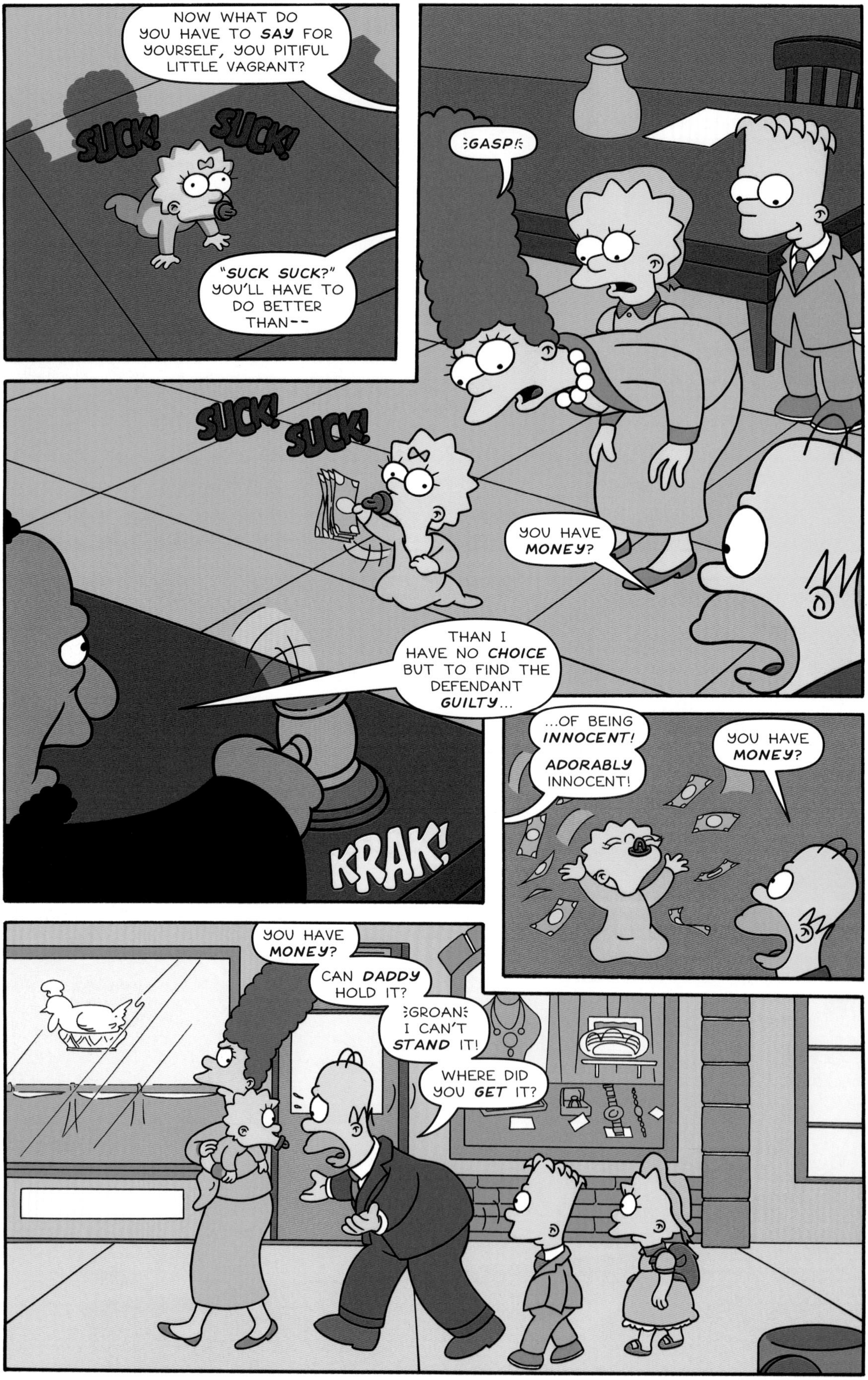

NOW WHAT DO YOU HAVE TO SAY FOR YOURSELF, YOU PITIFUL LITTLE VAGRANT?
SUCK! SUCK!
"SUCK SUCK?" YOU'LL HAVE TO DO BETTER THAN--
GASP!
SUCK! SUCK!
YOU HAVE MONEY?
THAN I HAVE NO CHOICE BUT TO FIND THE DEFENDANT GUILTY...
KRAK!
...OF BEING INNOCENT!
ADORABLY INNOCENT!
YOU HAVE MONEY?
YOU HAVE MONEY?
CAN DADDY HOLD IT?
GROAN I CAN'T STAND IT!
WHERE DID YOU GET IT?

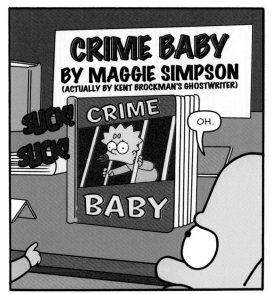

CRIME BABY
BY MAGGIE SIMPSON
(ACTUALLY BY KENT BROCKMAN'S GHOSTWRITER)

CRIME BABY

SUCK SUCK

OH.

BUT WHEN DID MAGGIE HAVE TIME TO GET INVOLVED WITH THIS BOOK WITHOUT OUR KNOWLEDGE?

I'LL *BET* IT HAPPENED THE DAY *YOUR FATHER* WATCHED HER.

WHA--?! OH, *THAT'S* WHY OPRAH WAS THERE!

CHAMBER OF ART

$124,999.99

LOOK! SHE WANTS THE *CALDER!*

THE *WHAT,* NOW?

IT'S A TYPE OF KINETIC SCULPTURE INVENTED BY *ALEXANDER CALDER,* IN WHICH DELICATELY BALANCED PARTS CAPABLE OF MOTION ARE SUSPENDED *FREELY* IN *SPACE!*

LIKE THE ONE OVER HER *CRIB...* BUT *NICER!*

BUT MAAA-ARGE! I HAD *PLANS* FOR THAT $125,000!

NO YOU *DIDN'T!* YOU DIDN'T EVEN *KNOW* ABOUT IT!

WELL, I *WOULD* HAVE IF I *DID!*

BUT YOU *DIDN'T!*

BUT IT WOULD MAKE ME FEEL SO MUCH BETTER AFTER MY *ORDEAL!*

MAGGIE'S THE ONE WHO HAD THE ORDEAL!

BUT MAAA-ARGE!

GO TO *SLEEP,* HOMIE!

THE END

BART SIMPSON in WINDOW OF OPPORTUNITY

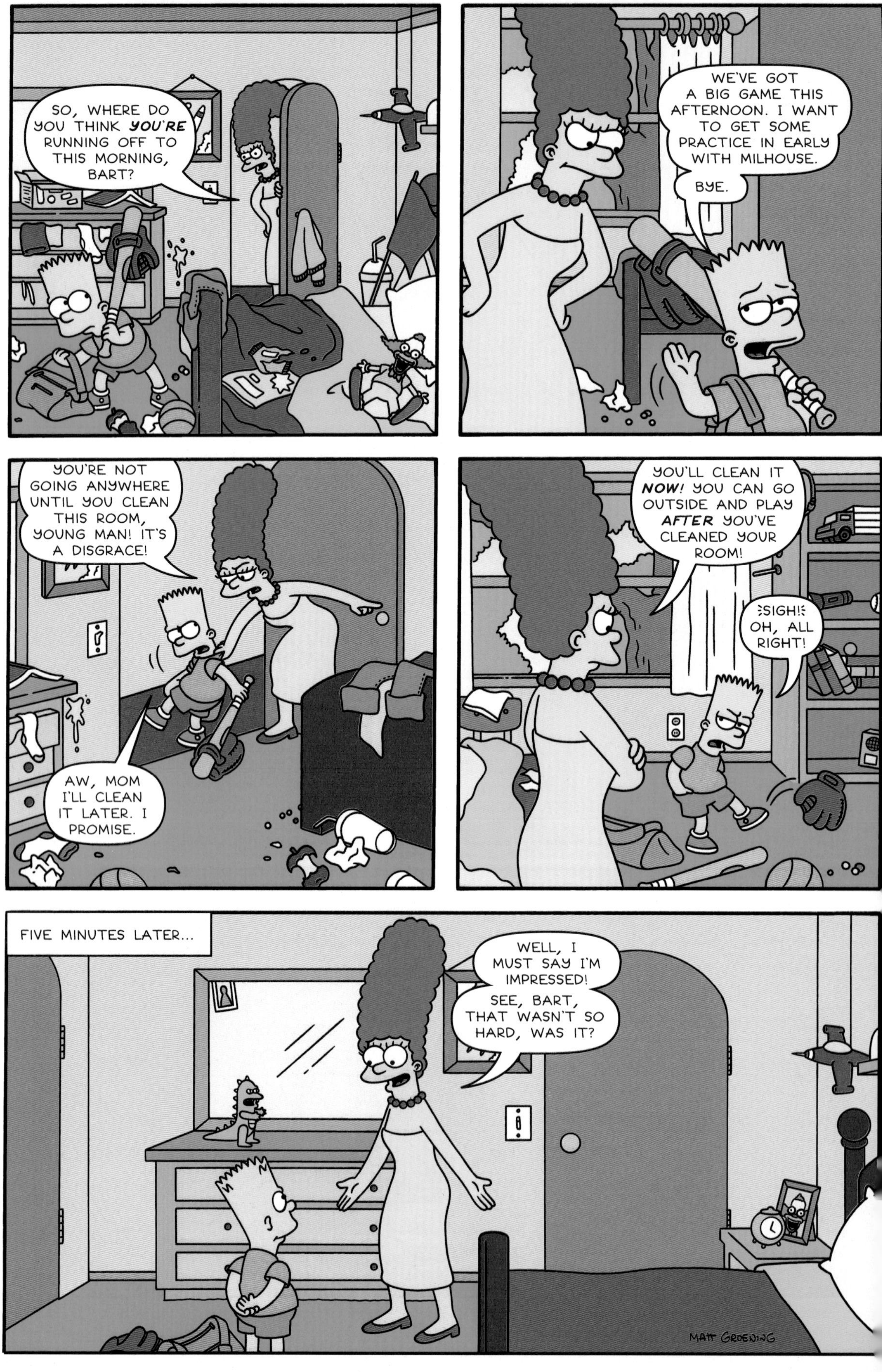

SO, WHERE DO YOU THINK YOU'RE RUNNING OFF TO THIS MORNING, BART?
WE'VE GOT A BIG GAME THIS AFTERNOON. I WANT TO GET SOME PRACTICE IN EARLY WITH MILHOUSE.
BYE.
YOU'RE NOT GOING ANYWHERE UNTIL YOU CLEAN THIS ROOM, YOUNG MAN! IT'S A DISGRACE!
AW, MOM I'LL CLEAN IT LATER. I PROMISE.
YOU'LL CLEAN IT NOW! YOU CAN GO OUTSIDE AND PLAY AFTER YOU'VE CLEANED YOUR ROOM!
SIGH! OH, ALL RIGHT!
FIVE MINUTES LATER...
WELL, I MUST SAY I'M IMPRESSED!
SEE, BART, THAT WASN'T SO HARD, WAS IT?
MATT GROENING

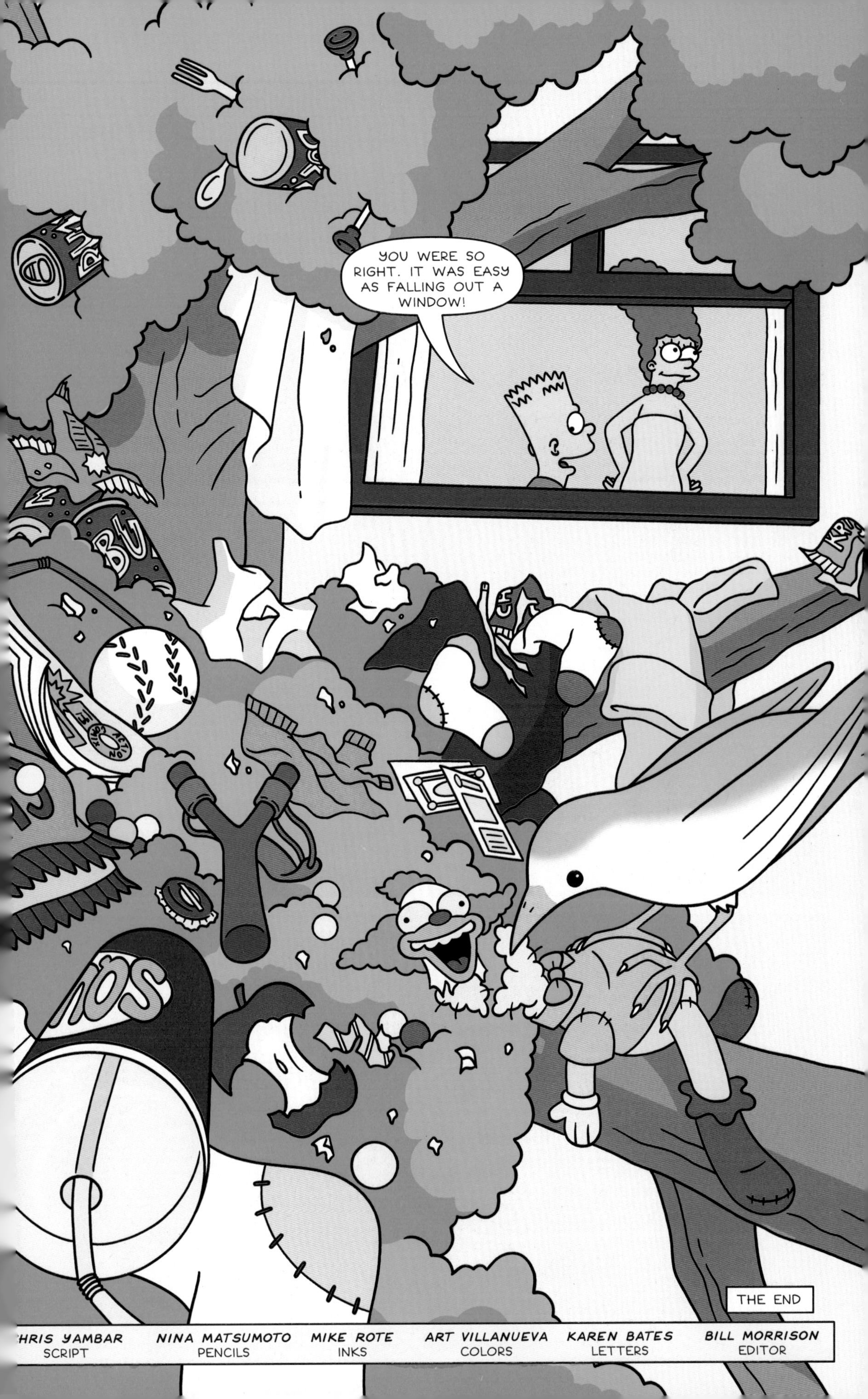
YOU WERE SO RIGHT. IT WAS EASY AS FALLING OUT A WINDOW!
THE END

CHRIS YAMBAR SCRIPT · NINA MATSUMOTO PENCILS · MIKE ROTE INKS · ART VILLANUEVA COLORS · KAREN BATES LETTERS · BILL MORRISON EDITOR

Li'L KRUSTY

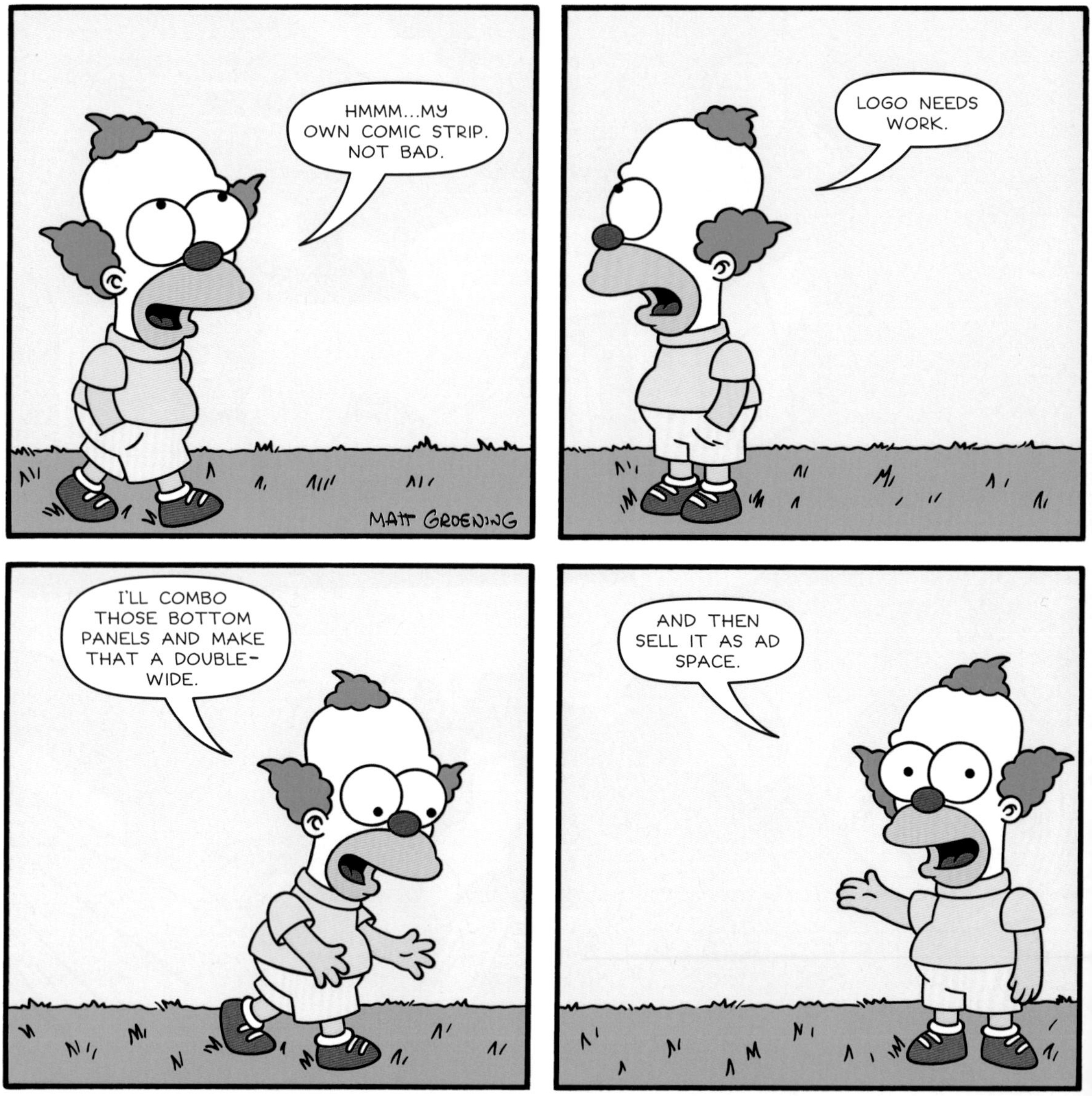
HMMM...MY OWN COMIC STRIP. NOT BAD.
MATT GROENING
LOGO NEEDS WORK.
I'LL COMBO THOSE BOTTOM PANELS AND MAKE THAT A DOUBLE-WIDE.
AND THEN SELL IT AS AD SPACE.

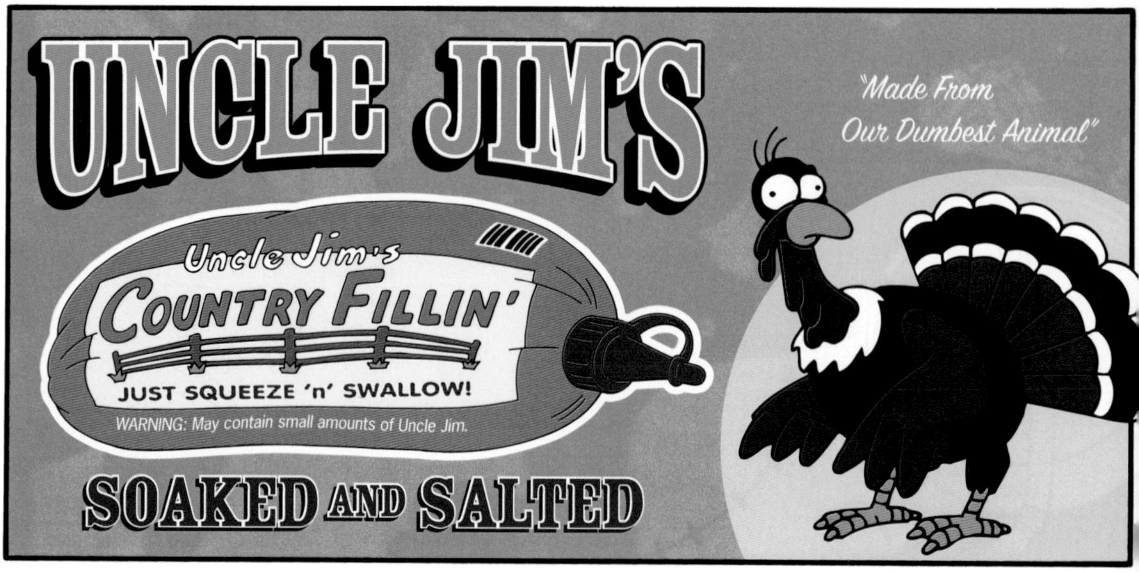
UNCLE JIM'S
"Made From Our Dumbest Animal"
Uncle Jim's
COUNTRY FILLIN'
JUST SQUEEZE 'n' SWALLOW!
WARNING: May contain small amounts of Uncle Jim.
SOAKED AND SALTED

BART SIMPSON in EASY WRITER

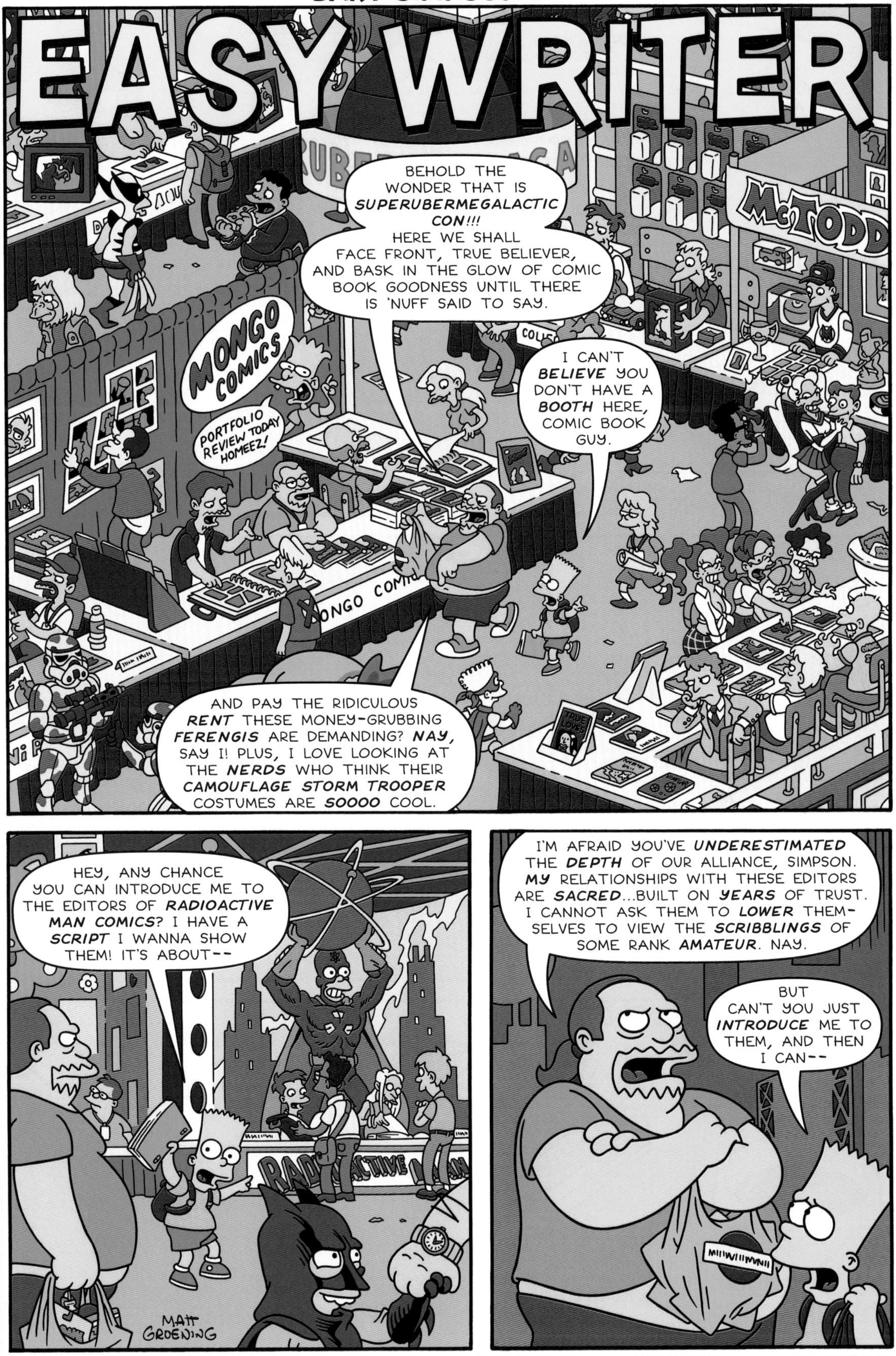

BEHOLD THE WONDER THAT IS SUPERUBERMEGALACTIC CON!!! HERE WE SHALL FACE FRONT, TRUE BELIEVER, AND BASK IN THE GLOW OF COMIC BOOK GOODNESS UNTIL THERE IS 'NUFF SAID TO SAY.
MONGO COMICS
PORTFOLIO REVIEW TODAY HOMEEZ!
McTODD
I CAN'T BELIEVE YOU DON'T HAVE A BOOTH HERE, COMIC BOOK GUY.
AND PAY THE RIDICULOUS RENT THESE MONEY-GRUBBING FERENGIS ARE DEMANDING? NAY, SAY I! PLUS, I LOVE LOOKING AT THE NERDS WHO THINK THEIR CAMOUFLAGE STORM TROOPER COSTUMES ARE SOOOO COOL.
HEY, ANY CHANCE YOU CAN INTRODUCE ME TO THE EDITORS OF RADIOACTIVE MAN COMICS? I HAVE A SCRIPT I WANNA SHOW THEM! IT'S ABOUT--
RADIOACTIVE MAN
MATT GROENING
I'M AFRAID YOU'VE UNDERESTIMATED THE DEPTH OF OUR ALLIANCE, SIMPSON. MY RELATIONSHIPS WITH THESE EDITORS ARE SACRED...BUILT ON YEARS OF TRUST. I CANNOT ASK THEM TO LOWER THEMSELVES TO VIEW THE SCRIBBLINGS OF SOME RANK AMATEUR. NAY.
BUT CAN'T YOU JUST INTRODUCE ME TO THEM, AND THEN I CAN--

TOM BELAND SCRIPT | *JAMES LLOYD* PENCILS | *STEVE STEERE, JR.* INKS | *NATHAN HAMILL* COLORS | *KAREN BATES* LETTERS | *BILL MORRISON* EDITOR

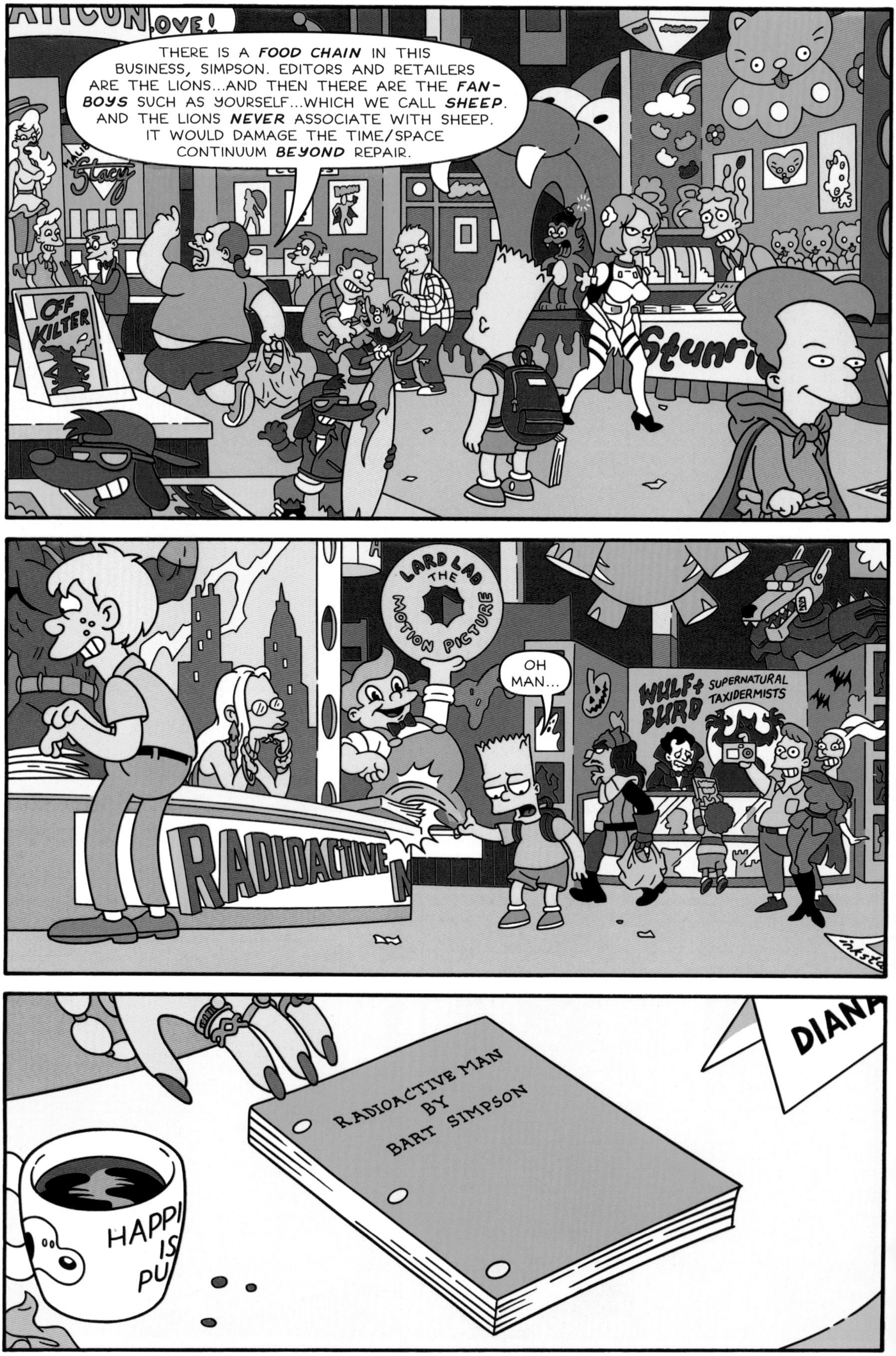
THERE IS A FOOD CHAIN IN THIS BUSINESS, SIMPSON. EDITORS AND RETAILERS ARE THE LIONS...AND THEN THERE ARE THE FAN-BOYS SUCH AS YOURSELF...WHICH WE CALL SHEEP. AND THE LIONS NEVER ASSOCIATE WITH SHEEP. IT WOULD DAMAGE THE TIME/SPACE CONTINUUM BEYOND REPAIR.
Stacy
OFF KILTER
Stunri
LARD LAD THE MOTION PICTURE
RADIOACTIVE
OH MAN...
WULF & BURD
SUPERNATURAL TAXIDERMISTS
DIANA
RADIOACTIVE MAN BY BART SIMPSON
HAPPI
IS
PU

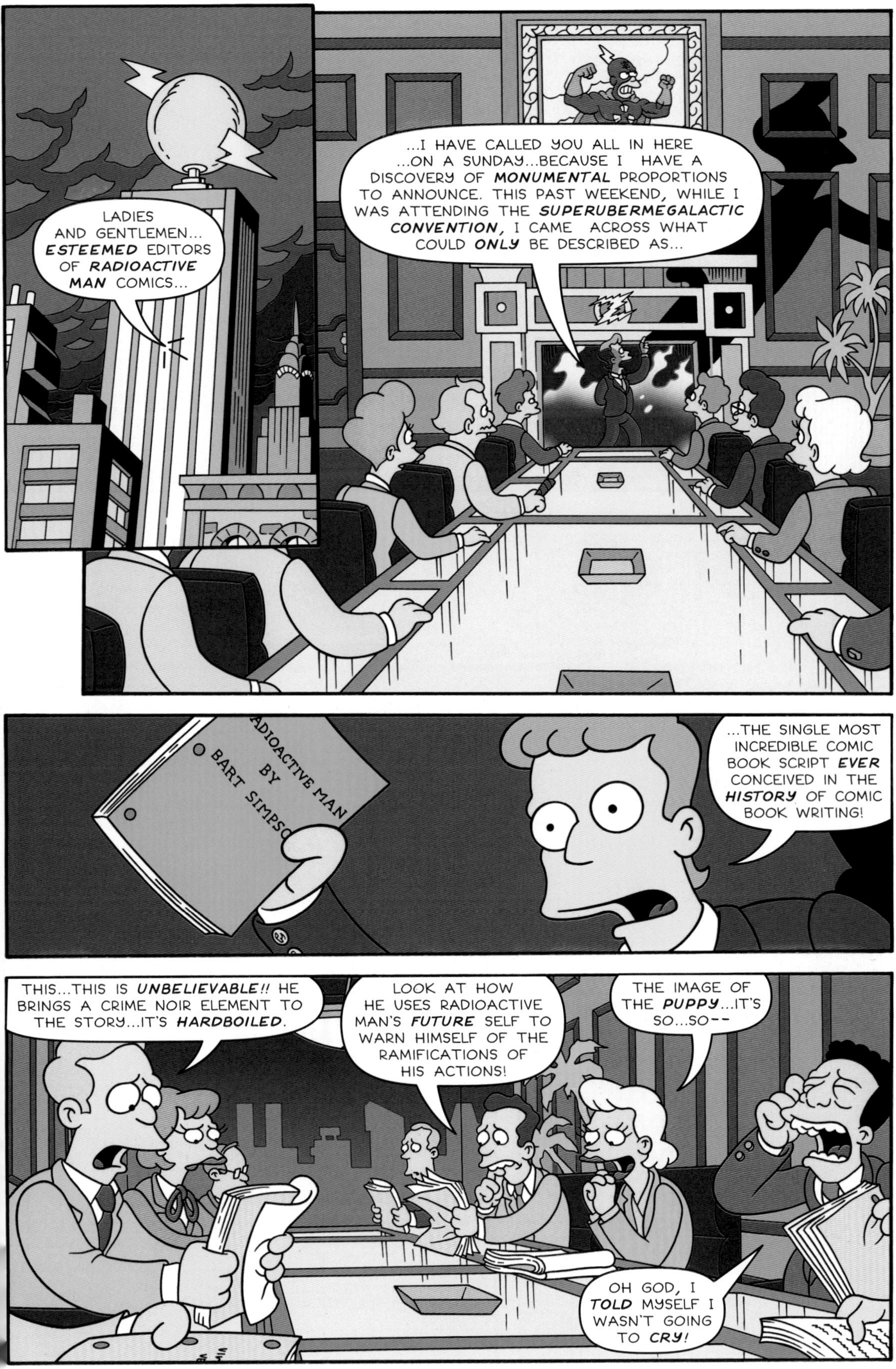
LADIES AND GENTLEMEN... ESTEEMED EDITORS OF RADIOACTIVE MAN COMICS...
...I HAVE CALLED YOU ALL IN HERE ...ON A SUNDAY...BECAUSE I HAVE A DISCOVERY OF MONUMENTAL PROPORTIONS TO ANNOUNCE. THIS PAST WEEKEND, WHILE I WAS ATTENDING THE SUPERUBERMEGALACTIC CONVENTION, I CAME ACROSS WHAT COULD ONLY BE DESCRIBED AS...
RADIOACTIVE MAN BY BART SIMPSO
...THE SINGLE MOST INCREDIBLE COMIC BOOK SCRIPT EVER CONCEIVED IN THE HISTORY OF COMIC BOOK WRITING!
THIS...THIS IS UNBELIEVABLE!! HE BRINGS A CRIME NOIR ELEMENT TO THE STORY...IT'S HARDBOILED.
LOOK AT HOW HE USES RADIOACTIVE MAN'S FUTURE SELF TO WARN HIMSELF OF THE RAMIFICATIONS OF HIS ACTIONS!
THE IMAGE OF THE PUPPY...IT'S SO...SO--
OH GOD, I TOLD MYSELF I WASN'T GOING TO CRY!

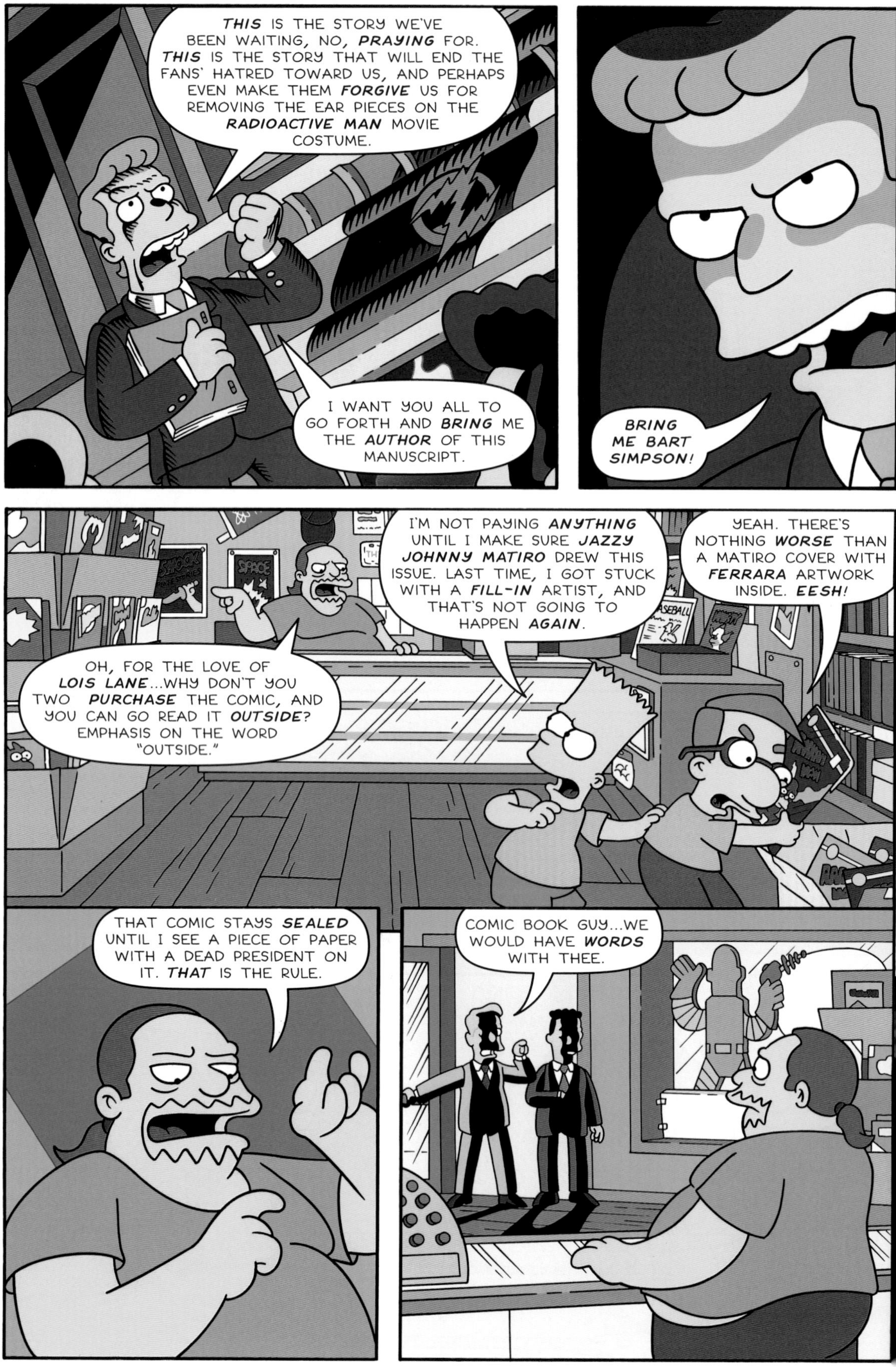
THIS IS THE STORY WE'VE BEEN WAITING, NO, PRAYING FOR. THIS IS THE STORY THAT WILL END THE FANS' HATRED TOWARD US, AND PERHAPS EVEN MAKE THEM FORGIVE US FOR REMOVING THE EAR PIECES ON THE RADIOACTIVE MAN MOVIE COSTUME.
I WANT YOU ALL TO GO FORTH AND BRING ME THE AUTHOR OF THIS MANUSCRIPT.
BRING ME BART SIMPSON!
I'M NOT PAYING ANYTHING UNTIL I MAKE SURE JAZZY JOHNNY MATIRO DREW THIS ISSUE. LAST TIME, I GOT STUCK WITH A FILL-IN ARTIST, AND THAT'S NOT GOING TO HAPPEN AGAIN.
YEAH. THERE'S NOTHING WORSE THAN A MATIRO COVER WITH FERRARA ARTWORK INSIDE. EESH!
OH, FOR THE LOVE OF LOIS LANE...WHY DON'T YOU TWO PURCHASE THE COMIC, AND YOU CAN GO READ IT OUTSIDE? EMPHASIS ON THE WORD "OUTSIDE."
THAT COMIC STAYS SEALED UNTIL I SEE A PIECE OF PAPER WITH A DEAD PRESIDENT ON IT. THAT IS THE RULE.
COMIC BOOK GUY...WE WOULD HAVE WORDS WITH THEE.

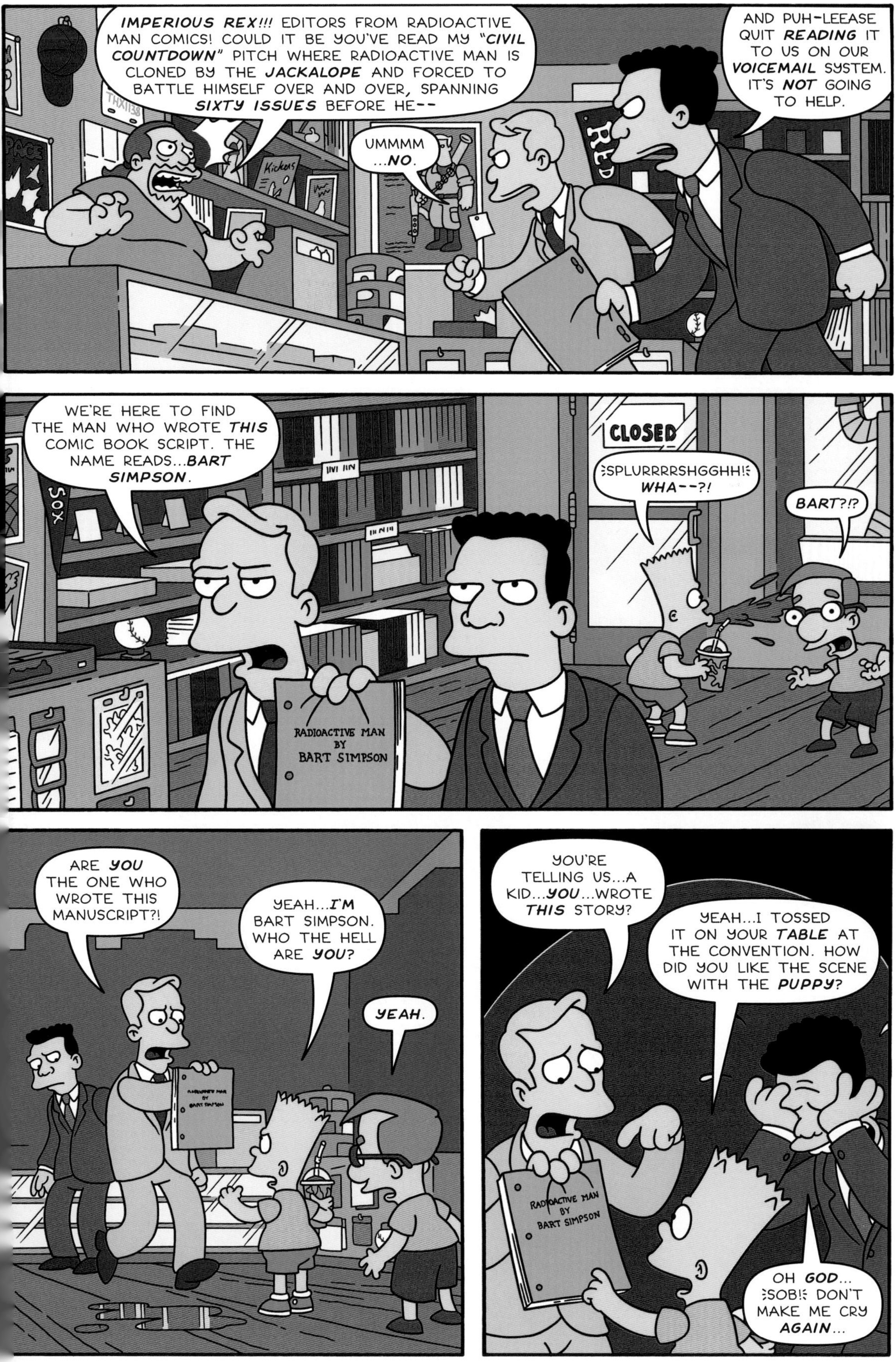
IMPERIOUS REX!!! EDITORS FROM RADIOACTIVE MAN COMICS! COULD IT BE YOU'VE READ MY "CIVIL COUNTDOWN" PITCH WHERE RADIOACTIVE MAN IS CLONED BY THE JACKALOPE AND FORCED TO BATTLE HIMSELF OVER AND OVER, SPANNING SIXTY ISSUES BEFORE HE--
UMMMM ...NO.
AND PUH-LEEASE QUIT READING IT TO US ON OUR VOICEMAIL SYSTEM. IT'S NOT GOING TO HELP.
WE'RE HERE TO FIND THE MAN WHO WROTE THIS COMIC BOOK SCRIPT. THE NAME READS...BART SIMPSON.
CLOSED
SPLURRRRSHGGHH! WHA--?!
BART?!?
RADIOACTIVE MAN BY BART SIMPSON
ARE YOU THE ONE WHO WROTE THIS MANUSCRIPT?!
YEAH...I'M BART SIMPSON. WHO THE HELL ARE YOU?
YEAH.
YOU'RE TELLING US...A KID...YOU...WROTE THIS STORY?
YEAH...I TOSSED IT ON YOUR TABLE AT THE CONVENTION. HOW DID YOU LIKE THE SCENE WITH THE PUPPY?
RADIOACTIVE MAN BY BART SIMPSON
OH GOD... SOB! DON'T MAKE ME CRY AGAIN...

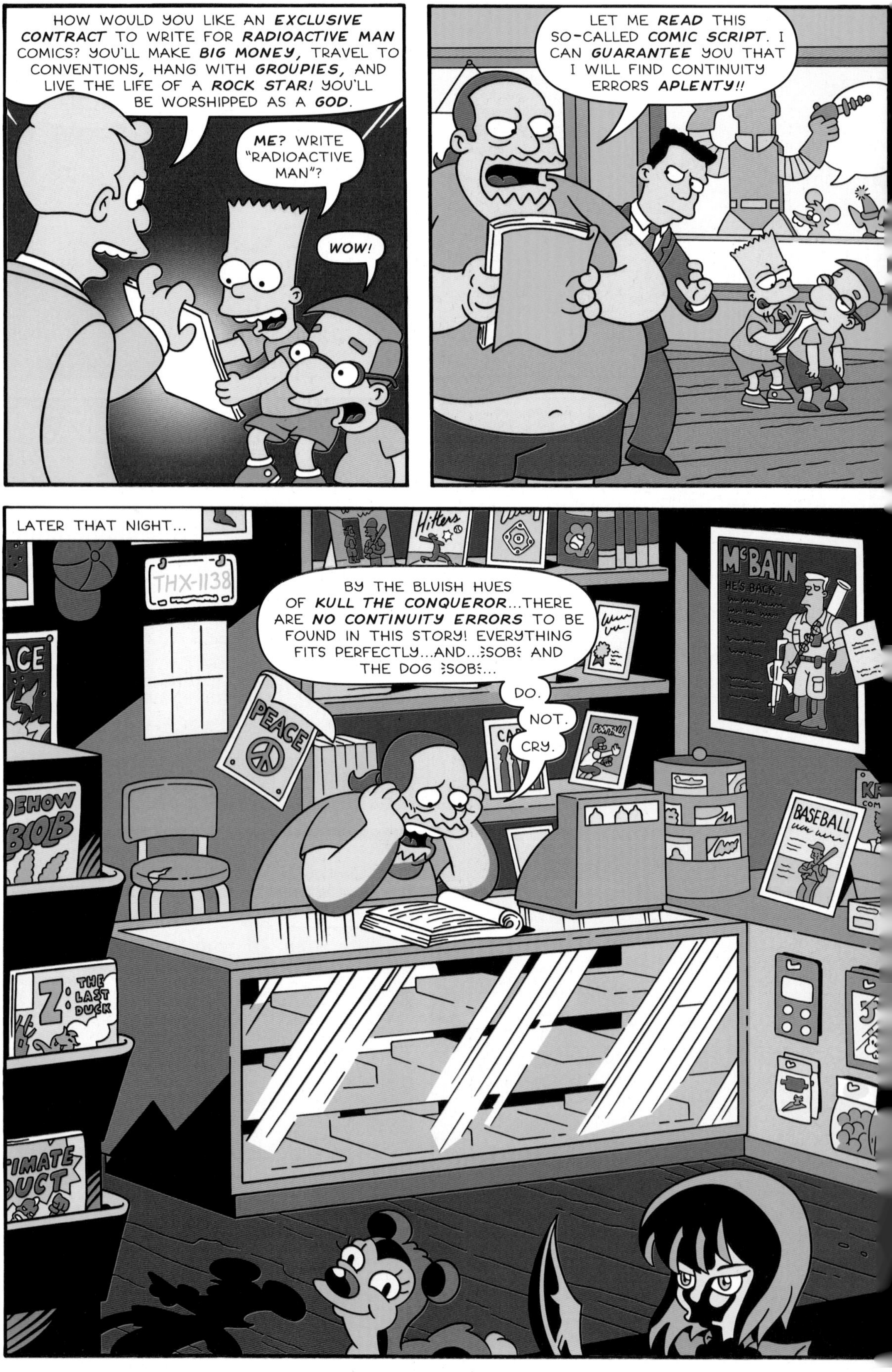
HOW WOULD YOU LIKE AN *EXCLUSIVE CONTRACT* TO WRITE FOR *RADIOACTIVE MAN* COMICS? YOU'LL MAKE *BIG MONEY*, TRAVEL TO CONVENTIONS, HANG WITH *GROUPIES*, AND LIVE THE LIFE OF A *ROCK STAR*! YOU'LL BE WORSHIPPED AS A *GOD*.
ME? WRITE "RADIOACTIVE MAN"?
WOW!
LET ME *READ* THIS SO-CALLED *COMIC SCRIPT*. I CAN *GUARANTEE* YOU THAT I WILL FIND CONTINUITY ERRORS *APLENTY*!!
LATER THAT NIGHT...
THX-1138
BY THE BLUISH HUES OF *KULL THE CONQUEROR*...THERE ARE *NO CONTINUITY ERRORS* TO BE FOUND IN THIS STORY! EVERYTHING FITS PERFECTLY...AND...SOB AND THE DOG SOB...
DO.
NOT.
CRY.
PEACE
McBAIN
HE'S BACK
BASEBALL
Z: THE LAST DUCK

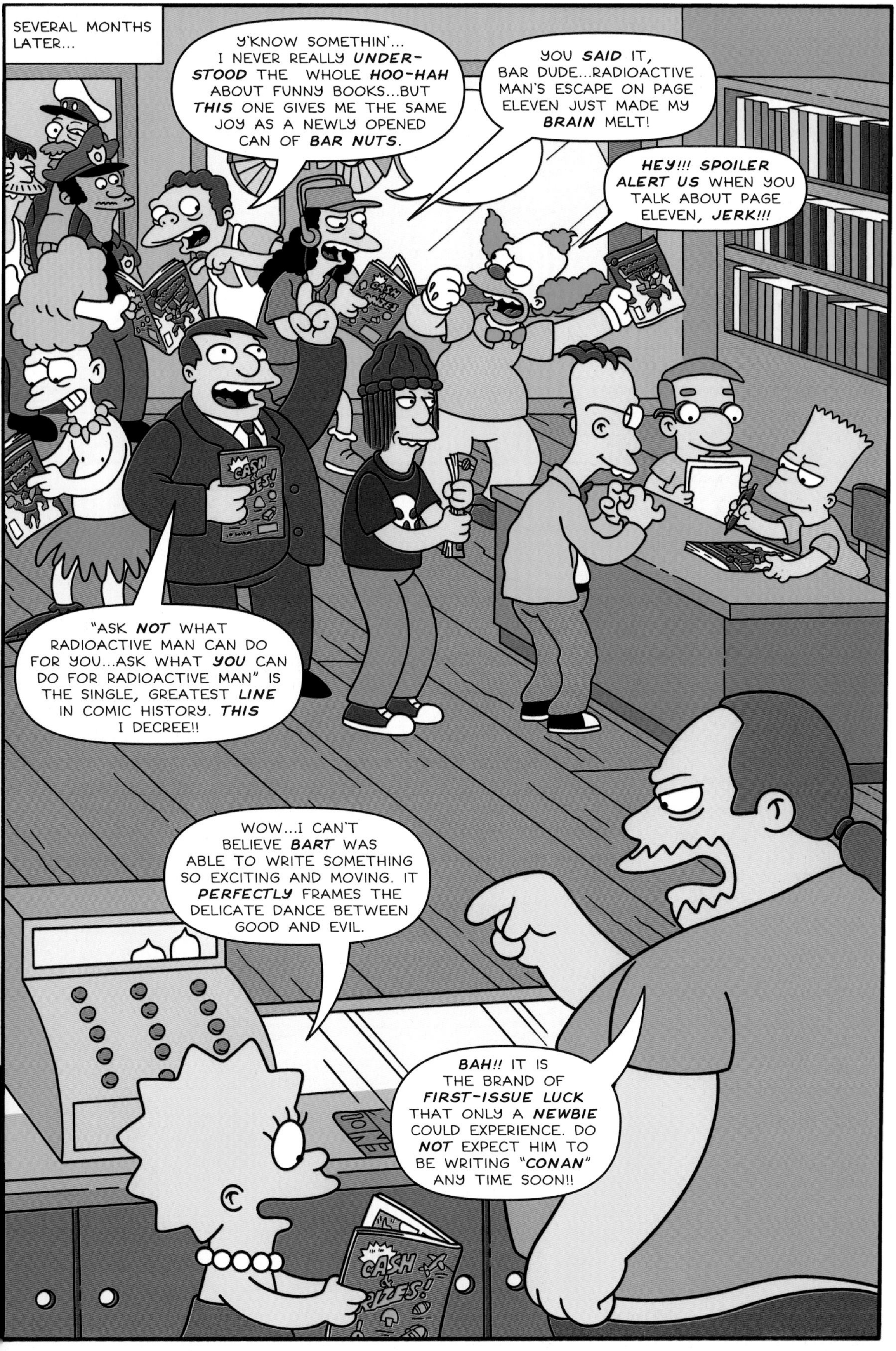
SEVERAL MONTHS LATER...
Y'KNOW SOMETHIN'... I NEVER REALLY UNDER-STOOD THE WHOLE HOO-HAH ABOUT FUNNY BOOKS...BUT THIS ONE GIVES ME THE SAME JOY AS A NEWLY OPENED CAN OF BAR NUTS.
YOU SAID IT, BAR DUDE...RADIOACTIVE MAN'S ESCAPE ON PAGE ELEVEN JUST MADE MY BRAIN MELT!
HEY!!! SPOILER ALERT US WHEN YOU TALK ABOUT PAGE ELEVEN, JERK!!!
"ASK NOT WHAT RADIOACTIVE MAN CAN DO FOR YOU...ASK WHAT YOU CAN DO FOR RADIOACTIVE MAN" IS THE SINGLE, GREATEST LINE IN COMIC HISTORY. THIS I DECREE!!
WOW...I CAN'T BELIEVE BART WAS ABLE TO WRITE SOMETHING SO EXCITING AND MOVING. IT PERFECTLY FRAMES THE DELICATE DANCE BETWEEN GOOD AND EVIL.
BAH!! IT IS THE BRAND OF FIRST-ISSUE LUCK THAT ONLY A NEWBIE COULD EXPERIENCE. DO NOT EXPECT HIM TO BE WRITING "CONAN" ANY TIME SOON!!

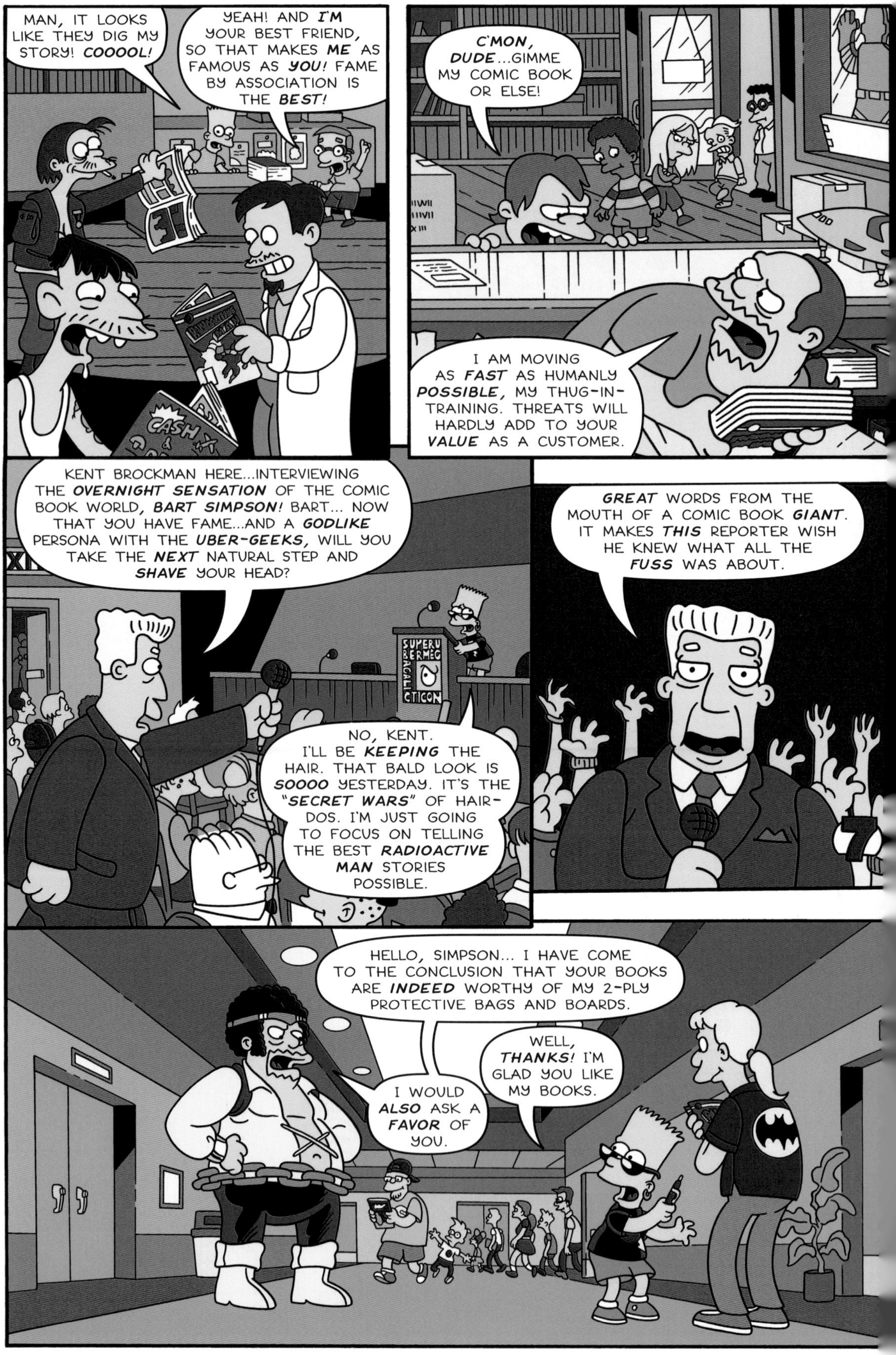
MAN, IT LOOKS LIKE THEY DIG MY STORY! COOOOL!
YEAH! AND I'M YOUR BEST FRIEND, SO THAT MAKES ME AS FAMOUS AS YOU! FAME BY ASSOCIATION IS THE BEST!
C'MON, DUDE...GIMME MY COMIC BOOK OR ELSE!
I AM MOVING AS FAST AS HUMANLY POSSIBLE, MY THUG-IN-TRAINING. THREATS WILL HARDLY ADD TO YOUR VALUE AS A CUSTOMER.
KENT BROCKMAN HERE...INTERVIEWING THE OVERNIGHT SENSATION OF THE COMIC BOOK WORLD, BART SIMPSON! BART... NOW THAT YOU HAVE FAME...AND A GODLIKE PERSONA WITH THE UBER-GEEKS, WILL YOU TAKE THE NEXT NATURAL STEP AND SHAVE YOUR HEAD?
NO, KENT. I'LL BE KEEPING THE HAIR. THAT BALD LOOK IS SOOOO YESTERDAY. IT'S THE "SECRET WARS" OF HAIR-DOS. I'M JUST GOING TO FOCUS ON TELLING THE BEST RADIOACTIVE MAN STORIES POSSIBLE.
GREAT WORDS FROM THE MOUTH OF A COMIC BOOK GIANT. IT MAKES THIS REPORTER WISH HE KNEW WHAT ALL THE FUSS WAS ABOUT.
HELLO, SIMPSON... I HAVE COME TO THE CONCLUSION THAT YOUR BOOKS ARE INDEED WORTHY OF MY 2-PLY PROTECTIVE BAGS AND BOARDS.
I WOULD ALSO ASK A FAVOR OF YOU.
WELL, THANKS! I'M GLAD YOU LIKE MY BOOKS.

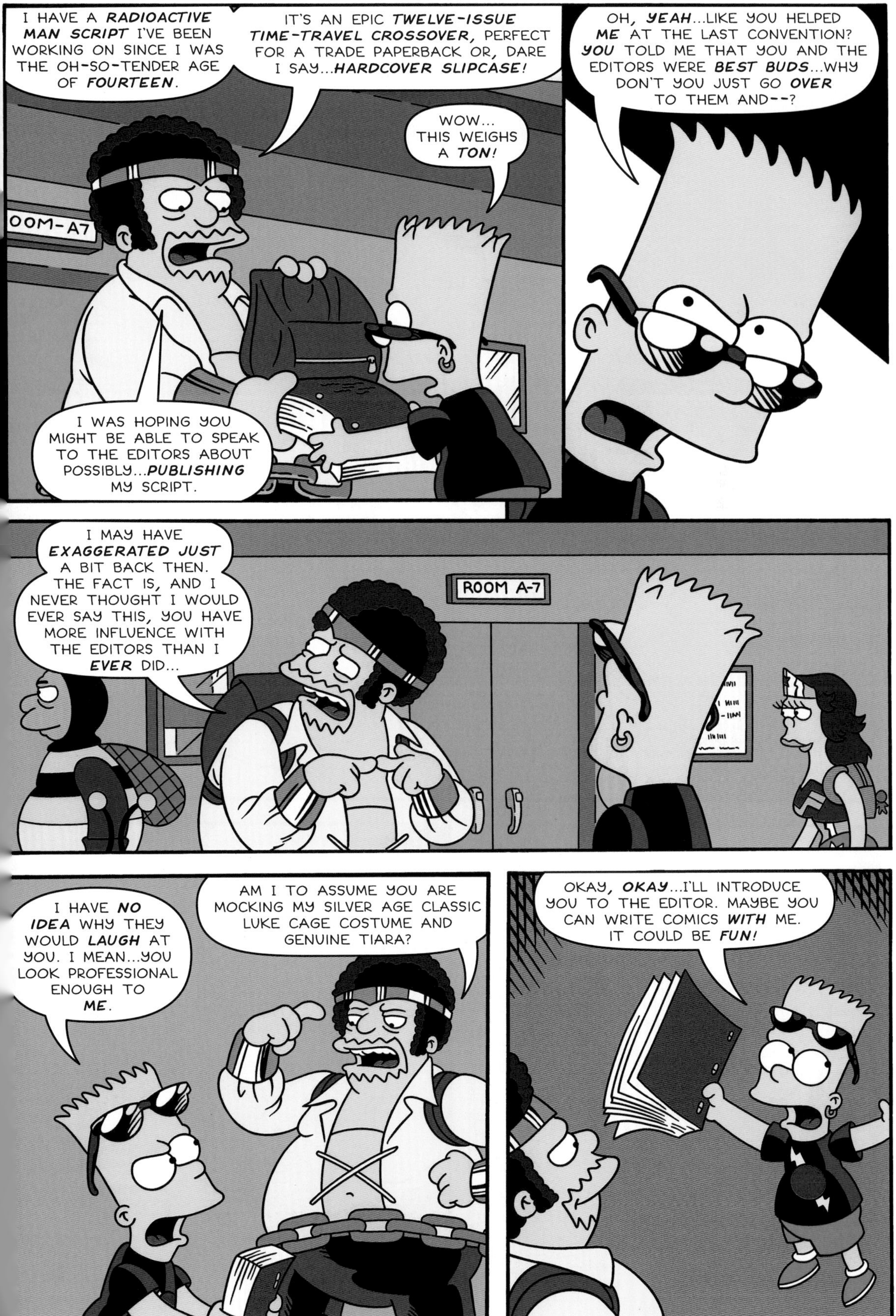
I HAVE A RADIOACTIVE MAN SCRIPT I'VE BEEN WORKING ON SINCE I WAS THE OH-SO-TENDER AGE OF FOURTEEN.
IT'S AN EPIC TWELVE-ISSUE TIME-TRAVEL CROSSOVER, PERFECT FOR A TRADE PAPERBACK OR, DARE I SAY...HARDCOVER SLIPCASE!
WOW... THIS WEIGHS A TON!
OOM-A7
I WAS HOPING YOU MIGHT BE ABLE TO SPEAK TO THE EDITORS ABOUT POSSIBLY...PUBLISHING MY SCRIPT.
OH, YEAH...LIKE YOU HELPED ME AT THE LAST CONVENTION? YOU TOLD ME THAT YOU AND THE EDITORS WERE BEST BUDS...WHY DON'T YOU JUST GO OVER TO THEM AND--?
I MAY HAVE EXAGGERATED JUST A BIT BACK THEN. THE FACT IS, AND I NEVER THOUGHT I WOULD EVER SAY THIS, YOU HAVE MORE INFLUENCE WITH THE EDITORS THAN I EVER DID...
ROOM A-7
I HAVE NO IDEA WHY THEY WOULD LAUGH AT YOU. I MEAN...YOU LOOK PROFESSIONAL ENOUGH TO ME.
AM I TO ASSUME YOU ARE MOCKING MY SILVER AGE CLASSIC LUKE CAGE COSTUME AND GENUINE TIARA?
OKAY, OKAY...I'LL INTRODUCE YOU TO THE EDITOR. MAYBE YOU CAN WRITE COMICS WITH ME. IT COULD BE FUN!

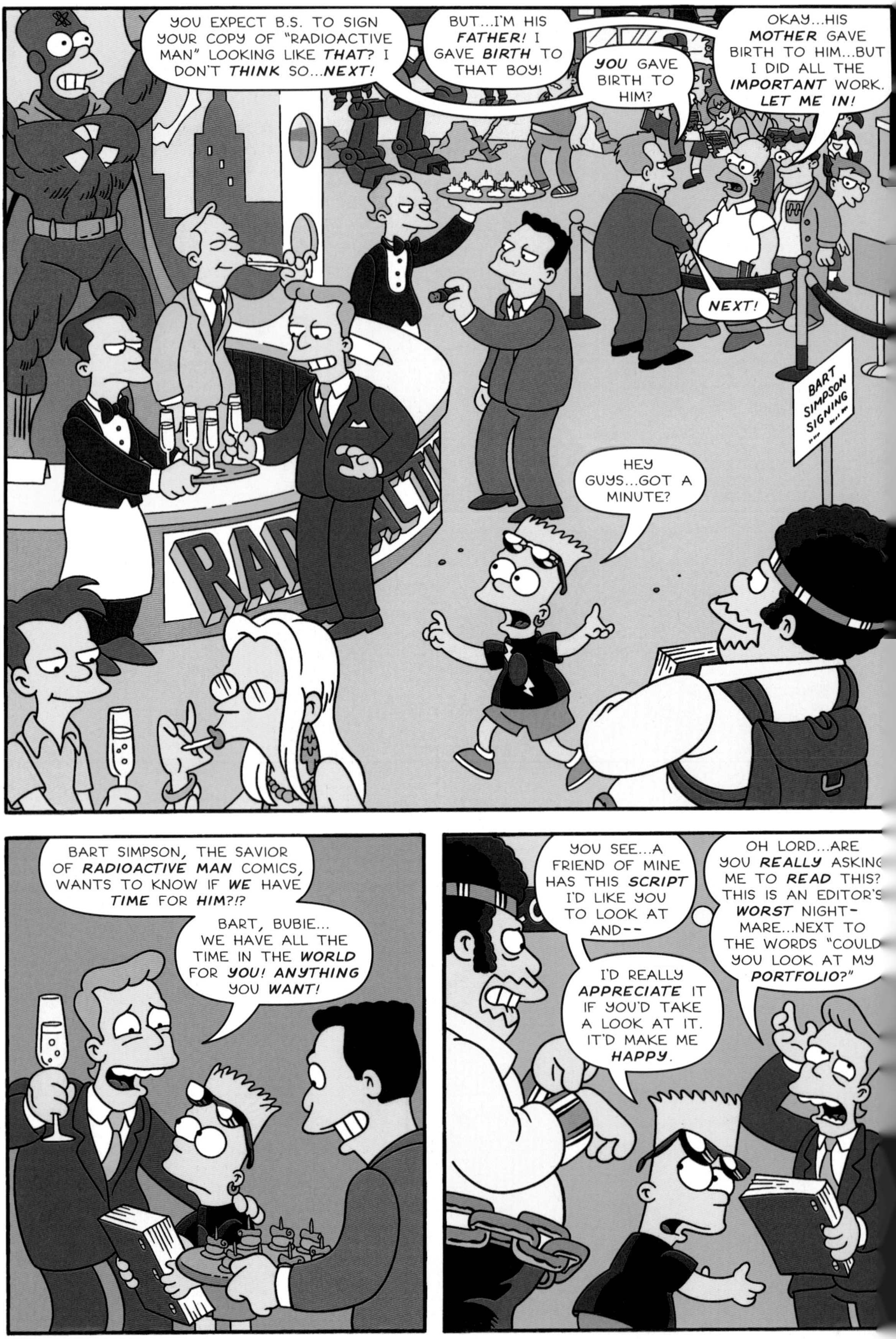
YOU EXPECT B.S. TO SIGN YOUR COPY OF "RADIOACTIVE MAN" LOOKING LIKE THAT? I DON'T THINK SO...NEXT!
BUT...I'M HIS FATHER! I GAVE BIRTH TO THAT BOY!
YOU GAVE BIRTH TO HIM?
OKAY...HIS MOTHER GAVE BIRTH TO HIM...BUT I DID ALL THE IMPORTANT WORK. LET ME IN!
NEXT!
BART SIMPSON SIGNING
HEY GUYS...GOT A MINUTE?
RAD
BART SIMPSON, THE SAVIOR OF RADIOACTIVE MAN COMICS, WANTS TO KNOW IF WE HAVE TIME FOR HIM?!?
BART, BUBIE... WE HAVE ALL THE TIME IN THE WORLD FOR YOU! ANYTHING YOU WANT!
YOU SEE...A FRIEND OF MINE HAS THIS SCRIPT I'D LIKE YOU TO LOOK AT AND--
I'D REALLY APPRECIATE IT IF YOU'D TAKE A LOOK AT IT. IT'D MAKE ME HAPPY.
OH LORD...ARE YOU REALLY ASKING ME TO READ THIS? THIS IS AN EDITOR'S WORST NIGHT-MARE...NEXT TO THE WORDS "COULD YOU LOOK AT MY PORTFOLIO?"

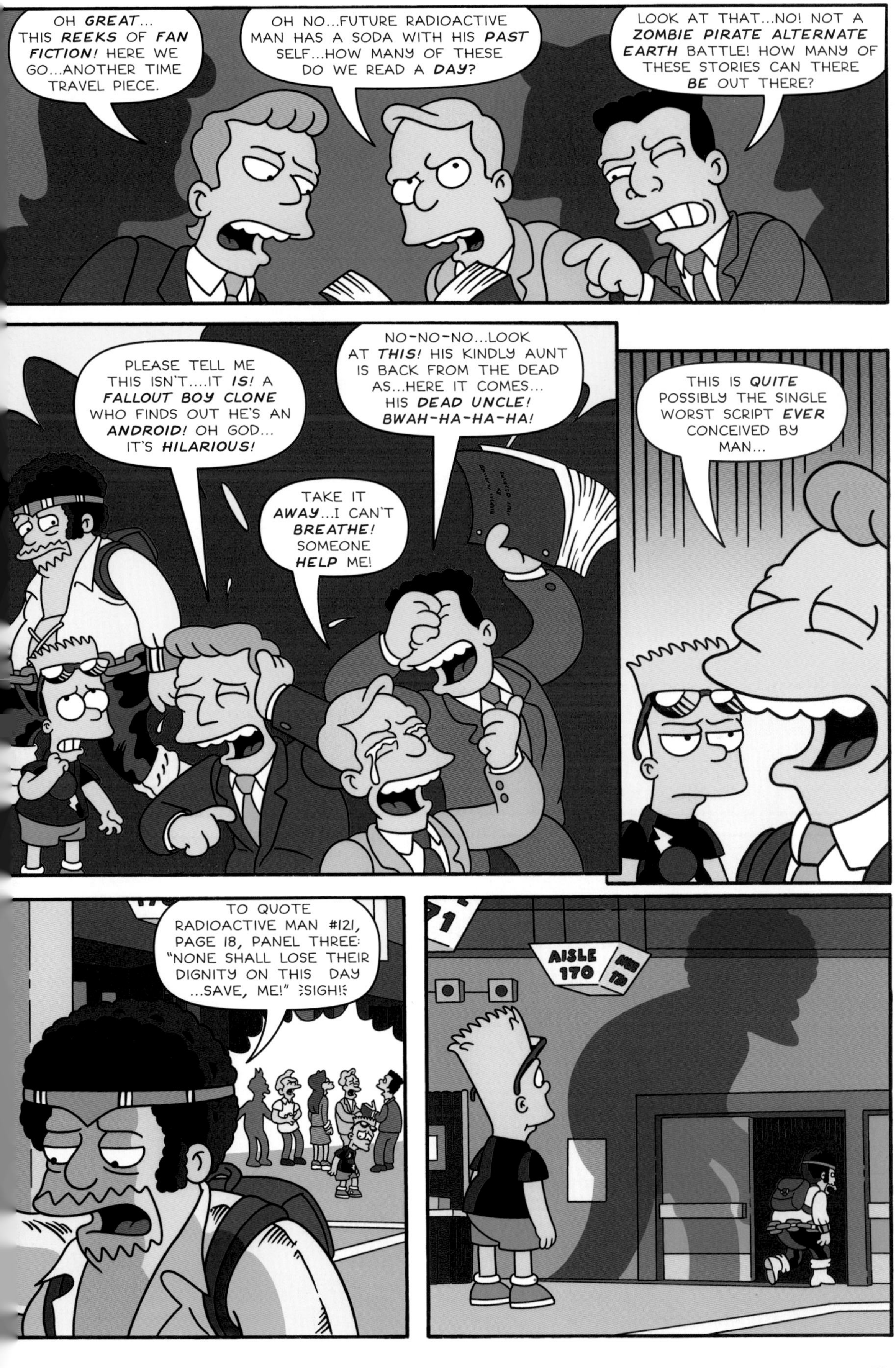
OH GREAT... THIS REEKS OF FAN FICTION! HERE WE GO...ANOTHER TIME TRAVEL PIECE.
OH NO...FUTURE RADIOACTIVE MAN HAS A SODA WITH HIS PAST SELF...HOW MANY OF THESE DO WE READ A DAY?
LOOK AT THAT...NO! NOT A ZOMBIE PIRATE ALTERNATE EARTH BATTLE! HOW MANY OF THESE STORIES CAN THERE BE OUT THERE?
PLEASE TELL ME THIS ISN'T....IT IS! A FALLOUT BOY CLONE WHO FINDS OUT HE'S AN ANDROID! OH GOD... IT'S HILARIOUS!
NO-NO-NO...LOOK AT THIS! HIS KINDLY AUNT IS BACK FROM THE DEAD AS...HERE IT COMES... HIS DEAD UNCLE! BWAH-HA-HA-HA!
TAKE IT AWAY...I CAN'T BREATHE! SOMEONE HELP ME!
THIS IS QUITE POSSIBLY THE SINGLE WORST SCRIPT EVER CONCEIVED BY MAN...
TO QUOTE RADIOACTIVE MAN #121, PAGE 18, PANEL THREE: "NONE SHALL LOSE THEIR DIGNITY ON THIS DAY ...SAVE, ME!" SIGH!
AISLE 170

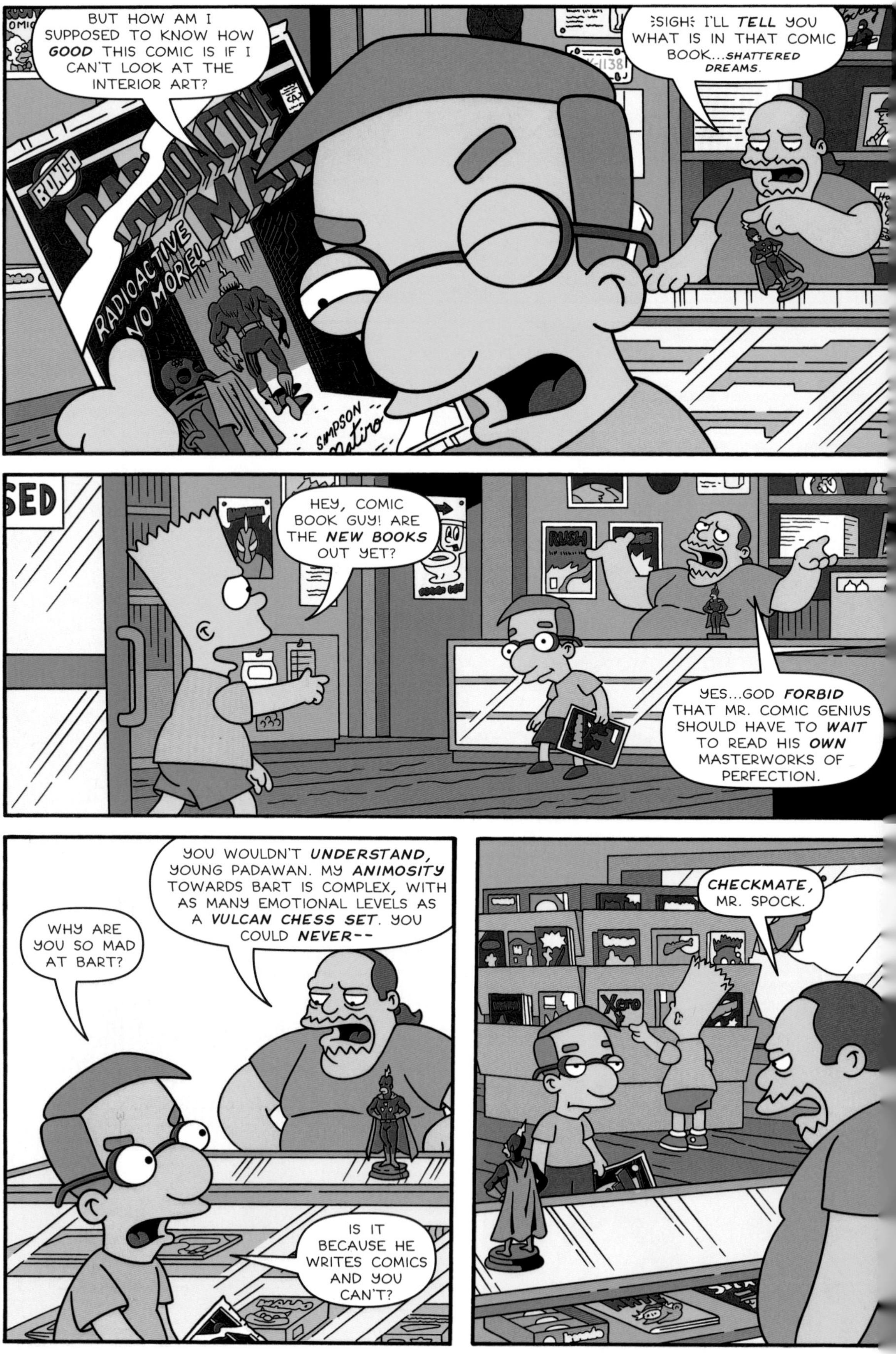
BUT HOW AM I SUPPOSED TO KNOW HOW GOOD THIS COMIC IS IF I CAN'T LOOK AT THE INTERIOR ART?
BONGO
RADIOACTIVE MAN
RADIOACTIVE NO MORE!
SIMPSON
:SIGH: I'LL TELL YOU WHAT IS IN THAT COMIC BOOK...SHATTERED DREAMS.
SED
HEY, COMIC BOOK GUY! ARE THE NEW BOOKS OUT YET?
RUSH
YES...GOD FORBID THAT MR. COMIC GENIUS SHOULD HAVE TO WAIT TO READ HIS OWN MASTERWORKS OF PERFECTION.
WHY ARE YOU SO MAD AT BART?
YOU WOULDN'T UNDERSTAND, YOUNG PADAWAN. MY ANIMOSITY TOWARDS BART IS COMPLEX, WITH AS MANY EMOTIONAL LEVELS AS A VULCAN CHESS SET. YOU COULD NEVER--
IS IT BECAUSE HE WRITES COMICS AND YOU CAN'T?
CHECKMATE, MR. SPOCK.
Xero

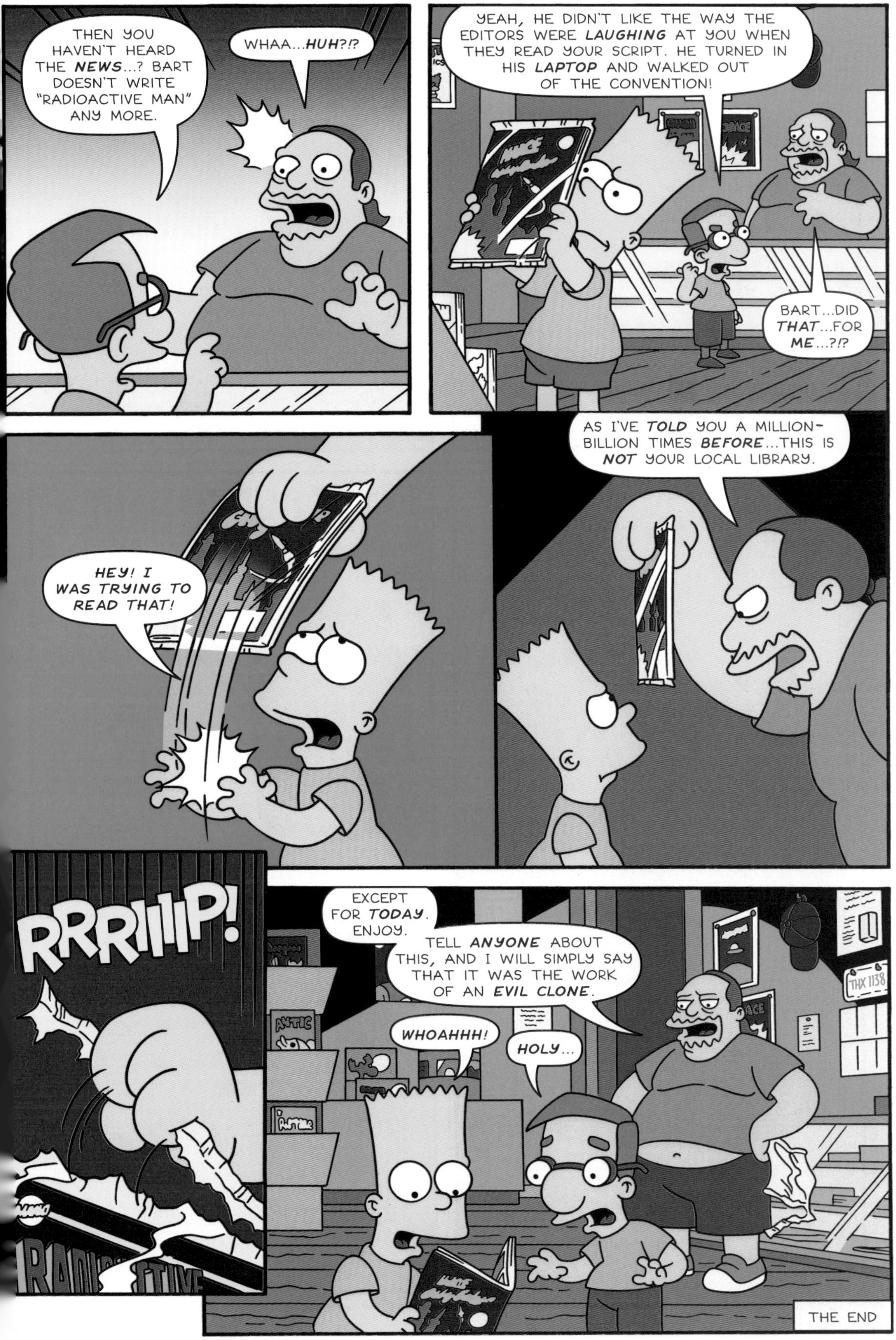

THEN YOU HAVEN'T HEARD THE NEWS...? BART DOESN'T WRITE "RADIOACTIVE MAN" ANY MORE.
WHAA...HUH?!?
YEAH, HE DIDN'T LIKE THE WAY THE EDITORS WERE LAUGHING AT YOU WHEN THEY READ YOUR SCRIPT. HE TURNED IN HIS LAPTOP AND WALKED OUT OF THE CONVENTION!
BART...DID THAT...FOR ME...?!?
HEY! I WAS TRYING TO READ THAT!
AS I'VE TOLD YOU A MILLION-BILLION TIMES BEFORE...THIS IS NOT YOUR LOCAL LIBRARY.
RRRIIIIP!
EXCEPT FOR TODAY. ENJOY.
TELL ANYONE ABOUT THIS, AND I WILL SIMPLY SAY THAT IT WAS THE WORK OF AN EVIL CLONE.
WHOAHHH!
HOLY...
THX 1138
THE END

LI'L KRUSTY

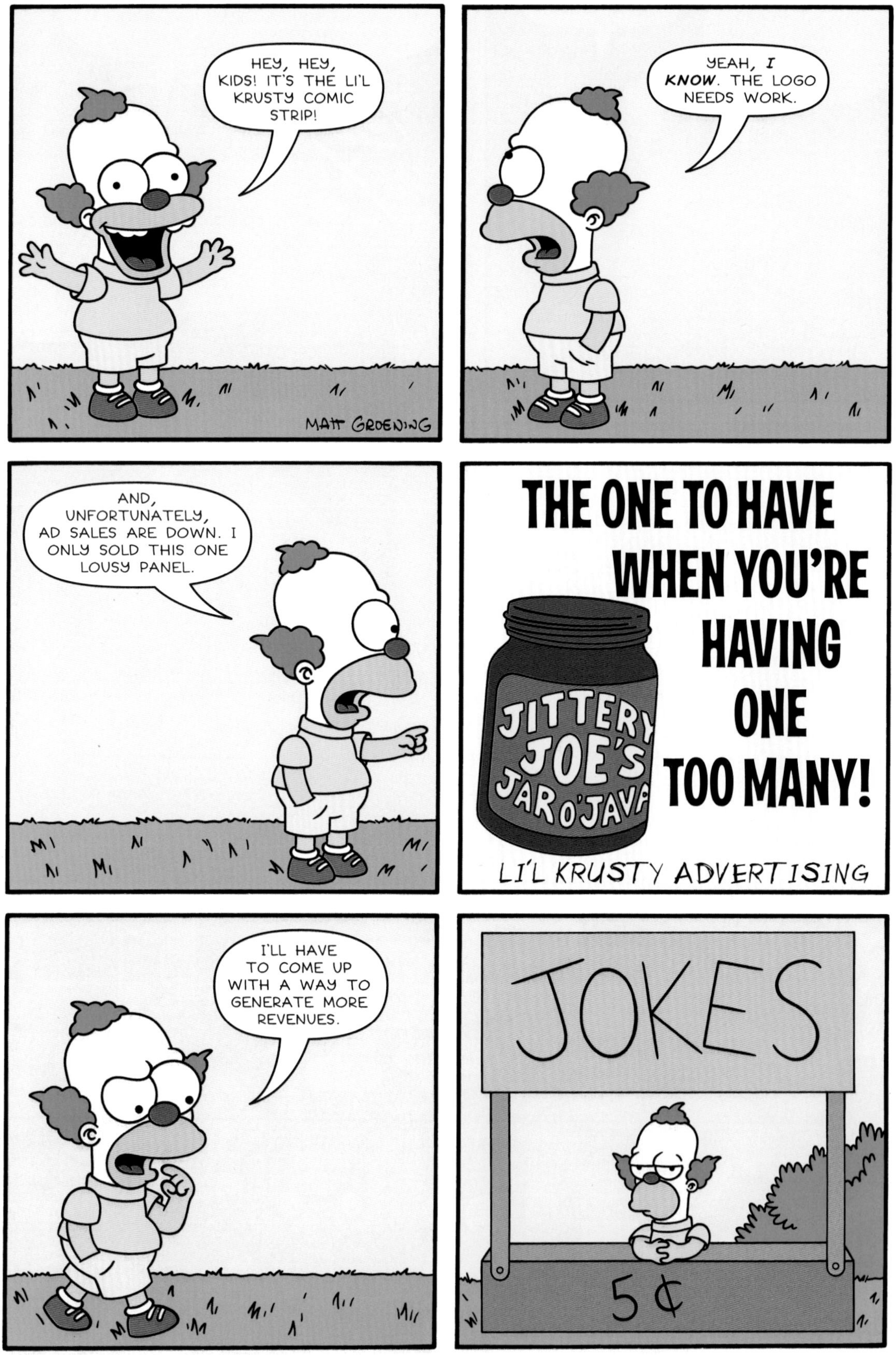

HEY, HEY, KIDS! IT'S THE LI'L KRUSTY COMIC STRIP!
MATT GROENING
YEAH, *I* ***KNOW***. THE LOGO NEEDS WORK.
AND, UNFORTUNATELY, AD SALES ARE DOWN. I ONLY SOLD THIS ONE LOUSY PANEL.
THE ONE TO HAVE WHEN YOU'RE HAVING ONE TOO MANY!
JITTERY JOE'S JAR O'JAVA
LI'L KRUSTY ADVERTISING
I'LL HAVE TO COME UP WITH A WAY TO GENERATE MORE REVENUES.
JOKES
5¢

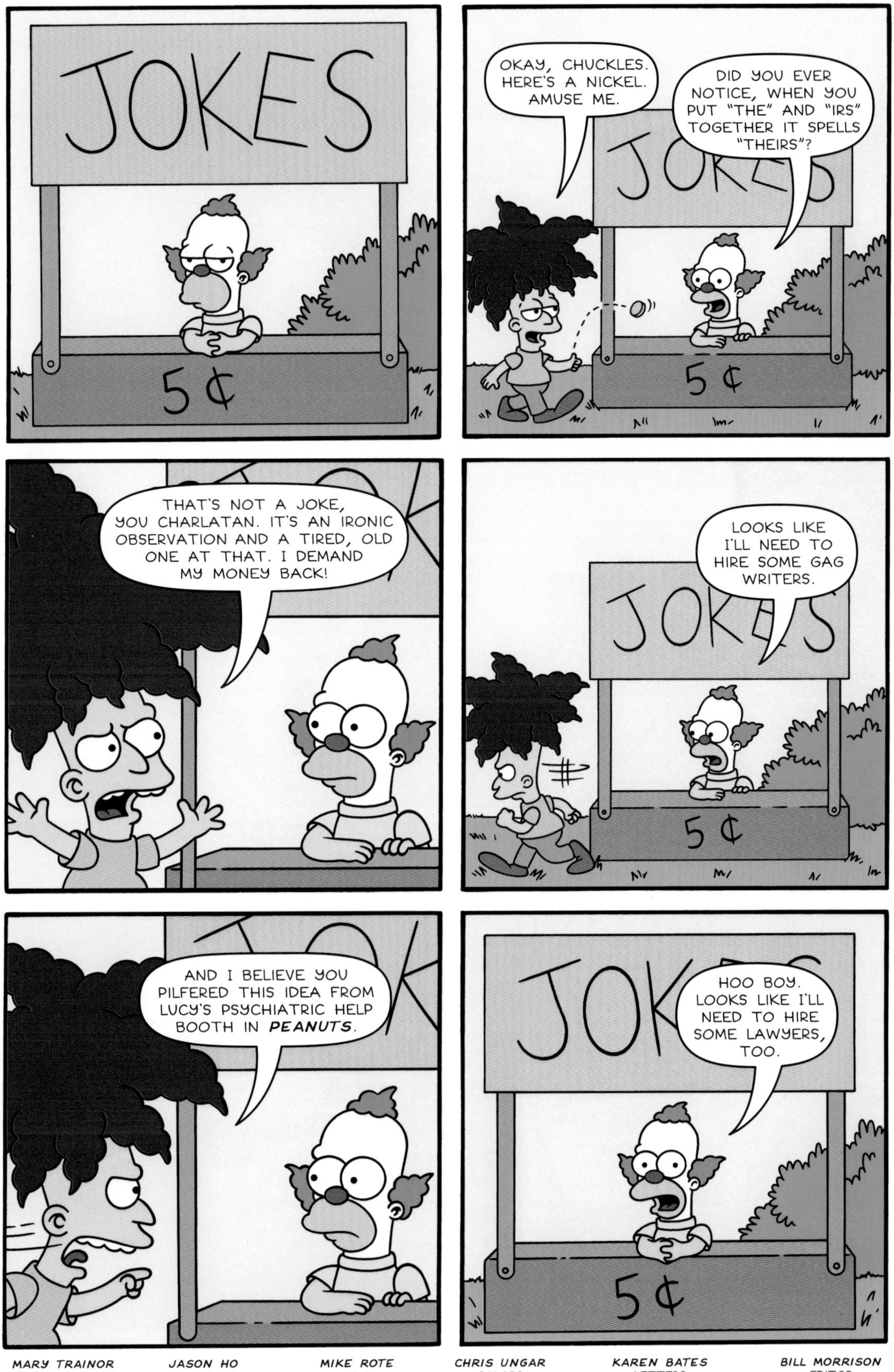
JOKES
5¢
OKAY, CHUCKLES. HERE'S A NICKEL. AMUSE ME.
DID YOU EVER NOTICE, WHEN YOU PUT "THE" AND "IRS" TOGETHER IT SPELLS "THEIRS"?
JOKES
5¢
THAT'S NOT A JOKE, YOU CHARLATAN. IT'S AN IRONIC OBSERVATION AND A TIRED, OLD ONE AT THAT. I DEMAND MY MONEY BACK!
LOOKS LIKE I'LL NEED TO HIRE SOME GAG WRITERS.
JOKES
5¢
AND I BELIEVE YOU PILFERED THIS IDEA FROM LUCY'S PSYCHIATRIC HELP BOOTH IN *PEANUTS*.
HOO BOY. LOOKS LIKE I'LL NEED TO HIRE SOME LAWYERS, TOO.
5¢

MARY TRAINOR SCRIPT | *JASON HO* PENCILS | *MIKE ROTE* INKS | *CHRIS UNGAR* COLORS | *KAREN BATES* LETTERS | *BILL MORRISON* EDITOR

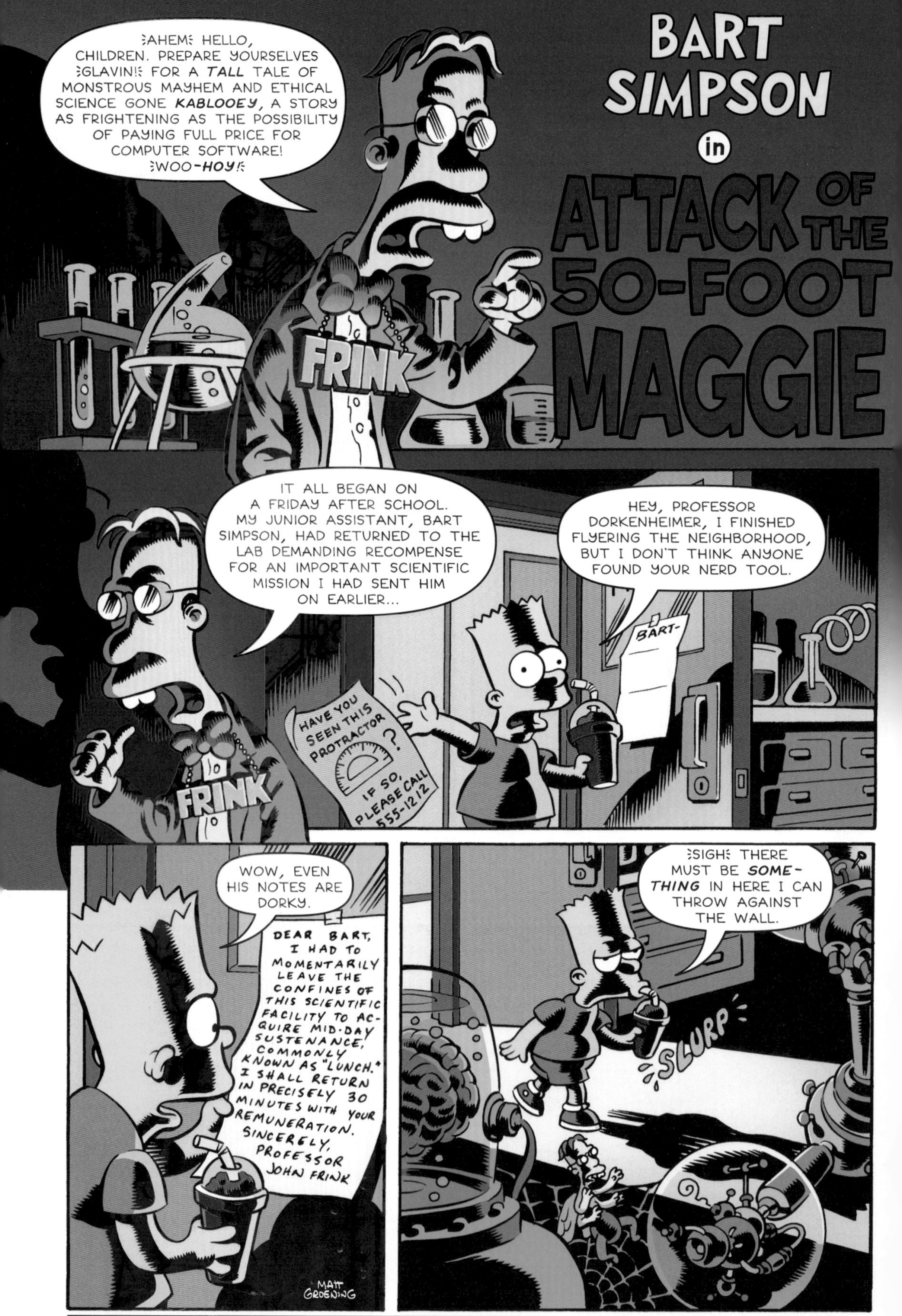
BART SIMPSON in ATTACK OF THE 50-FOOT MAGGIE
:AHEM: HELLO, CHILDREN. PREPARE YOURSELVES :GLAVIN!: FOR A TALL TALE OF MONSTROUS MAYHEM AND ETHICAL SCIENCE GONE KABLOOEY, A STORY AS FRIGHTENING AS THE POSSIBILITY OF PAYING FULL PRICE FOR COMPUTER SOFTWARE! :WOO-HOY!:
FRINK
IT ALL BEGAN ON A FRIDAY AFTER SCHOOL. MY JUNIOR ASSISTANT, BART SIMPSON, HAD RETURNED TO THE LAB DEMANDING RECOMPENSE FOR AN IMPORTANT SCIENTIFIC MISSION I HAD SENT HIM ON EARLIER...
HEY, PROFESSOR DORKENHEIMER, I FINISHED FLYERING THE NEIGHBORHOOD, BUT I DON'T THINK ANYONE FOUND YOUR NERD TOOL.
HAVE YOU SEEN THIS PROTRACTOR? IF SO, PLEASE CALL 555-1212
BART-
FRINK
WOW, EVEN HIS NOTES ARE DORKY.
DEAR BART, I HAD TO MOMENTARILY LEAVE THE CONFINES OF THIS SCIENTIFIC FACILITY TO ACQUIRE MID-DAY SUSTENANCE, COMMONLY KNOWN AS "LUNCH." I SHALL RETURN IN PRECISELY 30 MINUTES WITH YOUR REMUNERATION. SINCERELY, PROFESSOR JOHN FRINK
MATT GROENING
:SIGH: THERE MUST BE SOMETHING IN HERE I CAN THROW AGAINST THE WALL.
SLURP

TONY DIGEROLAMO	*HILARY BARTA*	*ROBERT STANLEY*	*KAREN BATES*	*BILL MORRISON*
SCRIPT	PENCILS & INKS	COLORS	LETTERS	EDITOR

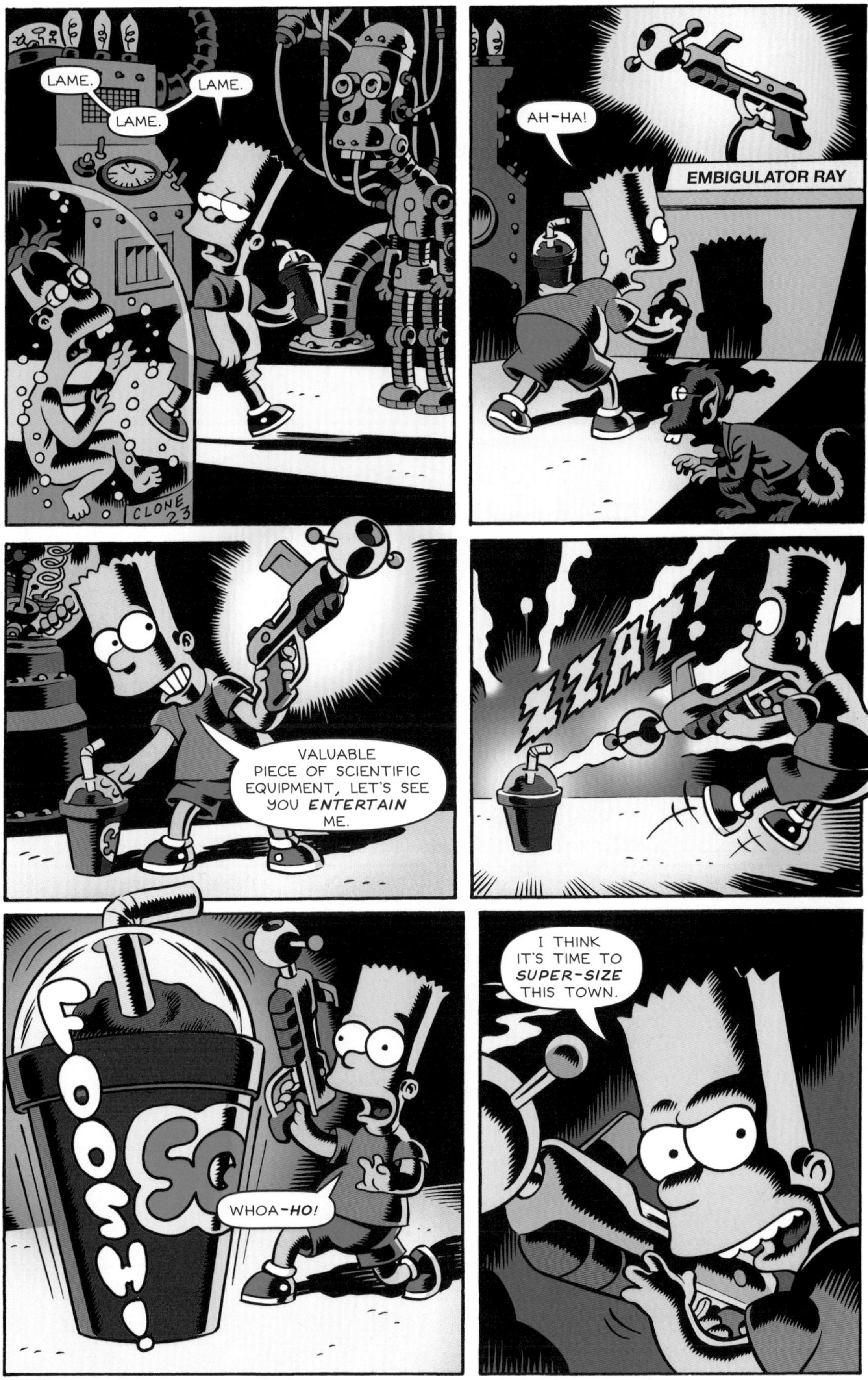
LAME.
LAME.
LAME.
CLONE 23
EMBIGULATOR RAY
AH-HA!
VALUABLE PIECE OF SCIENTIFIC EQUIPMENT, LET'S SEE YOU ENTERTAIN ME.
ZZAT!
FOOSH!
WHOA-HO!
I THINK IT'S TIME TO SUPER-SIZE THIS TOWN.

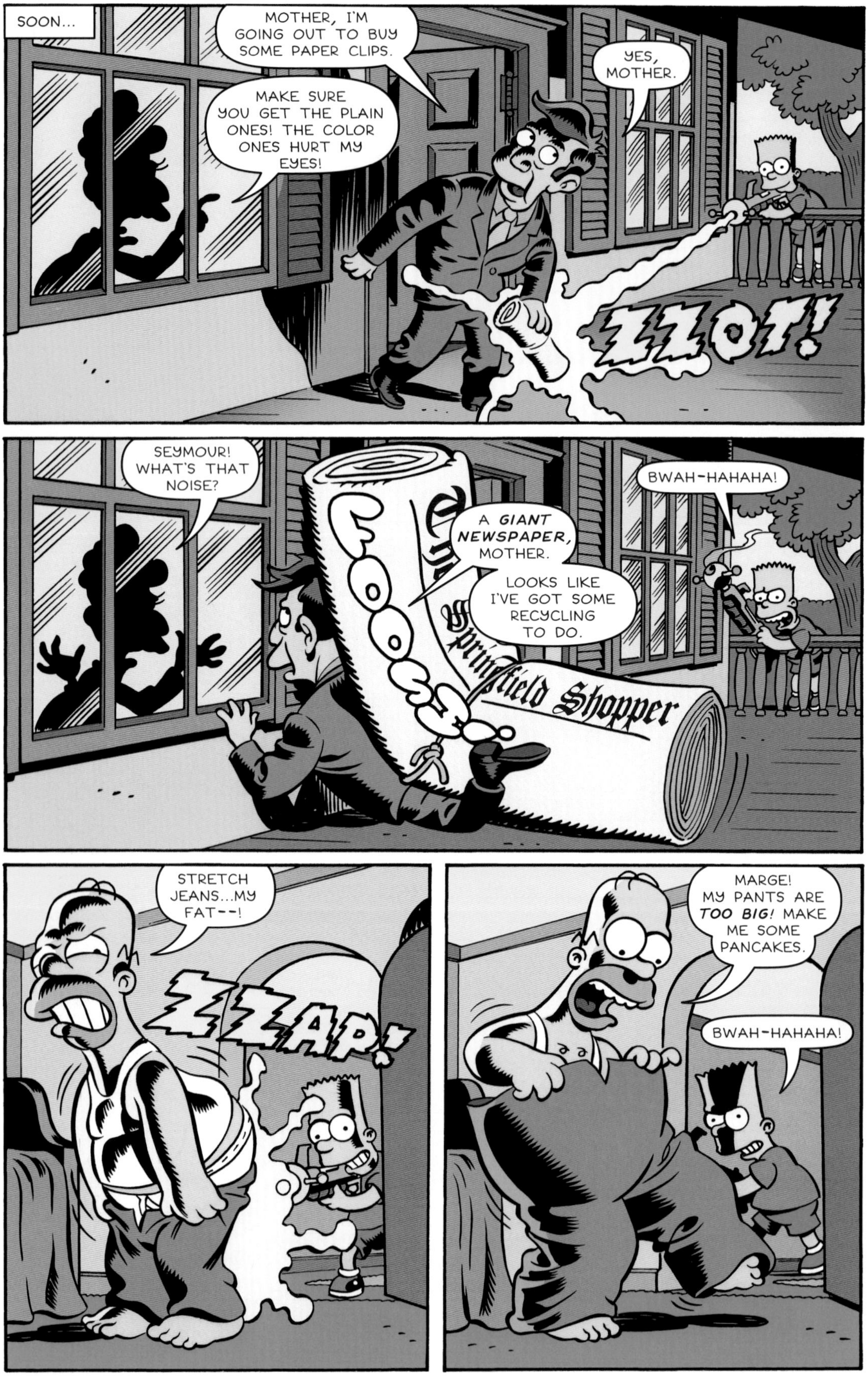
SOON...
MOTHER, I'M GOING OUT TO BUY SOME PAPER CLIPS.
MAKE SURE YOU GET THE PLAIN ONES! THE COLOR ONES HURT MY EYES!
YES, MOTHER.
ZZOT!
SEYMOUR! WHAT'S THAT NOISE?
A GIANT NEWSPAPER, MOTHER.
LOOKS LIKE I'VE GOT SOME RECYCLING TO DO.
Springfield Shopper
BWAH-HAHAHA!
STRETCH JEANS...MY FAT--!
ZZAP!
MARGE! MY PANTS ARE TOO BIG! MAKE ME SOME PANCAKES.
BWAH-HAHAHA!

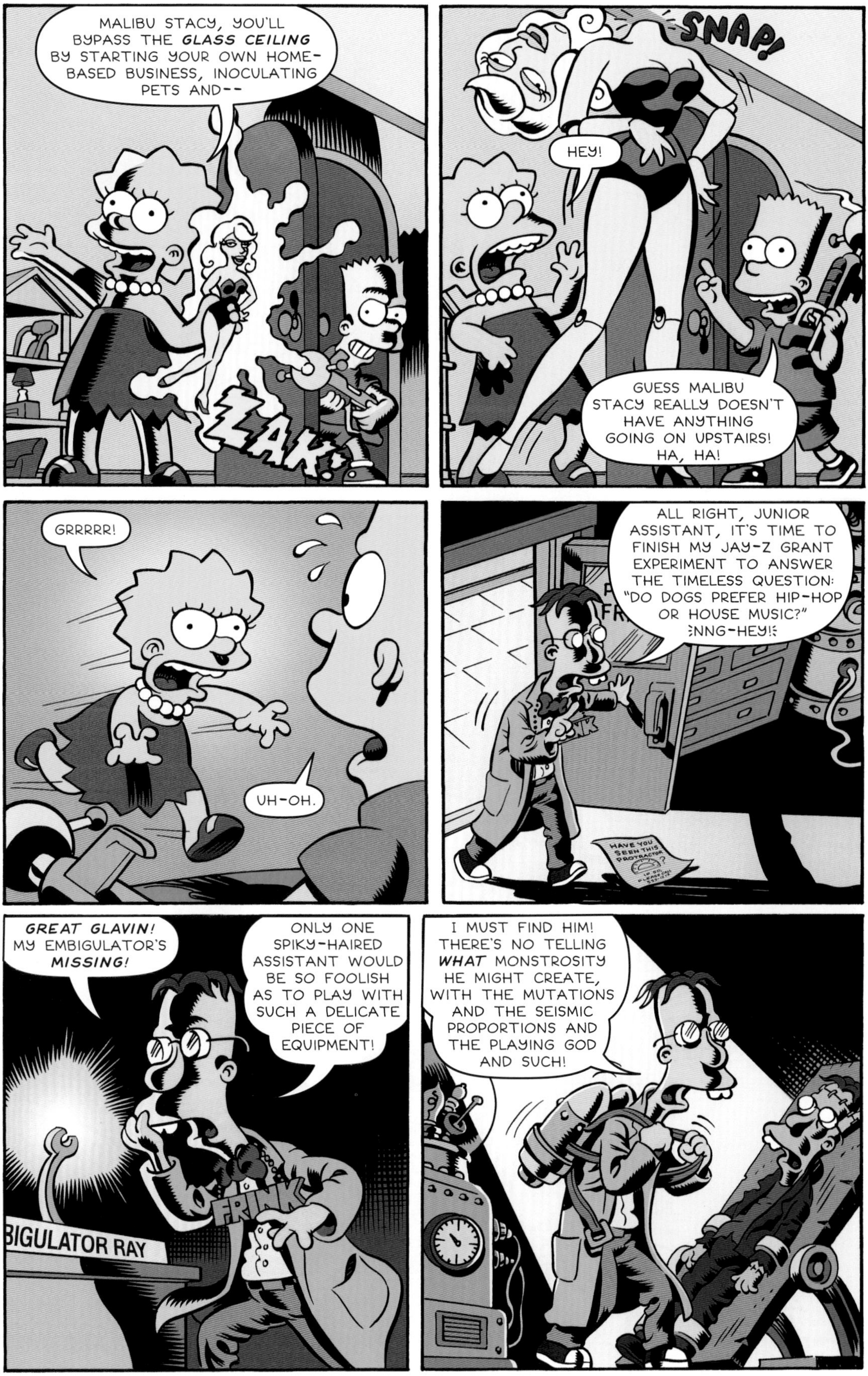
MALIBU STACY, YOU'LL BYPASS THE *GLASS CEILING* BY STARTING YOUR OWN HOME-BASED BUSINESS, INOCULATING PETS AND--
ZAK!
SNAP!
HEY!
GUESS MALIBU STACY REALLY DOESN'T HAVE ANYTHING GOING ON UPSTAIRS! HA, HA!
GRRRRR!
UH-OH.
ALL RIGHT, JUNIOR ASSISTANT, IT'S TIME TO FINISH MY JAY-Z GRANT EXPERIMENT TO ANSWER THE TIMELESS QUESTION: "DO DOGS PREFER HIP-HOP OR HOUSE MUSIC?" NNG-HEY!
HAVE YOU SEEN THIS PROTRACTOR?
GREAT GLAVIN! MY EMBIGULATOR'S *MISSING!*
ONLY ONE SPIKY-HAIRED ASSISTANT WOULD BE SO FOOLISH AS TO PLAY WITH SUCH A DELICATE PIECE OF EQUIPMENT!
BIGULATOR RAY
FRINK
I MUST FIND HIM! THERE'S NO TELLING *WHAT* MONSTROSITY HE MIGHT CREATE, WITH THE MUTATIONS AND THE SEISMIC PROPORTIONS AND THE PLAYING GOD AND SUCH!

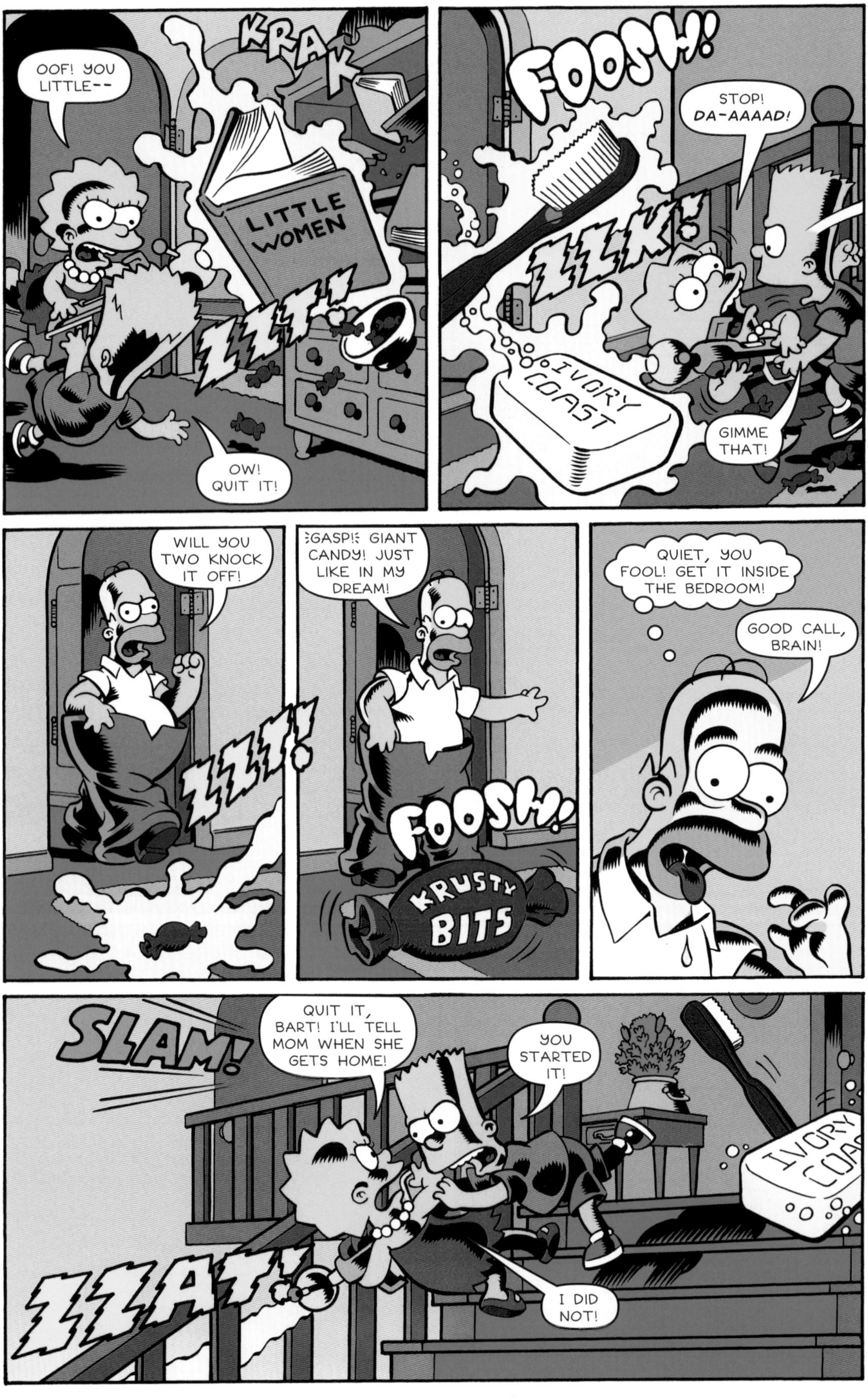
KRAK
OOF! YOU LITTLE--
LITTLE WOMEN
ZZZT!
OW! QUIT IT!
FOOSH!
STOP! DA-AAAAD!
ZZZK!
IVORY COAST
GIMME THAT!
WILL YOU TWO KNOCK IT OFF!
ZZZT!
:GASP!: GIANT CANDY! JUST LIKE IN MY DREAM!
FOOSH!
KRUSTY BITS
QUIET, YOU FOOL! GET IT INSIDE THE BEDROOM!
GOOD CALL, BRAIN!
SLAM!
QUIT IT, BART! I'LL TELL MOM WHEN SHE GETS HOME!
YOU STARTED IT!
IVORY COA
ZZAT!
I DID NOT!

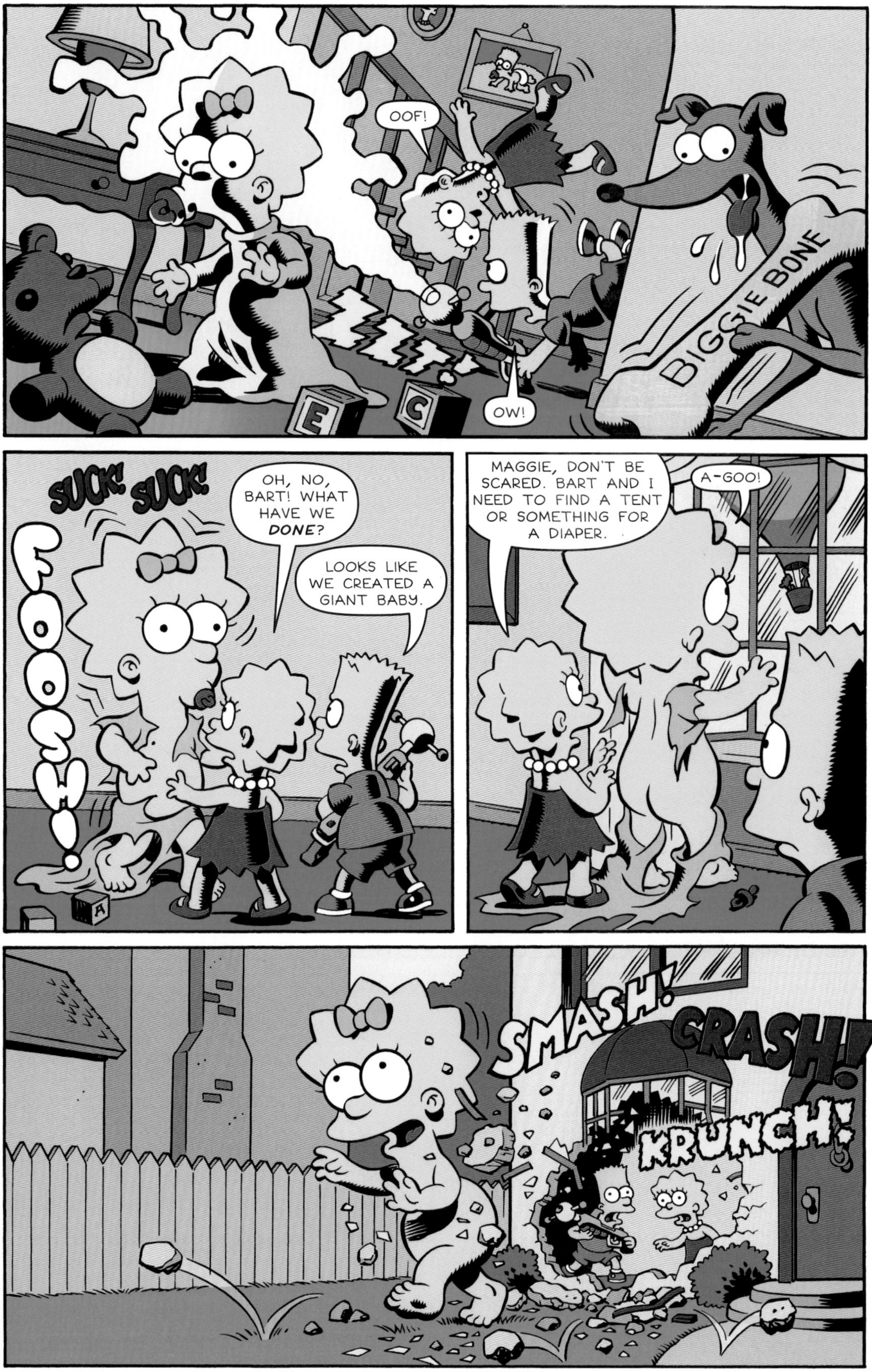
OOF!
BIGGIE BONE
OW!
SUCK! SUCK!
FOOSH!
OH, NO, BART! WHAT HAVE WE ***DONE***?
LOOKS LIKE WE CREATED A GIANT BABY.
MAGGIE, DON'T BE SCARED. BART AND I NEED TO FIND A TENT OR SOMETHING FOR A DIAPER.
A-GOO!
SMASH!
CRASH!
KRUNCH!

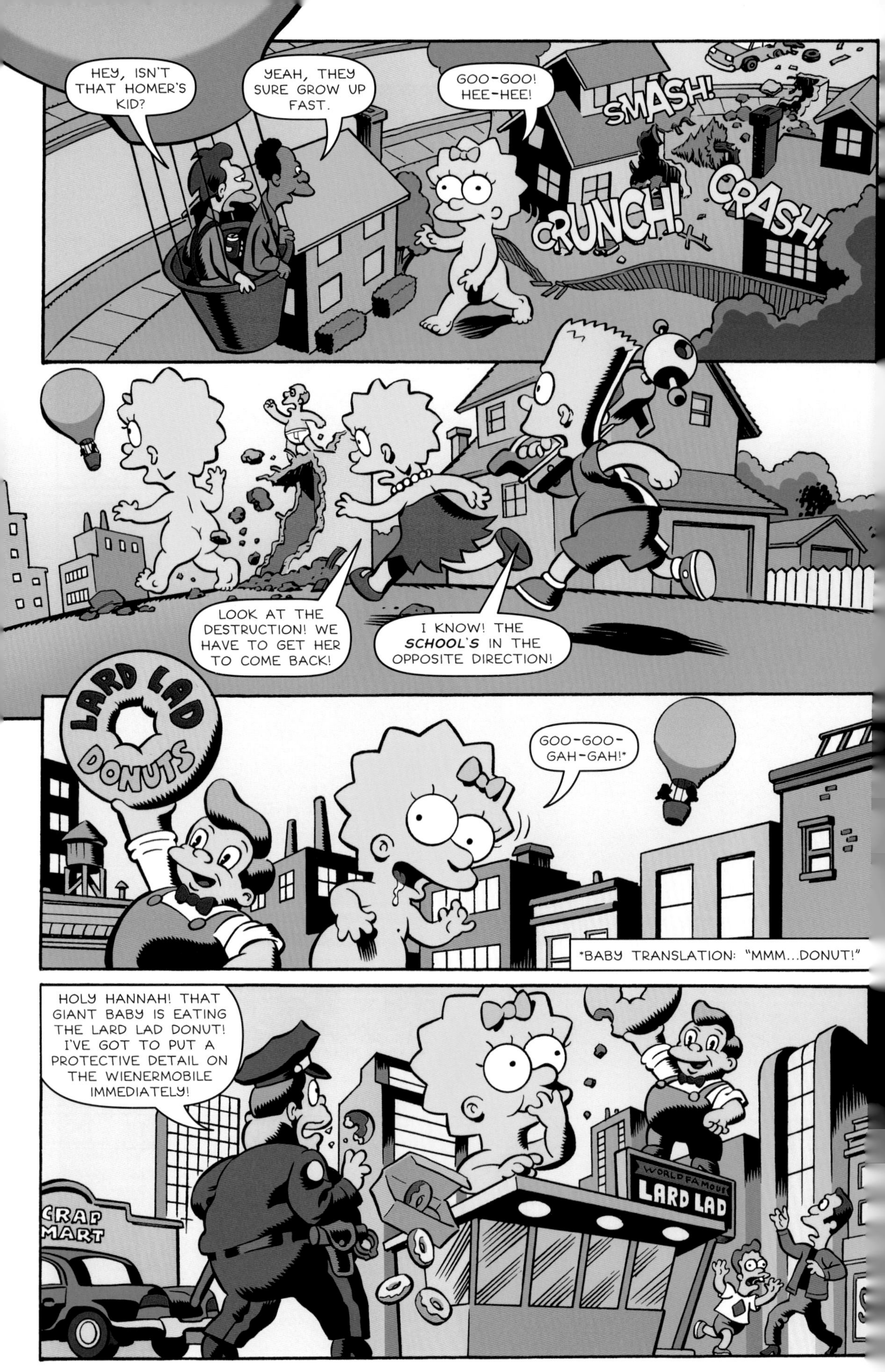
HEY, ISN'T THAT HOMER'S KID?
YEAH, THEY SURE GROW UP FAST.
GOO-GOO! HEE-HEE!
SMASH!
CRUNCH!
CRASH!
LOOK AT THE DESTRUCTION! WE HAVE TO GET HER TO COME BACK!
I KNOW! THE *SCHOOL'S* IN THE OPPOSITE DIRECTION!
LARD LAD DONUTS
GOO-GOO-GAH-GAH!*
*BABY TRANSLATION: "MMM...DONUT!"
HOLY HANNAH! THAT GIANT BABY IS EATING THE LARD LAD DONUT! I'VE GOT TO PUT A PROTECTIVE DETAIL ON THE WIENERMOBILE IMMEDIATELY!
WORLD FAMOUS
LARD LAD
CRAP MART

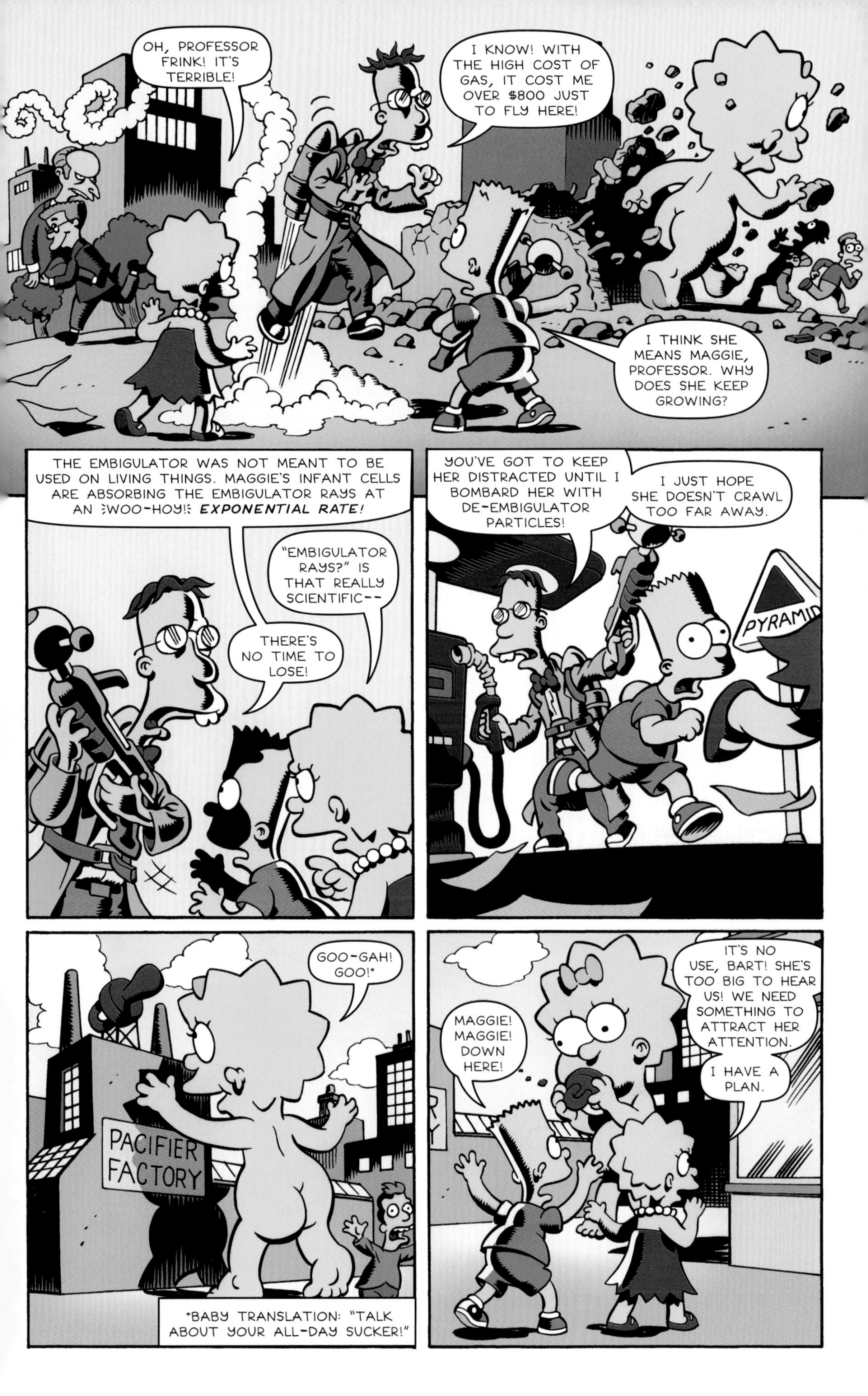
OH, PROFESSOR FRINK! IT'S TERRIBLE!
I KNOW! WITH THE HIGH COST OF GAS, IT COST ME OVER $800 JUST TO FLY HERE!
I THINK SHE MEANS MAGGIE, PROFESSOR. WHY DOES SHE KEEP GROWING?
THE EMBIGULATOR WAS NOT MEANT TO BE USED ON LIVING THINGS. MAGGIE'S INFANT CELLS ARE ABSORBING THE EMBIGULATOR RAYS AT AN ;WOO-HOY!; EXPONENTIAL RATE!
"EMBIGULATOR RAYS?" IS THAT REALLY SCIENTIFIC--
THERE'S NO TIME TO LOSE!
YOU'VE GOT TO KEEP HER DISTRACTED UNTIL I BOMBARD HER WITH DE-EMBIGULATOR PARTICLES!
I JUST HOPE SHE DOESN'T CRAWL TOO FAR AWAY.
PYRAMID
GOO-GAH! GOO!*
PACIFIER FACTORY
*BABY TRANSLATION: "TALK ABOUT YOUR ALL-DAY SUCKER!"
MAGGIE! MAGGIE! DOWN HERE!
IT'S NO USE, BART! SHE'S TOO BIG TO HEAR US! WE NEED SOMETHING TO ATTRACT HER ATTENTION.
I HAVE A PLAN.

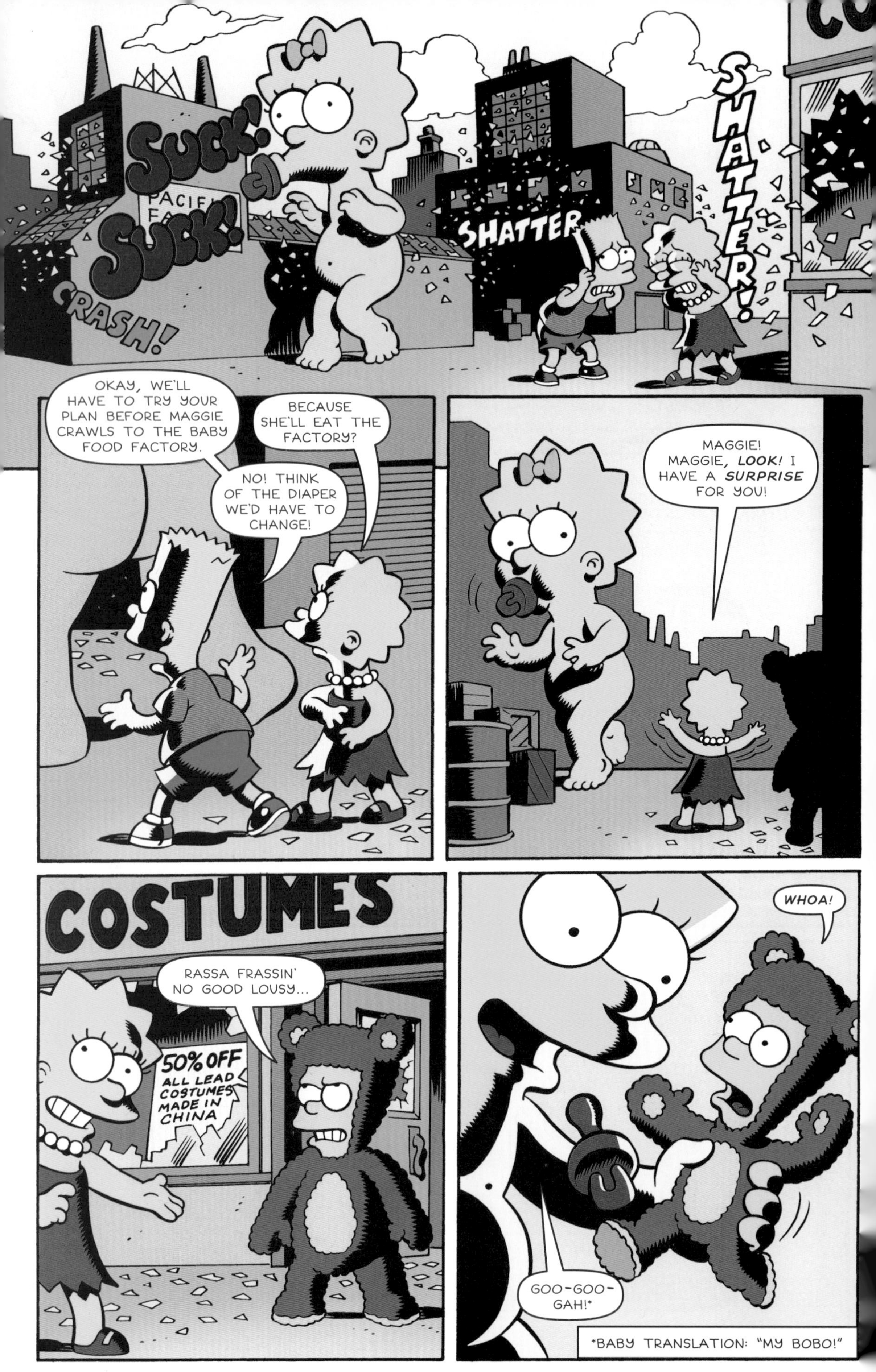
SUCK!
SUCK!
PACIFI
F
CRASH!
SHATTER
SHATTER!
OKAY, WE'LL HAVE TO TRY YOUR PLAN BEFORE MAGGIE CRAWLS TO THE BABY FOOD FACTORY.
BECAUSE SHE'LL EAT THE FACTORY?
NO! THINK OF THE DIAPER WE'D HAVE TO CHANGE!
MAGGIE! MAGGIE, **LOOK!** I HAVE A ***SURPRISE*** FOR YOU!
COSTUMES
RASSA FRASSIN' NO GOOD LOUSY...
50% OFF ALL LEAD COSTUMES MADE IN CHINA
WHOA!
GOO-GOO-GAH!*
*BABY TRANSLATION: "MY BOBO!"

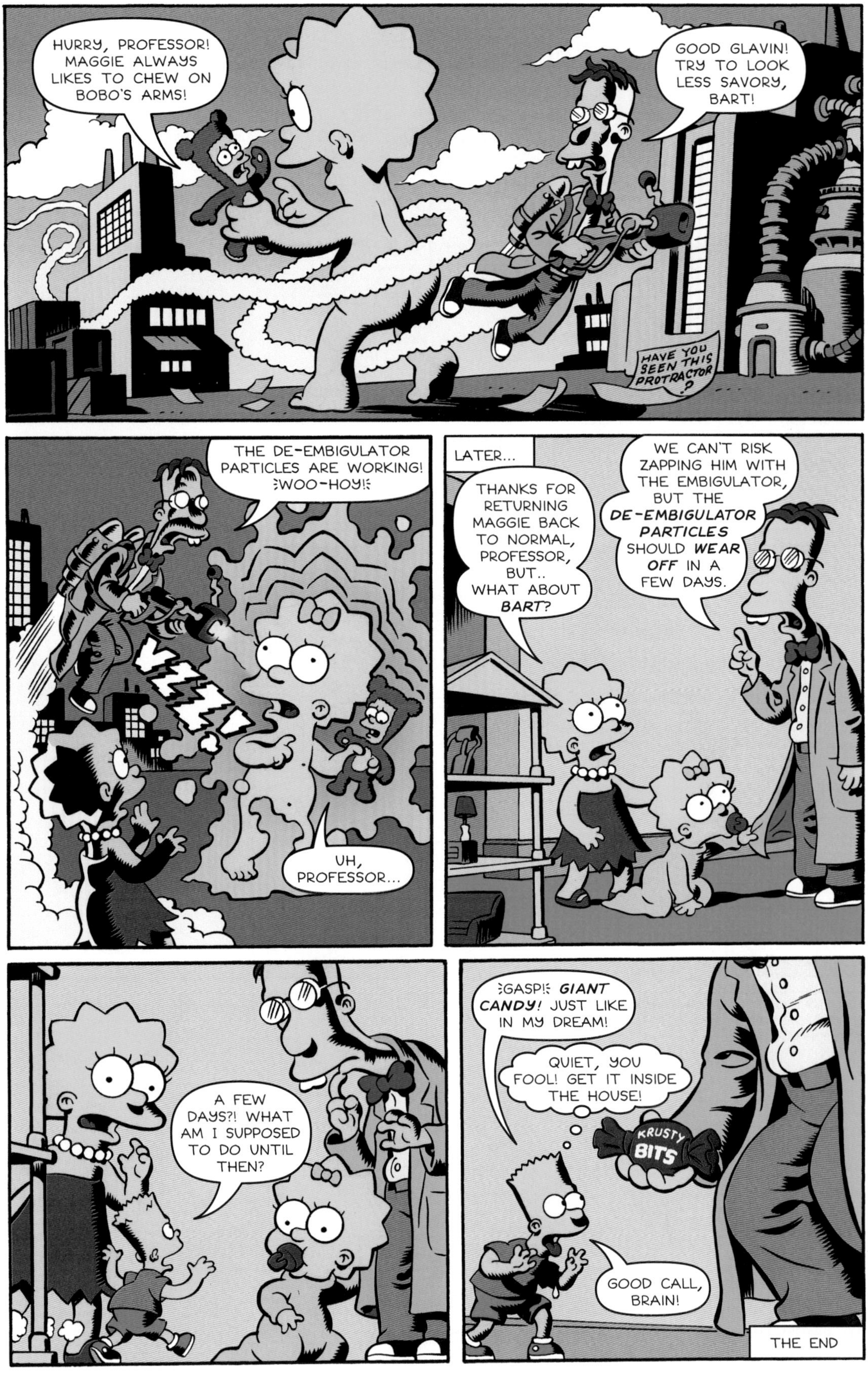
HURRY, PROFESSOR! MAGGIE ALWAYS LIKES TO CHEW ON BOBO'S ARMS!
GOOD GLAVIN! TRY TO LOOK LESS SAVORY, BART!
HAVE YOU SEEN THIS PROTRACTOR ?
THE DE-EMBIGULATOR PARTICLES ARE WORKING! WOO-HOY!
UH, PROFESSOR...
LATER...
THANKS FOR RETURNING MAGGIE BACK TO NORMAL, PROFESSOR, BUT.. WHAT ABOUT BART?
WE CAN'T RISK ZAPPING HIM WITH THE EMBIGULATOR, BUT THE DE-EMBIGULATOR PARTICLES SHOULD WEAR OFF IN A FEW DAYS.
A FEW DAYS?! WHAT AM I SUPPOSED TO DO UNTIL THEN?
GASP! GIANT CANDY! JUST LIKE IN MY DREAM!
QUIET, YOU FOOL! GET IT INSIDE THE HOUSE!
KRUSTY BITS
GOOD CALL, BRAIN!
THE END

BART SIMPSON (IN)

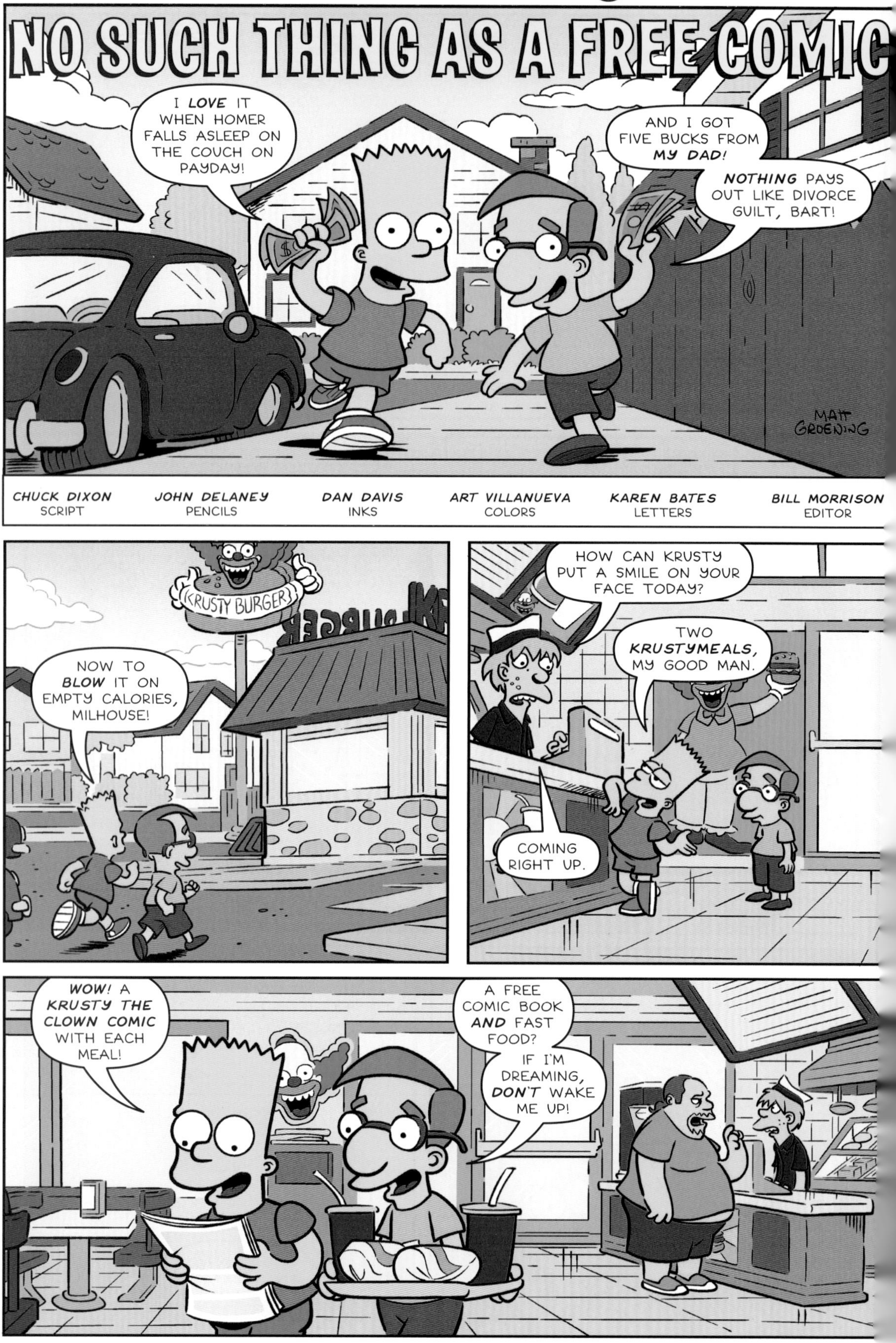
NO SUCH THING AS A FREE COMIC
I LOVE IT WHEN HOMER FALLS ASLEEP ON THE COUCH ON PAYDAY!
AND I GOT FIVE BUCKS FROM MY DAD!
NOTHING PAYS OUT LIKE DIVORCE GUILT, BART!
MATT GROENING
CHUCK DIXON SCRIPT
JOHN DELANEY PENCILS
DAN DAVIS INKS
ART VILLANUEVA COLORS
KAREN BATES LETTERS
BILL MORRISON EDITOR
KRUSTY BURGER
NOW TO BLOW IT ON EMPTY CALORIES, MILHOUSE!
HOW CAN KRUSTY PUT A SMILE ON YOUR FACE TODAY?
TWO KRUSTYMEALS, MY GOOD MAN.
COMING RIGHT UP.
WOW! A KRUSTY THE CLOWN COMIC WITH EACH MEAL!
A FREE COMIC BOOK AND FAST FOOD?
IF I'M DREAMING, DON'T WAKE ME UP!

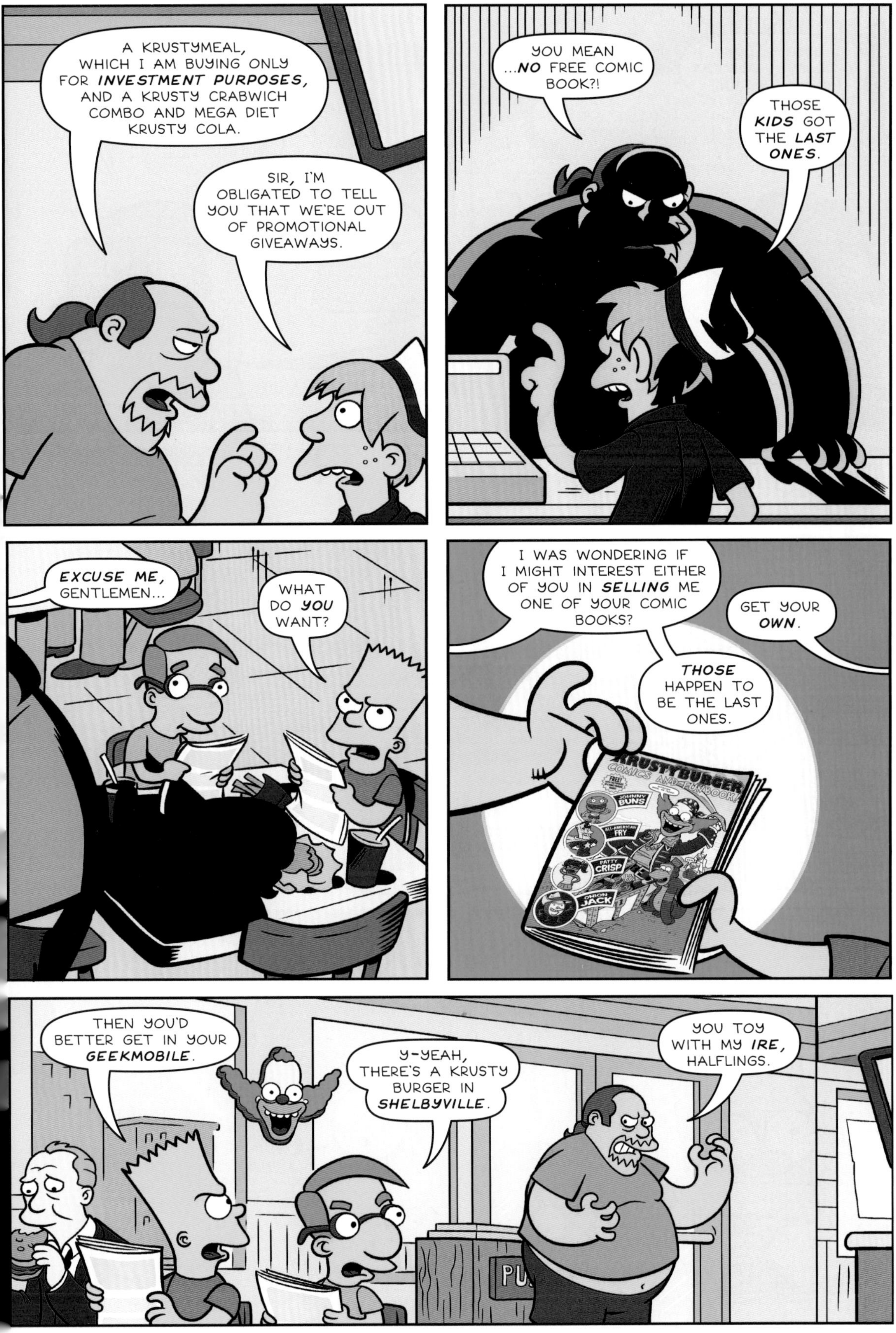
A KRUSTYMEAL, WHICH I AM BUYING ONLY FOR INVESTMENT PURPOSES, AND A KRUSTY CRABWICH COMBO AND MEGA DIET KRUSTY COLA.
SIR, I'M OBLIGATED TO TELL YOU THAT WE'RE OUT OF PROMOTIONAL GIVEAWAYS.
YOU MEAN ...NO FREE COMIC BOOK?!
THOSE KIDS GOT THE LAST ONES.
EXCUSE ME, GENTLEMEN...
WHAT DO YOU WANT?
I WAS WONDERING IF I MIGHT INTEREST EITHER OF YOU IN SELLING ME ONE OF YOUR COMIC BOOKS?
GET YOUR OWN.
THOSE HAPPEN TO BE THE LAST ONES.
KRUSTYBURGER COMICS AND FUNBOOK!
FREE!
JOHNNY BUNS
ALL-AMERICAN FRY
PATTY CRISP
ONION JACK
THEN YOU'D BETTER GET IN YOUR GEEKMOBILE.
Y-YEAH, THERE'S A KRUSTY BURGER IN SHELBYVILLE.
YOU TOY WITH MY IRE, HALFLINGS.

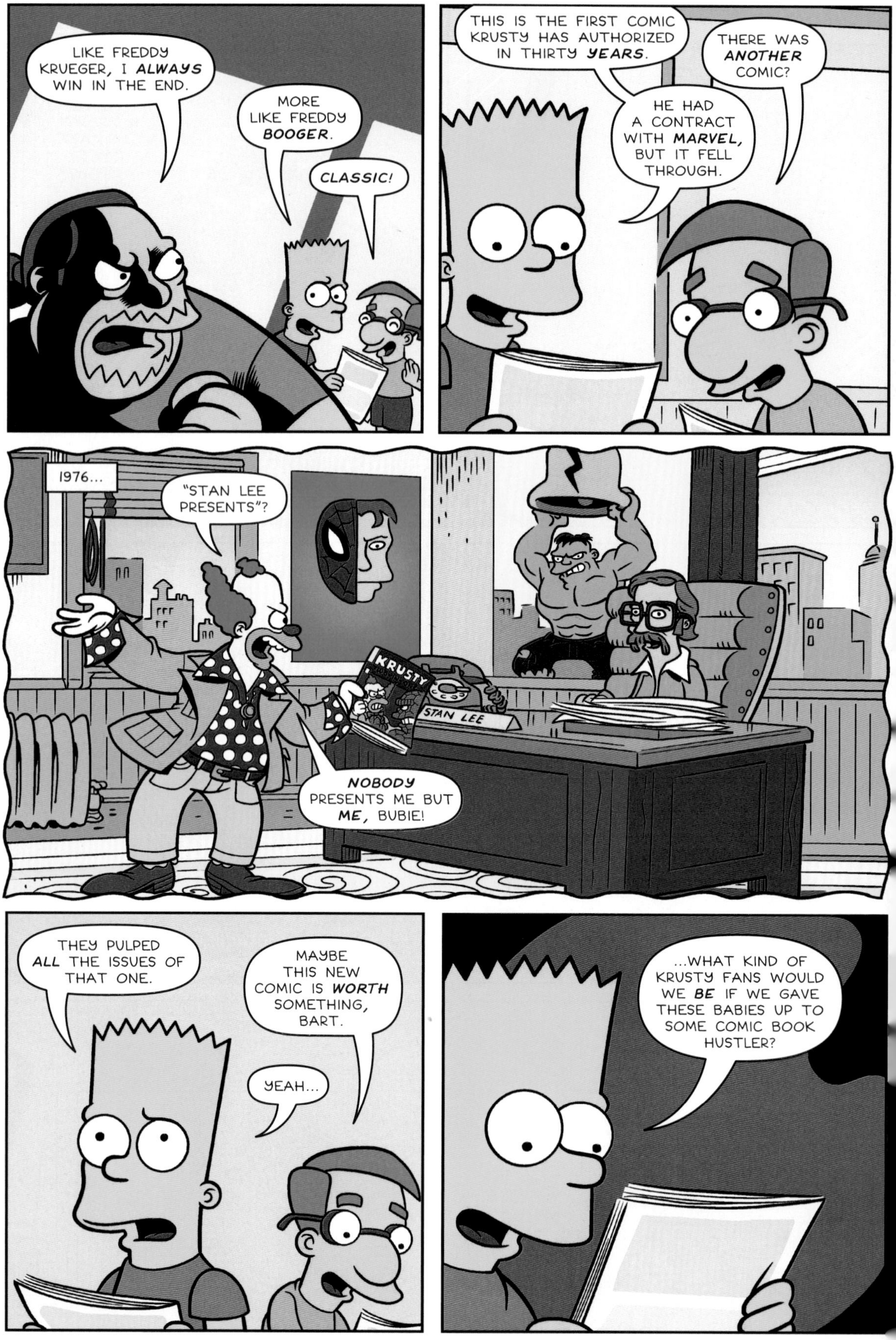
LIKE FREDDY KRUEGER, I ALWAYS WIN IN THE END.
MORE LIKE FREDDY BOOGER.
CLASSIC!
THIS IS THE FIRST COMIC KRUSTY HAS AUTHORIZED IN THIRTY YEARS.
THERE WAS ANOTHER COMIC?
HE HAD A CONTRACT WITH MARVEL, BUT IT FELL THROUGH.
1976...
"STAN LEE PRESENTS"?
KRUSTY
STAN LEE
NOBODY PRESENTS ME BUT ME, BUBIE!
THEY PULPED ALL THE ISSUES OF THAT ONE.
MAYBE THIS NEW COMIC IS WORTH SOMETHING, BART.
YEAH...
...WHAT KIND OF KRUSTY FANS WOULD WE BE IF WE GAVE THESE BABIES UP TO SOME COMIC BOOK HUSTLER?

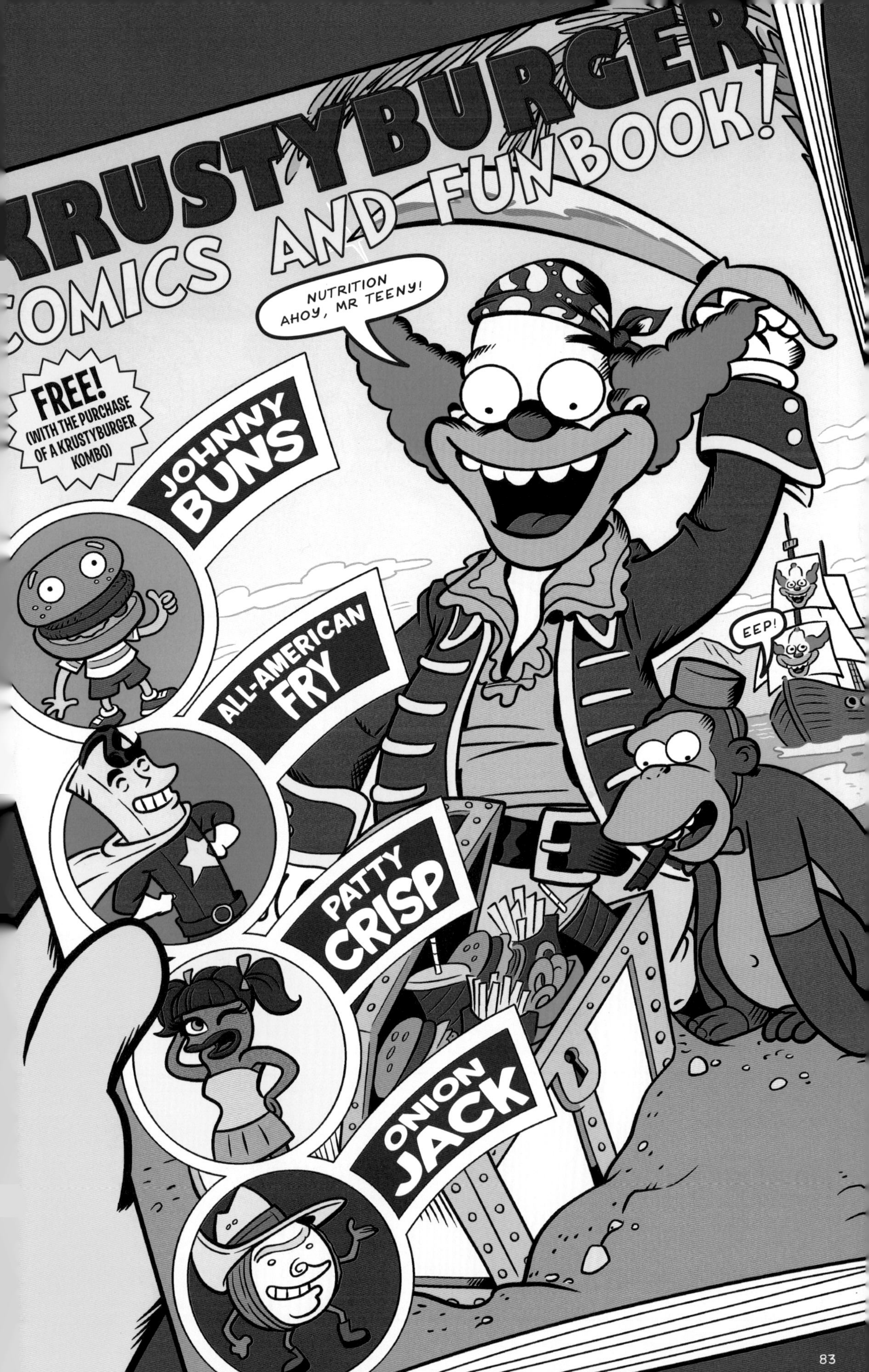
KRUSTYBURGER COMICS AND FUNBOOK!
NUTRITION AHOY, MR TEENY!
FREE! (WITH THE PURCHASE OF A KRUSTYBURGER KOMBO)
JOHNNY BUNS
ALL-AMERICAN FRY
PATTY CRISP
ONION JACK
EEP!

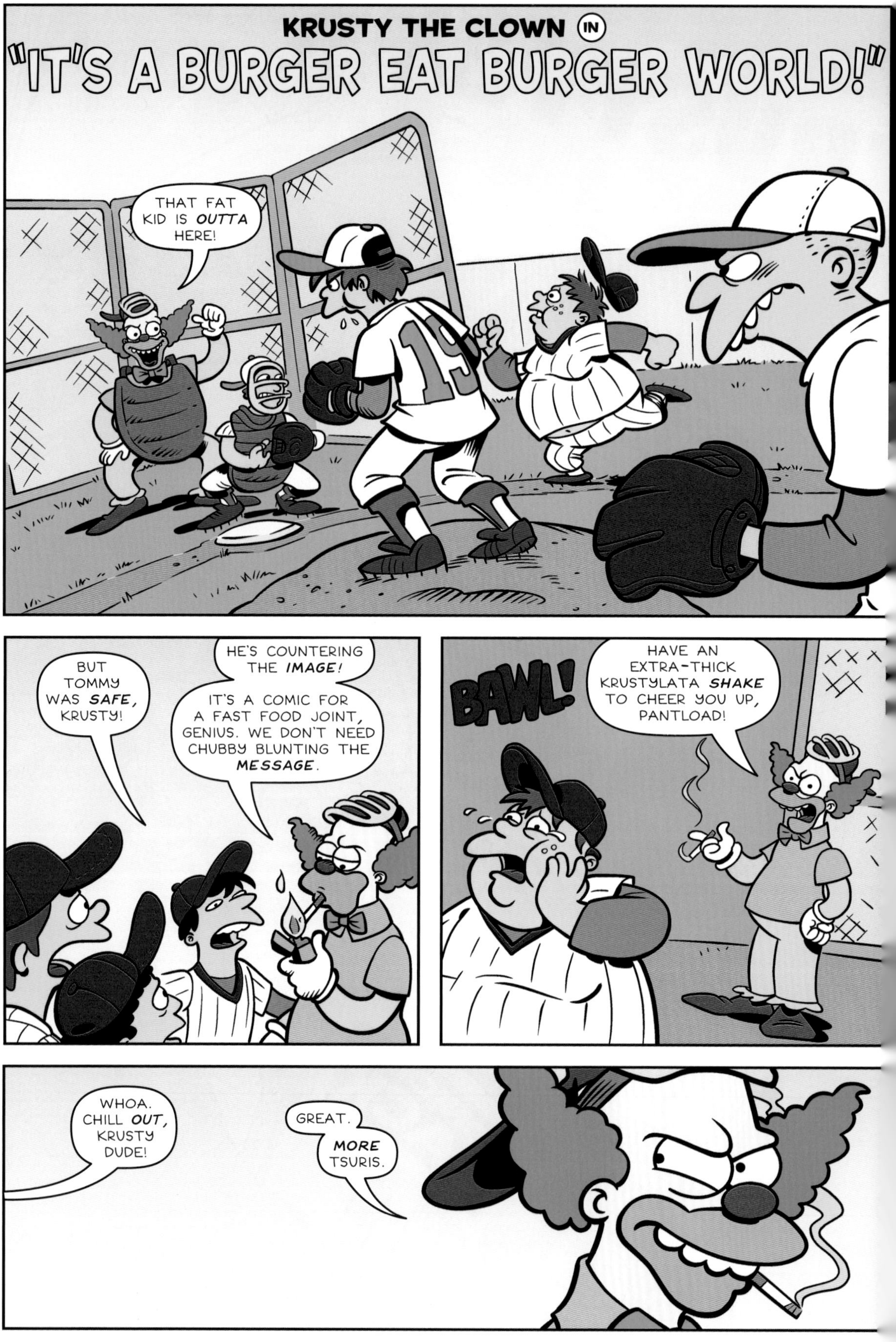
KRUSTY THE CLOWN IN
"IT'S A BURGER EAT BURGER WORLD!"
THAT FAT KID IS OUTTA HERE!
BUT TOMMY WAS SAFE, KRUSTY!
HE'S COUNTERING THE IMAGE!
IT'S A COMIC FOR A FAST FOOD JOINT, GENIUS. WE DON'T NEED CHUBBY BLUNTING THE MESSAGE.
BAWL!
HAVE AN EXTRA-THICK KRUSTYLATA SHAKE TO CHEER YOU UP, PANTLOAD!
WHOA. CHILL OUT, KRUSTY DUDE!
GREAT.
MORE TSURIS.

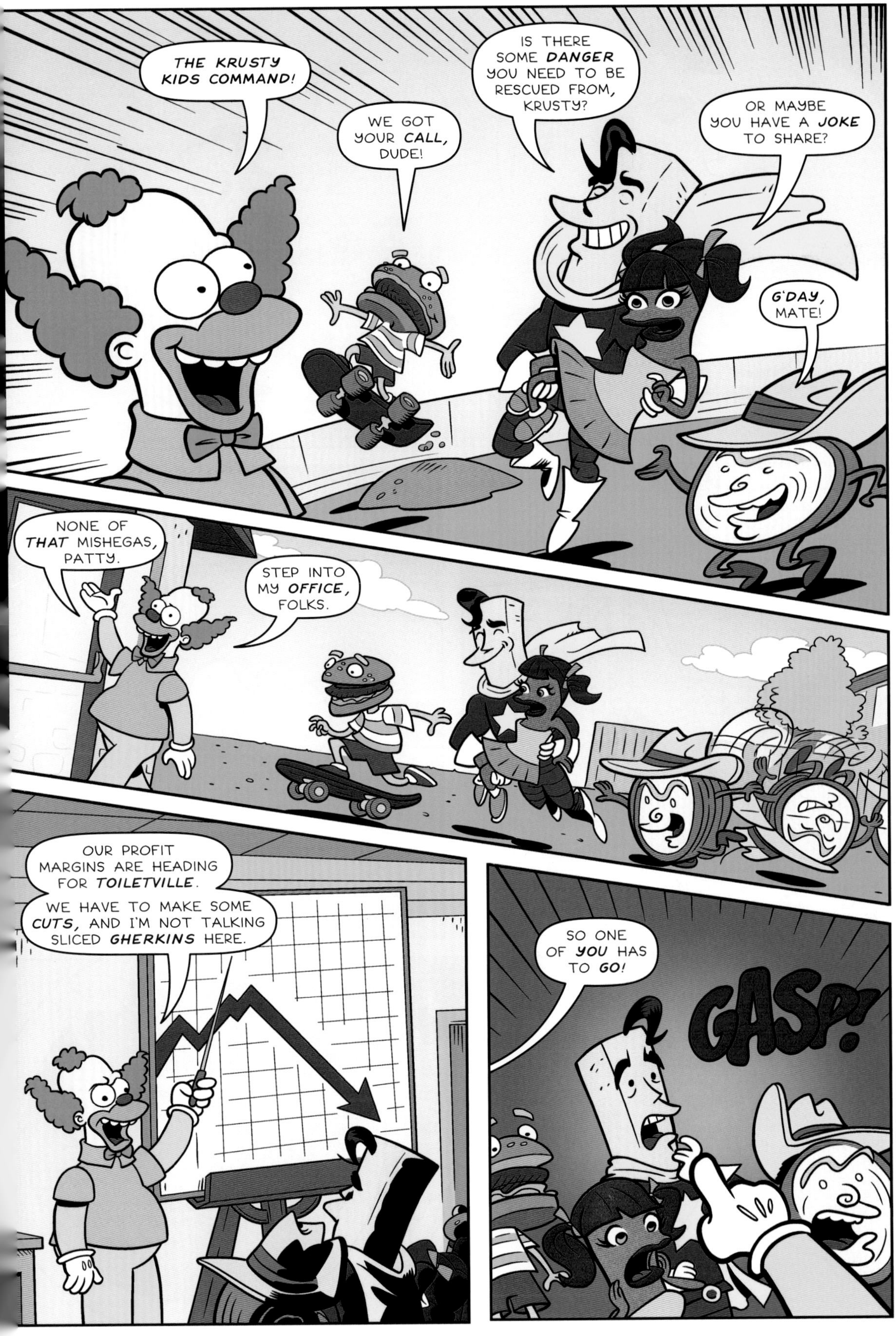
THE KRUSTY KIDS COMMAND!
WE GOT YOUR CALL, DUDE!
IS THERE SOME DANGER YOU NEED TO BE RESCUED FROM, KRUSTY?
OR MAYBE YOU HAVE A JOKE TO SHARE?
G'DAY, MATE!
NONE OF THAT MISHEGAS, PATTY.
STEP INTO MY OFFICE, FOLKS.
OUR PROFIT MARGINS ARE HEADING FOR TOILETVILLE.
WE HAVE TO MAKE SOME CUTS, AND I'M NOT TALKING SLICED GHERKINS HERE.
SO ONE OF YOU HAS TO GO!
GASP!

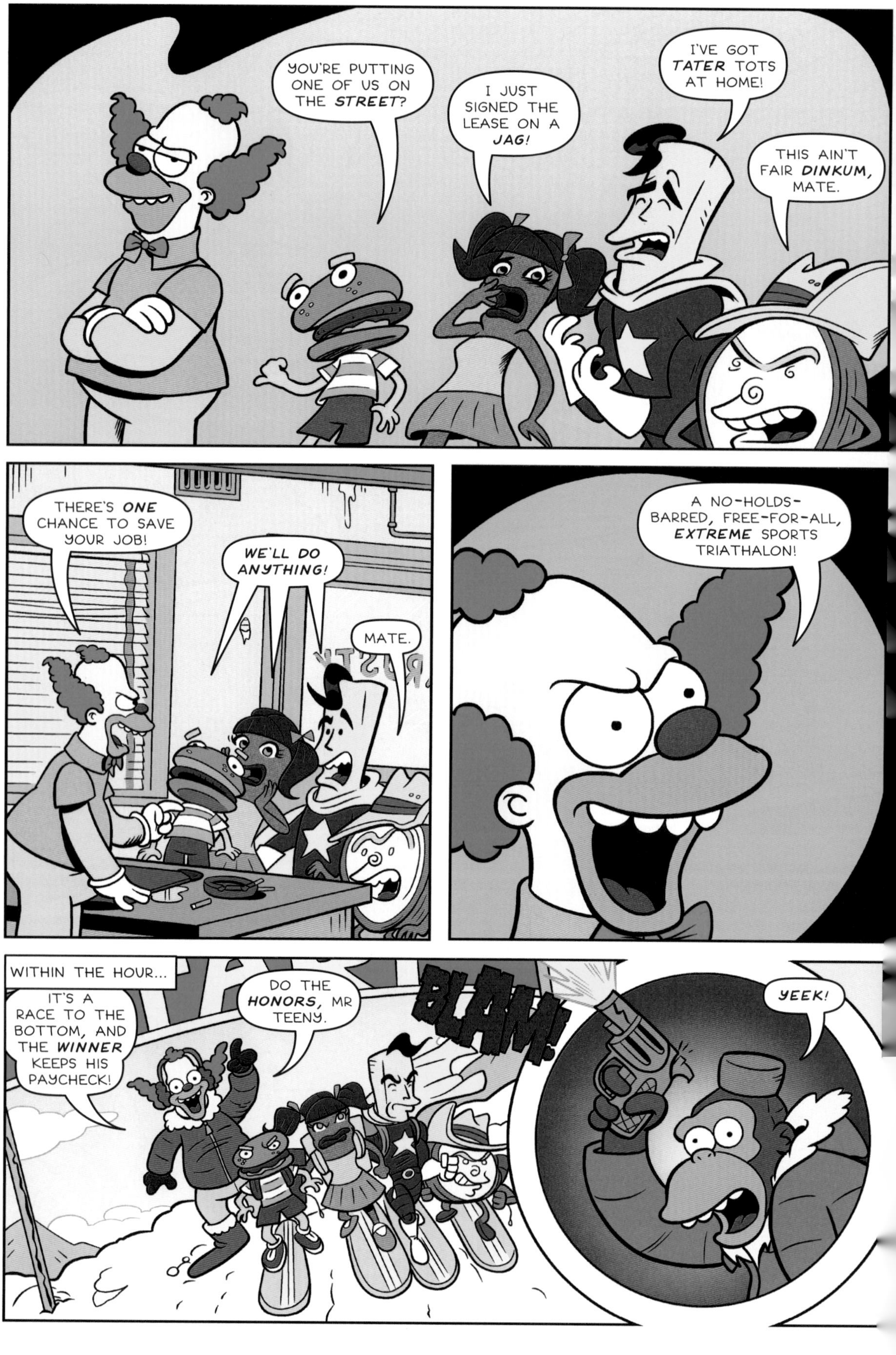

YOU'RE PUTTING ONE OF US ON THE STREET?
I JUST SIGNED THE LEASE ON A JAG!
I'VE GOT TATER TOTS AT HOME!
THIS AIN'T FAIR DINKUM, MATE.
THERE'S ONE CHANCE TO SAVE YOUR JOB!
WE'LL DO ANYTHING!
MATE.
A NO-HOLDS-BARRED, FREE-FOR-ALL, EXTREME SPORTS TRIATHALON!
WITHIN THE HOUR...
IT'S A RACE TO THE BOTTOM, AND THE WINNER KEEPS HIS PAYCHECK!
DO THE HONORS, MR TEENY.
BLAM!
YEEK!

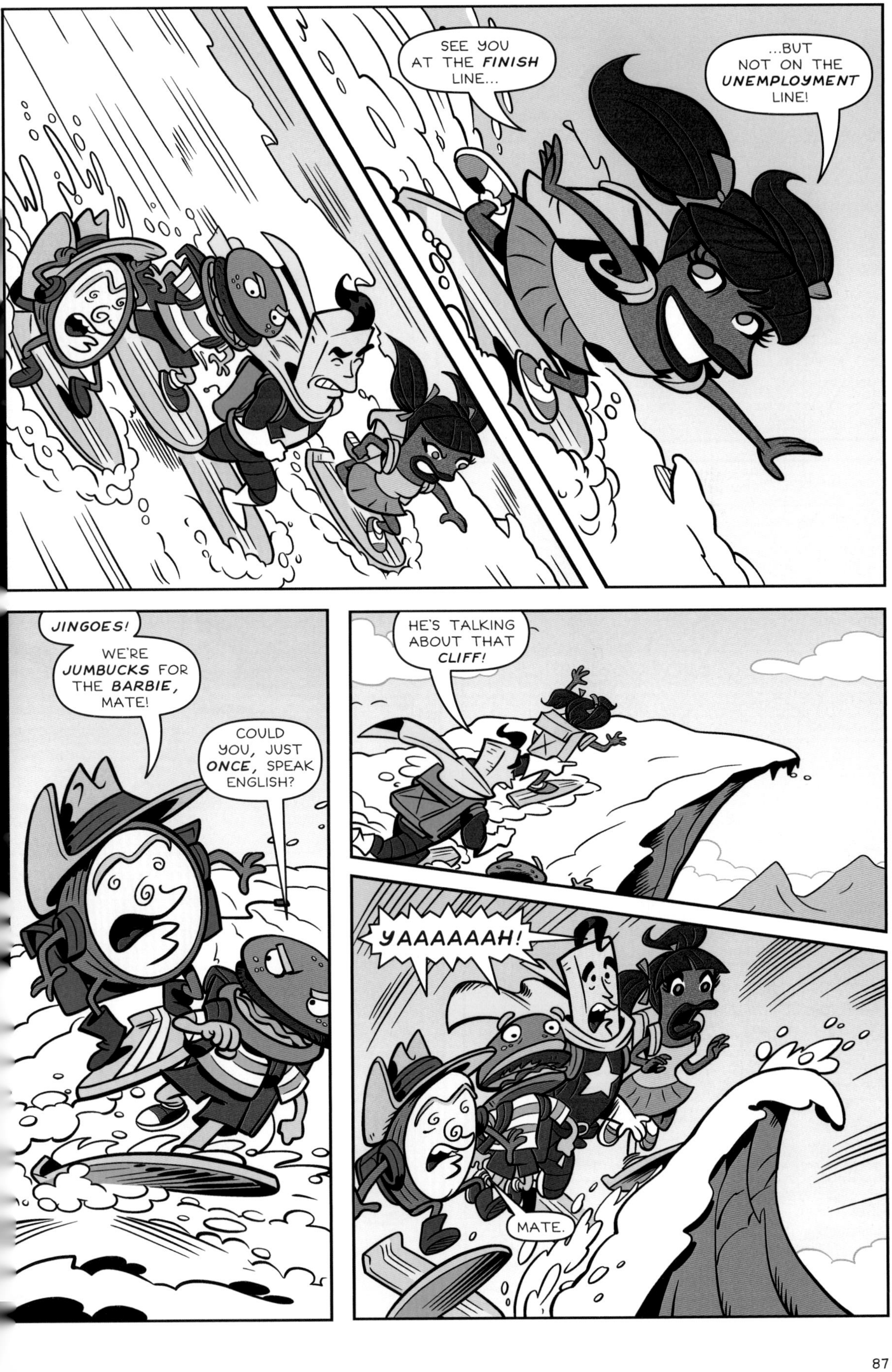
SEE YOU AT THE FINISH LINE...
...BUT NOT ON THE UNEMPLOYMENT LINE!
JINGOES!
WE'RE JUMBUCKS FOR THE BARBIE, MATE!
COULD YOU, JUST ONCE, SPEAK ENGLISH?
HE'S TALKING ABOUT THAT CLIFF!
YAAAAAAH!
MATE.

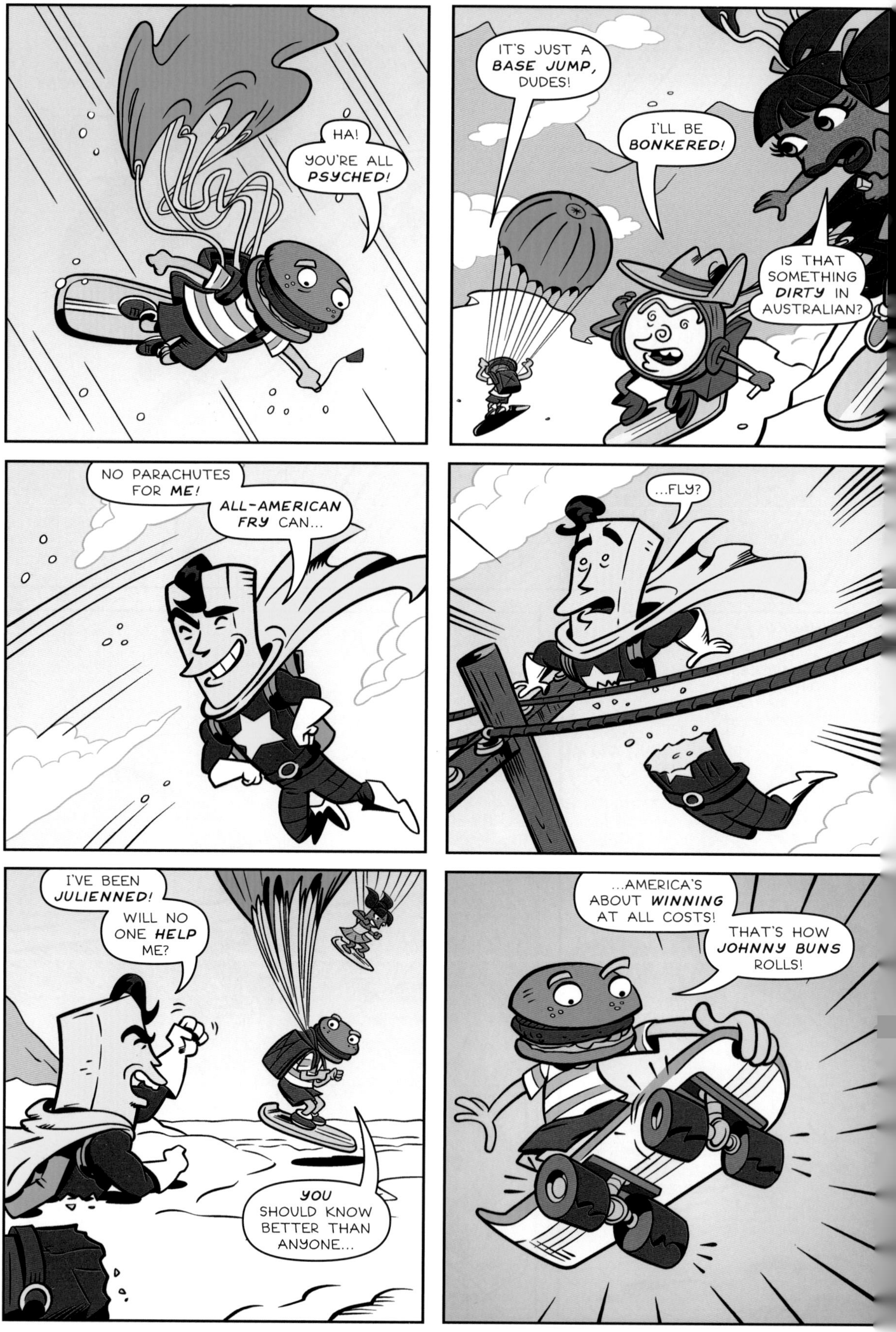
HA!
YOU'RE ALL PSYCHED!
IT'S JUST A BASE JUMP, DUDES!
I'LL BE BONKERED!
IS THAT SOMETHING DIRTY IN AUSTRALIAN?
NO PARACHUTES FOR ME!
ALL-AMERICAN FRY CAN...
...FLY?
I'VE BEEN JULIENNED!
WILL NO ONE HELP ME?
YOU SHOULD KNOW BETTER THAN ANYONE...
...AMERICA'S ABOUT WINNING AT ALL COSTS!
THAT'S HOW JOHNNY BUNS ROLLS!

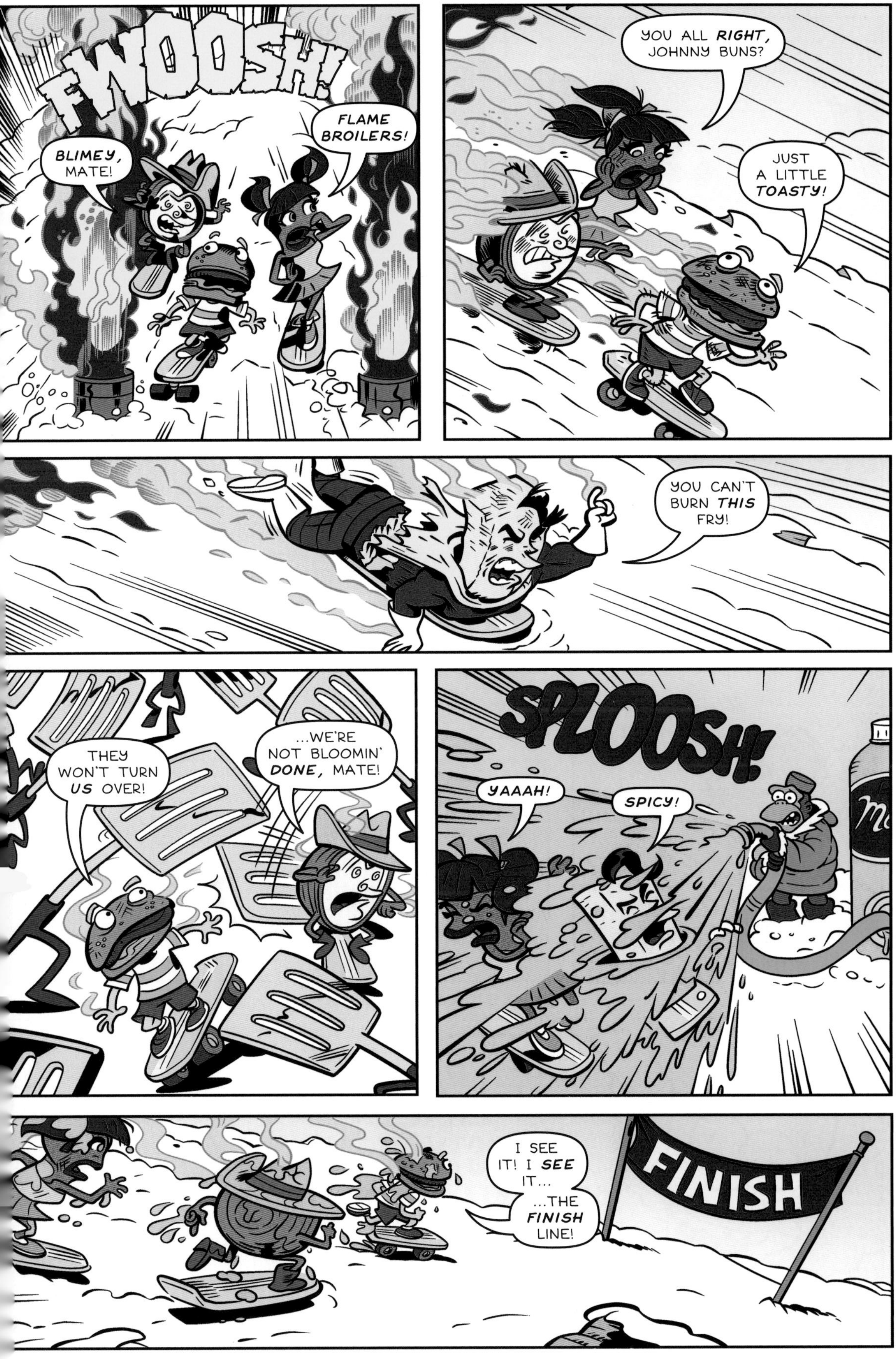
FWOOSH!
BLIMEY, MATE!
FLAME BROILERS!
YOU ALL RIGHT, JOHNNY BUNS?
JUST A LITTLE TOASTY!
YOU CAN'T BURN THIS FRY!
THEY WON'T TURN US OVER!
...WE'RE NOT BLOOMIN' DONE, MATE!
SPLOOSH!
YAAAH!
SPICY!
I SEE IT! I SEE IT...
...THE FINISH LINE!
FINISH

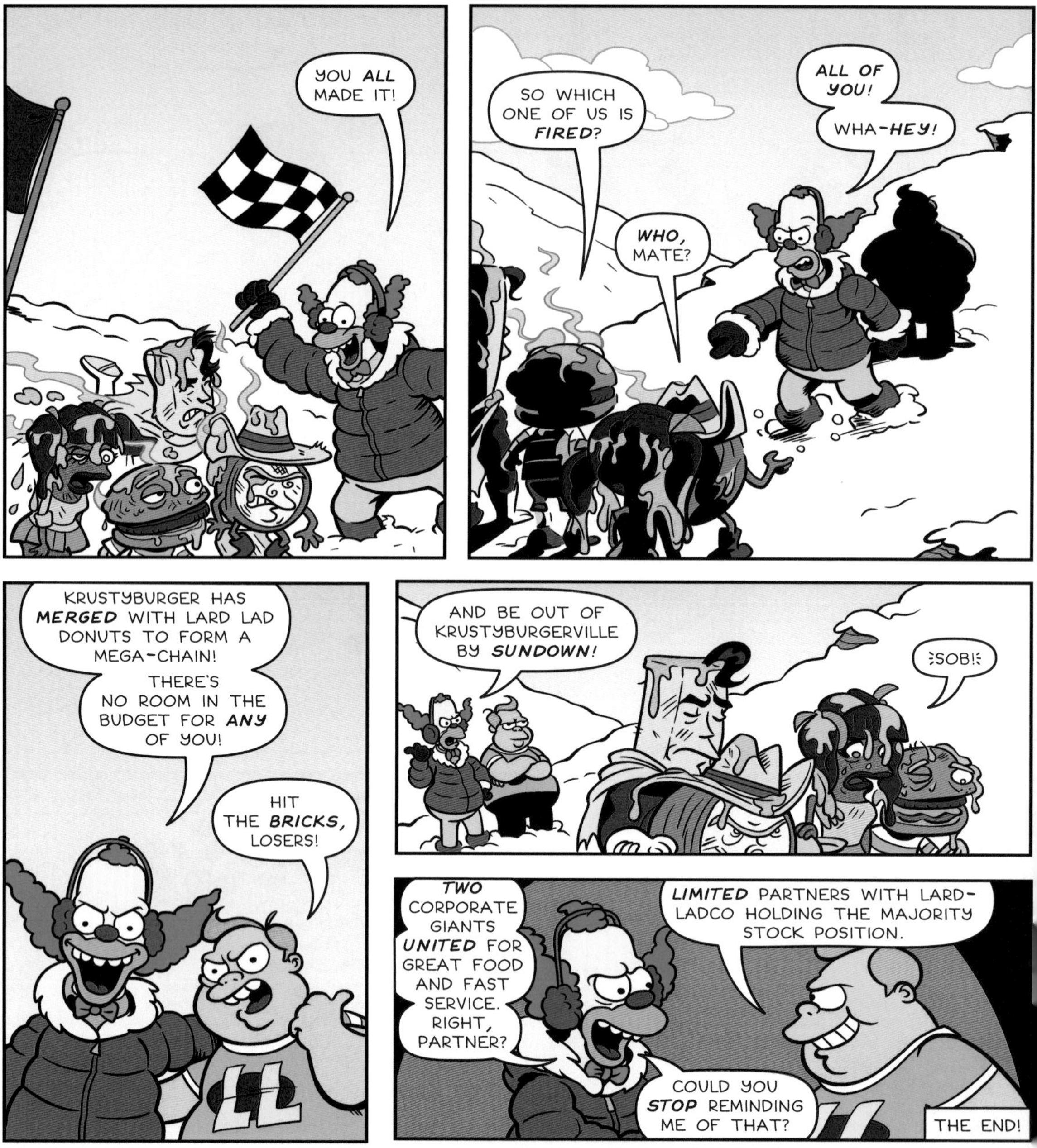
YOU ALL MADE IT!
SO WHICH ONE OF US IS FIRED?
ALL OF YOU!
WHA-HEY!
WHO, MATE?
KRUSTYBURGER HAS MERGED WITH LARD LAD DONUTS TO FORM A MEGA-CHAIN!
THERE'S NO ROOM IN THE BUDGET FOR ANY OF YOU!
HIT THE BRICKS, LOSERS!
AND BE OUT OF KRUSTYBURGERVILLE BY SUNDOWN!
SOB!
TWO CORPORATE GIANTS UNITED FOR GREAT FOOD AND FAST SERVICE. RIGHT, PARTNER?
LIMITED PARTNERS WITH LARD-LADCO HOLDING THE MAJORITY STOCK POSITION.
COULD YOU STOP REMINDING ME OF THAT?
THE END!

CLIP 'N' SAVE COUPON

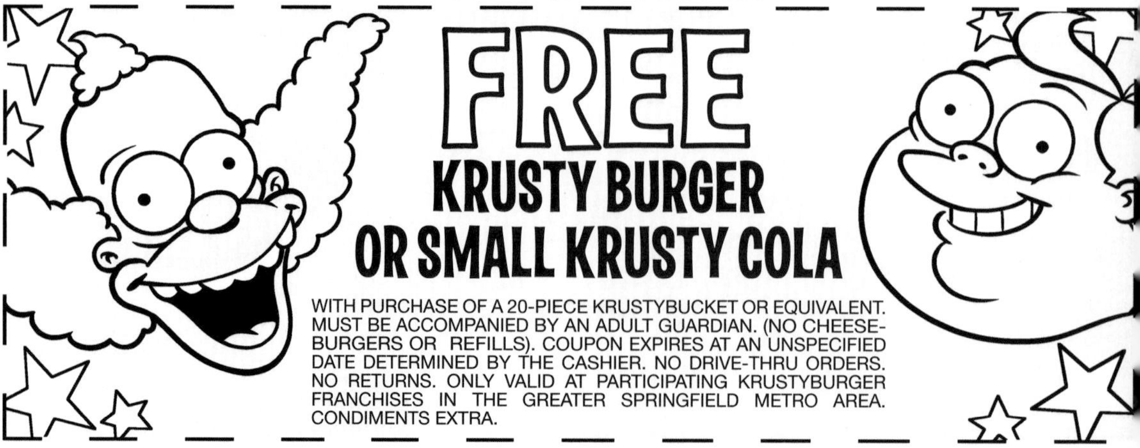
FREE
KRUSTY BURGER
OR SMALL KRUSTY COLA
WITH PURCHASE OF A 20-PIECE KRUSTYBUCKET OR EQUIVALENT. MUST BE ACCOMPANIED BY AN ADULT GUARDIAN. (NO CHEESE-BURGERS OR REFILLS). COUPON EXPIRES AT AN UNSPECIFIED DATE DETERMINED BY THE CASHIER. NO DRIVE-THRU ORDERS. NO RETURNS. ONLY VALID AT PARTICIPATING KRUSTYBURGER FRANCHISES IN THE GREATER SPRINGFIELD METRO AREA. CONDIMENTS EXTRA.

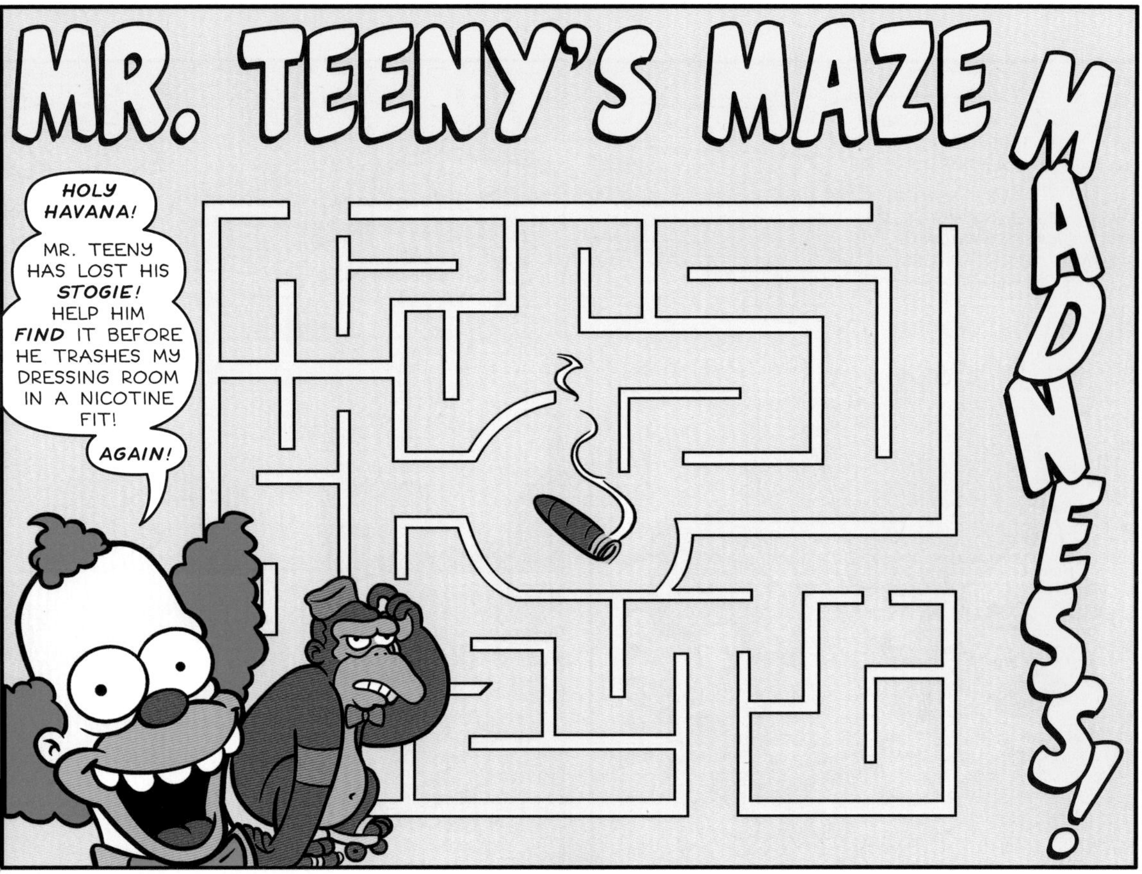
MR. TEENY'S MAZE MADNESS!
HOLY HAVANA!
MR. TEENY HAS LOST HIS STOGIE! HELP HIM FIND IT BEFORE HE TRASHES MY DRESSING ROOM IN A NICOTINE FIT!
AGAIN!

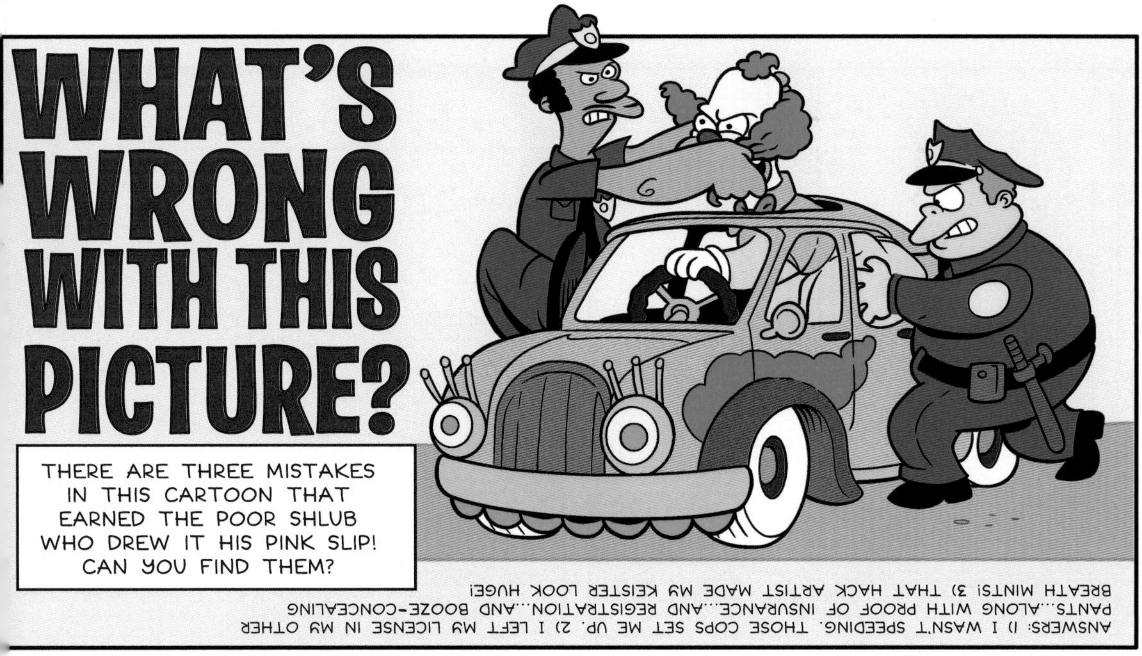
WHAT'S WRONG WITH THIS PICTURE?
THERE ARE THREE MISTAKES IN THIS CARTOON THAT EARNED THE POOR SHLUB WHO DREW IT HIS PINK SLIP! CAN YOU FIND THEM?
ANSWERS: 1) I WASN'T SPEEDING. THOSE COPS SET ME UP. 2) I LEFT MY LICENSE IN MY OTHER PANTS...ALONG WITH PROOF OF INSURANCE...AND REGISTRATION...AND BOOZE-CONCEALING BREATH MINTS! 3) THAT HACK ARTIST MADE MY KEISTER LOOK HUGE!

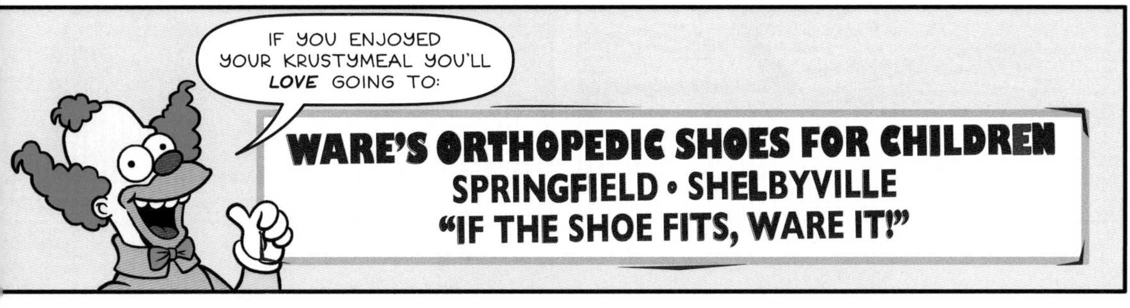
IF YOU ENJOYED YOUR KRUSTYMEAL YOU'LL LOVE GOING TO:
WARE'S ORTHOPEDIC SHOES FOR CHILDREN
SPRINGFIELD • SHELBYVILLE
"IF THE SHOE FITS, WARE IT!"

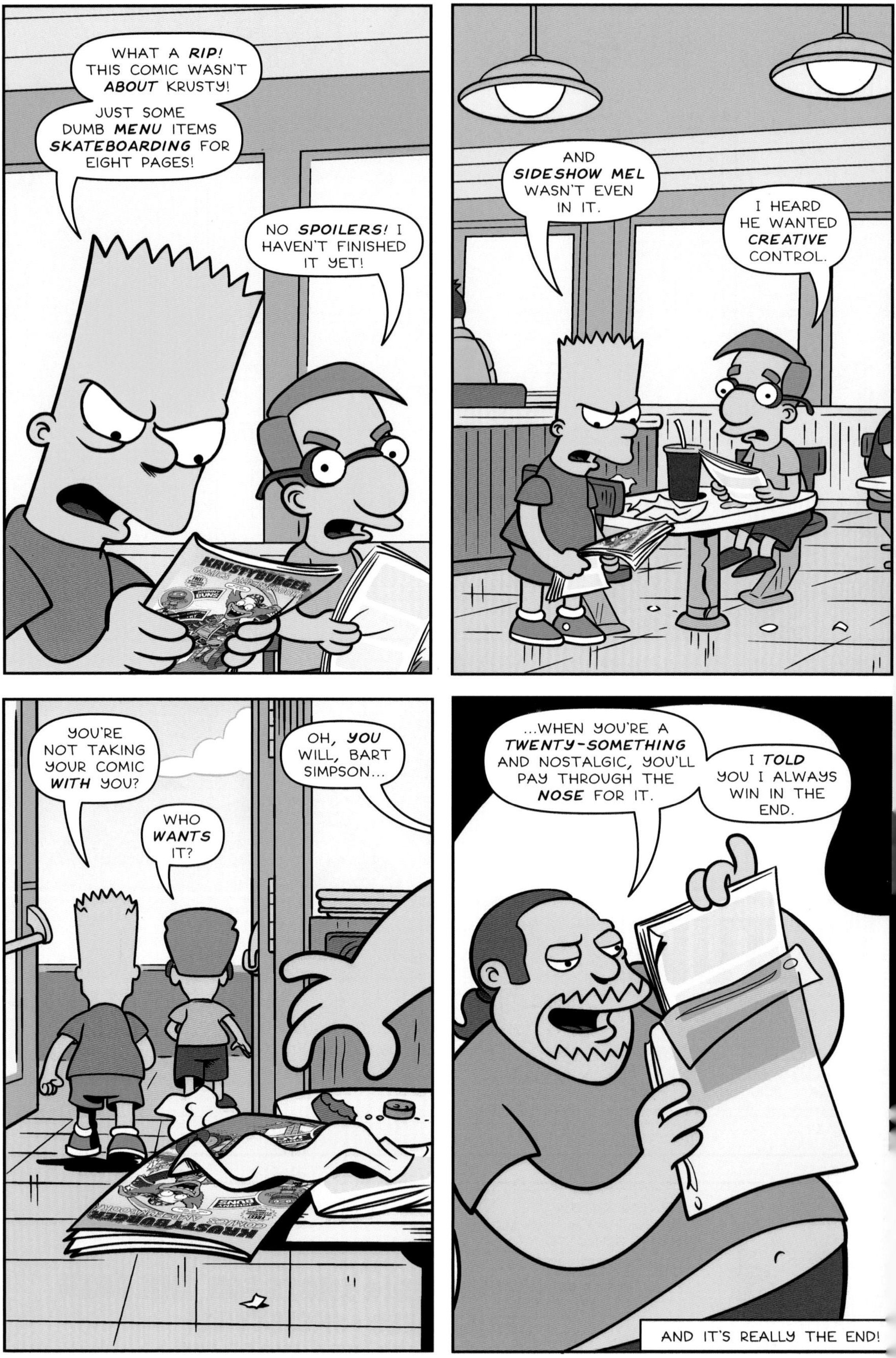
WHAT A RIP! THIS COMIC WASN'T ABOUT KRUSTY!
JUST SOME DUMB MENU ITEMS SKATEBOARDING FOR EIGHT PAGES!
NO SPOILERS! I HAVEN'T FINISHED IT YET!
AND SIDESHOW MEL WASN'T EVEN IN IT.
I HEARD HE WANTED CREATIVE CONTROL.
YOU'RE NOT TAKING YOUR COMIC WITH YOU?
WHO WANTS IT?
OH, YOU WILL, BART SIMPSON...
...WHEN YOU'RE A TWENTY-SOMETHING AND NOSTALGIC, YOU'LL PAY THROUGH THE NOSE FOR IT.
I TOLD YOU I ALWAYS WIN IN THE END.
AND IT'S REALLY THE END!

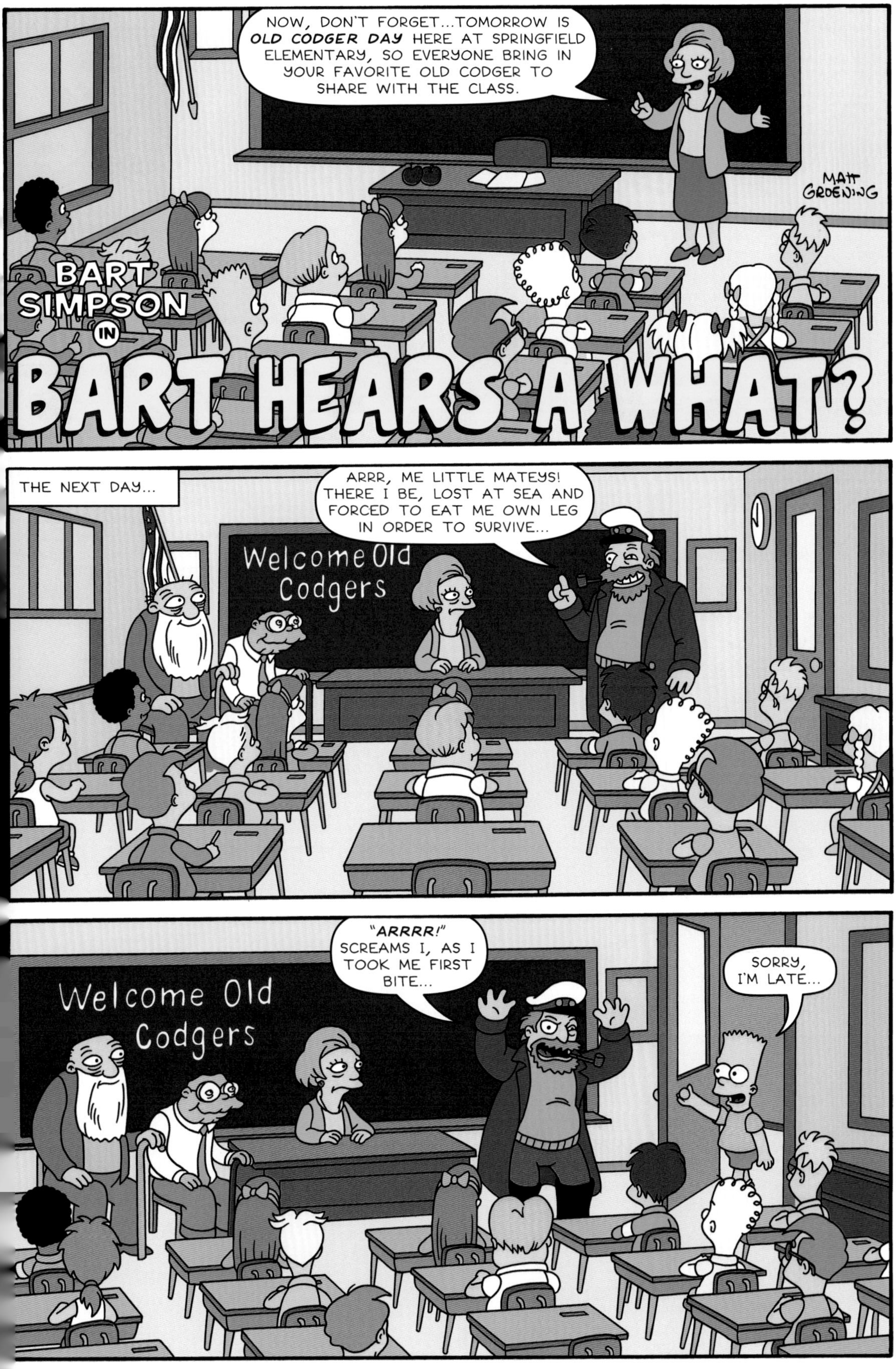
NOW, DON'T FORGET...TOMORROW IS OLD CODGER DAY HERE AT SPRINGFIELD ELEMENTARY, SO EVERYONE BRING IN YOUR FAVORITE OLD CODGER TO SHARE WITH THE CLASS.
MATT GROENING
BART SIMPSON IN
BART HEARS A WHAT?
THE NEXT DAY...
ARRR, ME LITTLE MATEYS! THERE I BE, LOST AT SEA AND FORCED TO EAT ME OWN LEG IN ORDER TO SURVIVE...
Welcome Old Codgers
"ARRRR!" SCREAMS I, AS I TOOK ME FIRST BITE...
SORRY, I'M LATE...
Welcome Old Codgers

MARY TRAINOR SCRIPT *MARCOS ASPREC* PENCILS *STEVE STEERE, JR.* INKS *NATHAN HAMILL* COLORS *KAREN BATES* LETTERS *BILL MORRISON* EDITOR

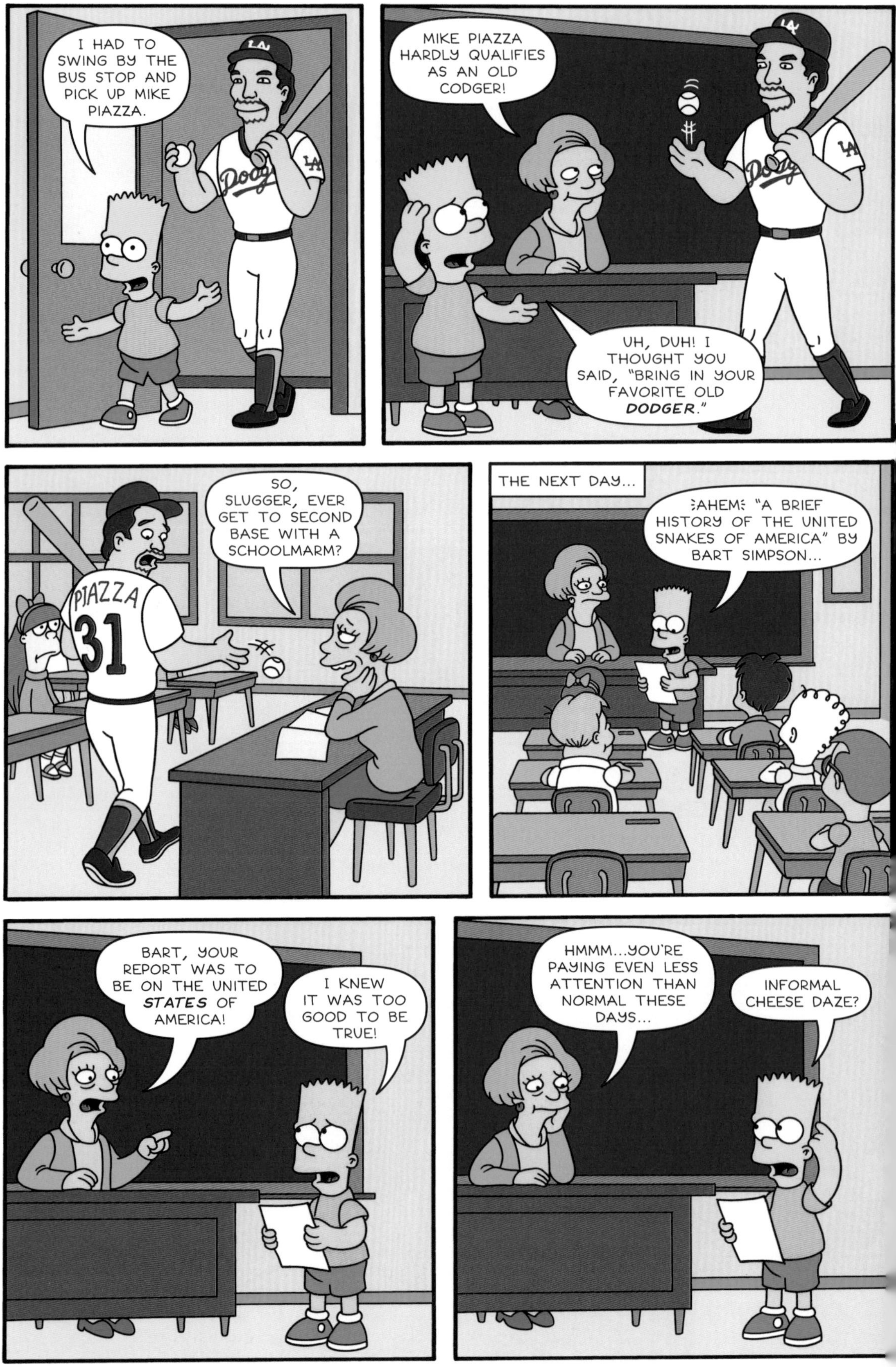
I HAD TO SWING BY THE BUS STOP AND PICK UP MIKE PIAZZA.
MIKE PIAZZA HARDLY QUALIFIES AS AN OLD CODGER!
UH, DUH! I THOUGHT YOU SAID, "BRING IN YOUR FAVORITE OLD DODGER."
SO, SLUGGER, EVER GET TO SECOND BASE WITH A SCHOOLMARM?
PIAZZA 31
THE NEXT DAY...
AHEM "A BRIEF HISTORY OF THE UNITED SNAKES OF AMERICA" BY BART SIMPSON...
BART, YOUR REPORT WAS TO BE ON THE UNITED STATES OF AMERICA!
I KNEW IT WAS TOO GOOD TO BE TRUE!
HMMM...YOU'RE PAYING EVEN LESS ATTENTION THAN NORMAL THESE DAYS...
INFORMAL CHEESE DAZE?

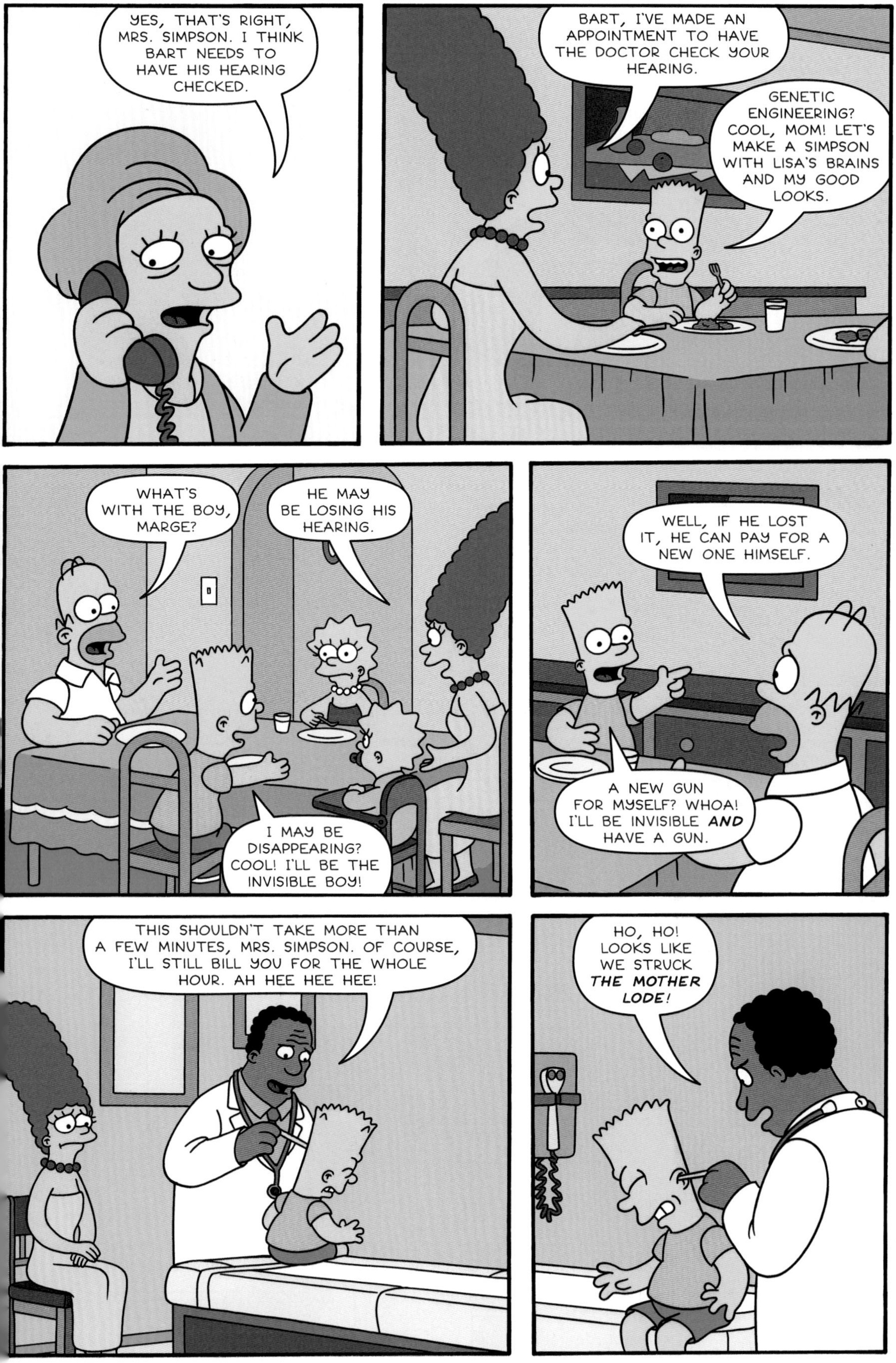
YES, THAT'S RIGHT, MRS. SIMPSON. I THINK BART NEEDS TO HAVE HIS HEARING CHECKED.
BART, I'VE MADE AN APPOINTMENT TO HAVE THE DOCTOR CHECK YOUR HEARING.
GENETIC ENGINEERING? COOL, MOM! LET'S MAKE A SIMPSON WITH LISA'S BRAINS AND MY GOOD LOOKS.
WHAT'S WITH THE BOY, MARGE?
HE MAY BE LOSING HIS HEARING.
I MAY BE DISAPPEARING? COOL! I'LL BE THE INVISIBLE BOY!
WELL, IF HE LOST IT, HE CAN PAY FOR A NEW ONE HIMSELF.
A NEW GUN FOR MYSELF? WHOA! I'LL BE INVISIBLE **AND** HAVE A GUN.
THIS SHOULDN'T TAKE MORE THAN A FEW MINUTES, MRS. SIMPSON. OF COURSE, I'LL STILL BILL YOU FOR THE WHOLE HOUR. AH HEE HEE HEE!
HO, HO! LOOKS LIKE WE STRUCK ***THE MOTHER LODE***!

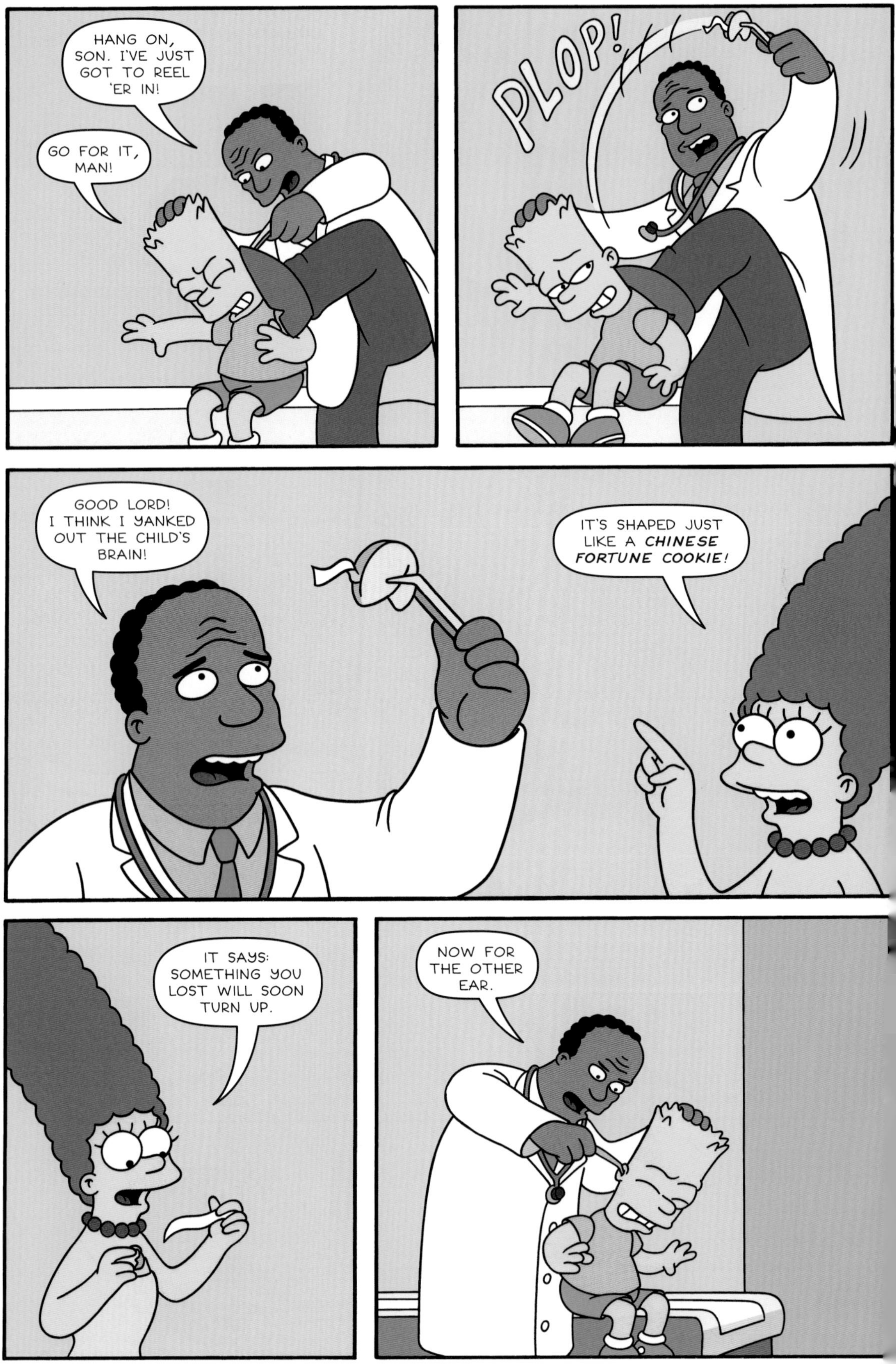
HANG ON, SON. I'VE JUST GOT TO REEL 'ER IN!
GO FOR IT, MAN!
PLOP!
GOOD LORD! I THINK I YANKED OUT THE CHILD'S BRAIN!
IT'S SHAPED JUST LIKE A ***CHINESE FORTUNE COOKIE***!
IT SAYS: SOMETHING YOU LOST WILL SOON TURN UP.
NOW FOR THE OTHER EAR.

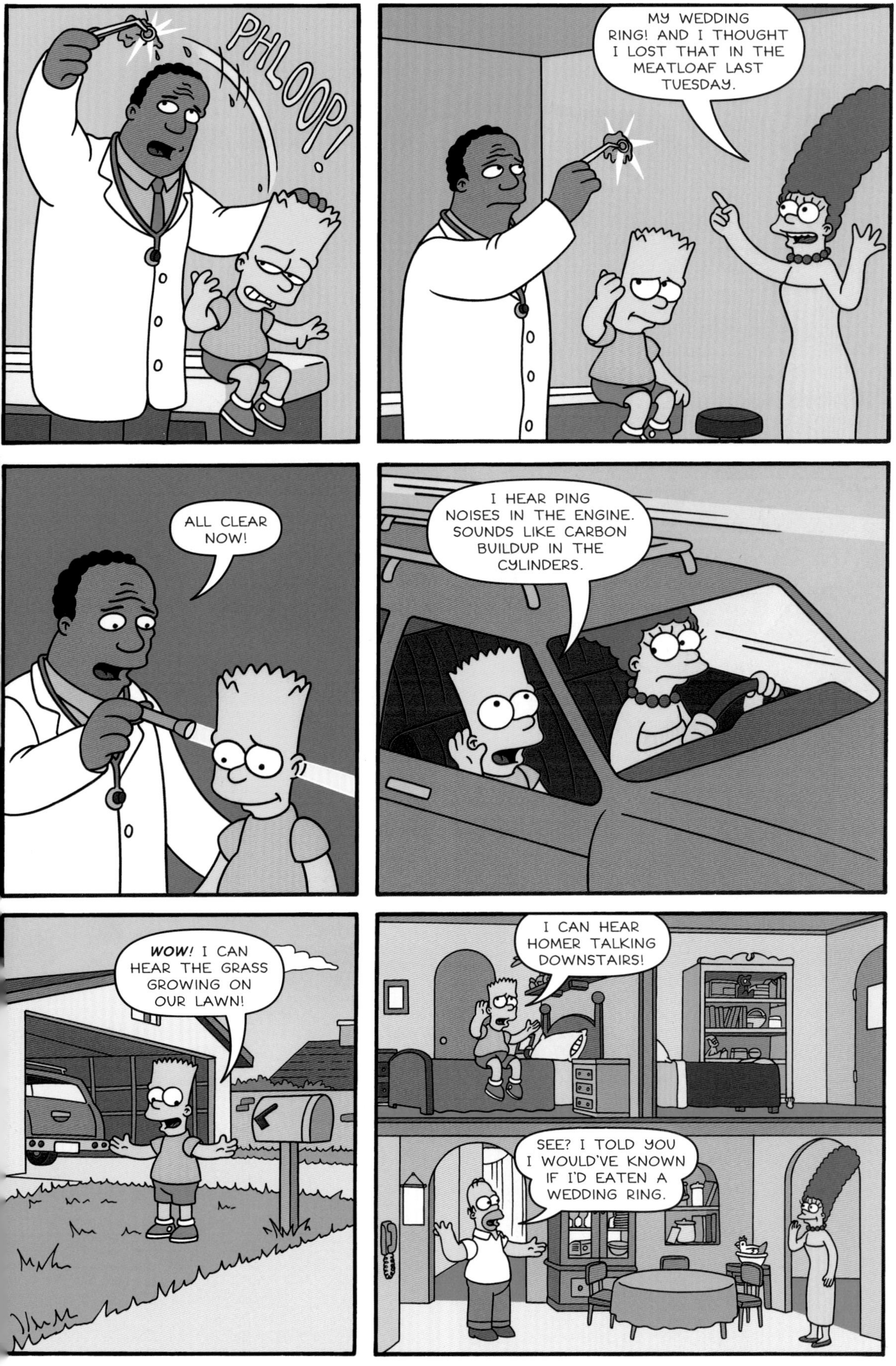
PHLOOP!
MY WEDDING RING! AND I THOUGHT I LOST THAT IN THE MEATLOAF LAST TUESDAY.
ALL CLEAR NOW!
I HEAR PING NOISES IN THE ENGINE. SOUNDS LIKE CARBON BUILDUP IN THE CYLINDERS.
WOW! I CAN HEAR THE GRASS GROWING ON OUR LAWN!
I CAN HEAR HOMER TALKING DOWNSTAIRS!
SEE? I TOLD YOU I WOULD'VE KNOWN IF I'D EATEN A WEDDING RING.

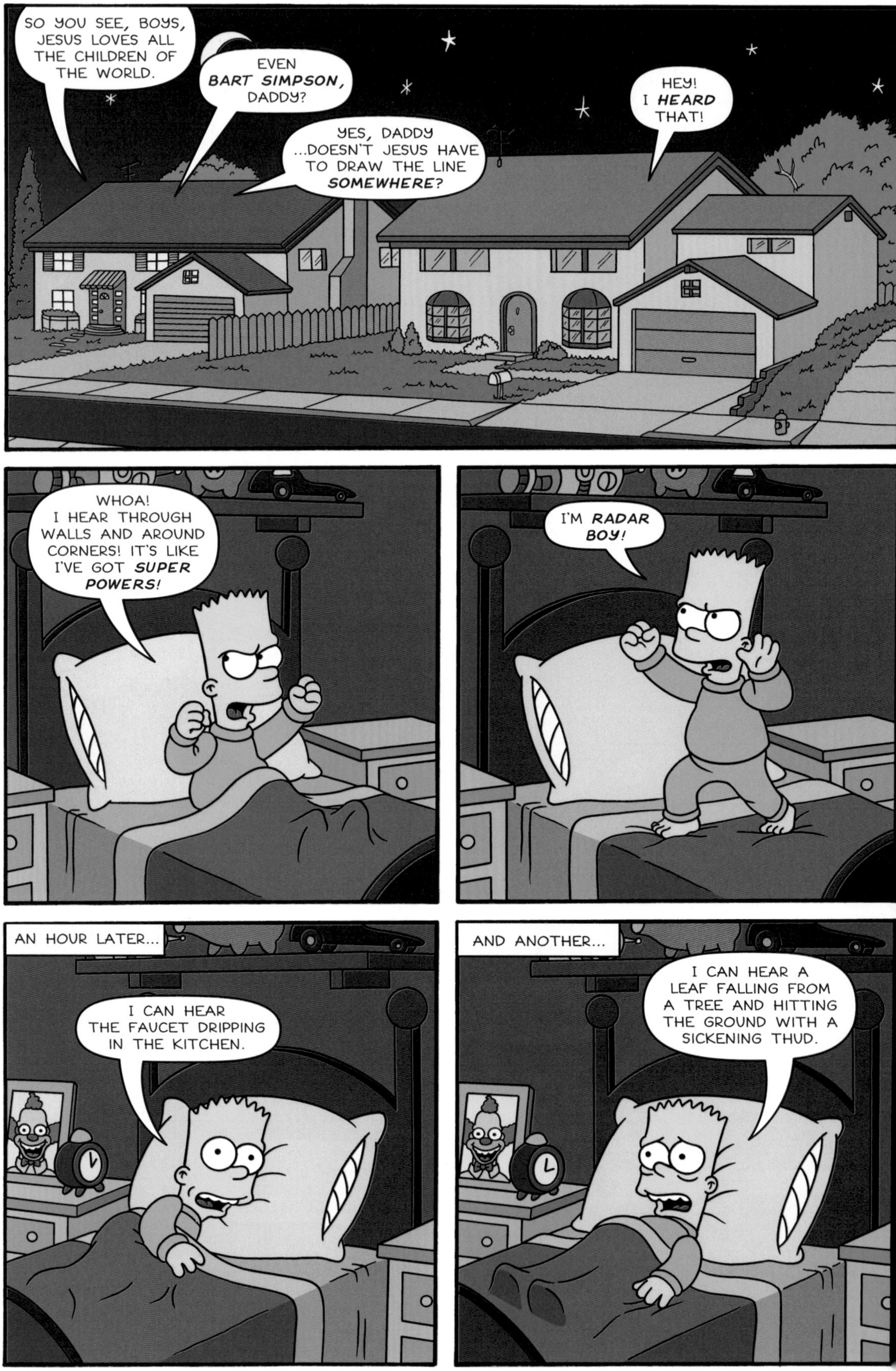
SO YOU SEE, BOYS, JESUS LOVES ALL THE CHILDREN OF THE WORLD.
EVEN **BART SIMPSON,** DADDY?
YES, DADDY ...DOESN'T JESUS HAVE TO DRAW THE LINE **SOMEWHERE?**
HEY! I **HEARD** THAT!
WHOA! I HEAR THROUGH WALLS AND AROUND CORNERS! IT'S LIKE I'VE GOT **SUPER POWERS!**
I'M **RADAR BOY!**
AN HOUR LATER...
I CAN HEAR THE FAUCET DRIPPING IN THE KITCHEN.
AND ANOTHER...
I CAN HEAR A LEAF FALLING FROM A TREE AND HITTING THE GROUND WITH A SICKENING THUD.

AND ANOTHER...

I CAN HEAR THE SPIDERS BREATHING IN THE WALLS.

AND ANOTHER...

OH, MAN! I CAN'T TAKE THIS!

SO LONG, RADAR BOY. I'M PUTTING A LOAD OF WAX BACK IN MY EARS!

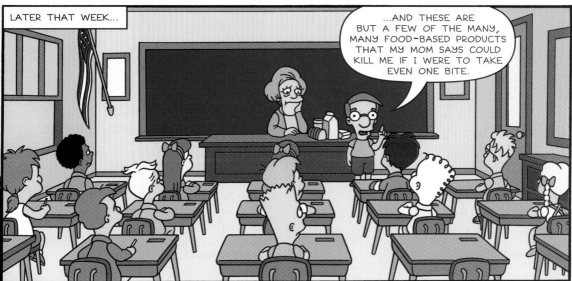

LATER THAT WEEK...

...AND THESE ARE BUT A FEW OF THE MANY, MANY FOOD-BASED PRODUCTS THAT MY MOM SAYS COULD KILL ME IF I WERE TO TAKE EVEN ONE BITE.

FASCINATING, MILHOUSE. NOW, BART, WHAT DID YOU BRING FOR *SHOW AND TELL DAY*?

UH, DUH! I THOUGHT YOU SAID SHOW AND *SMELL* DAY!

THE END

99

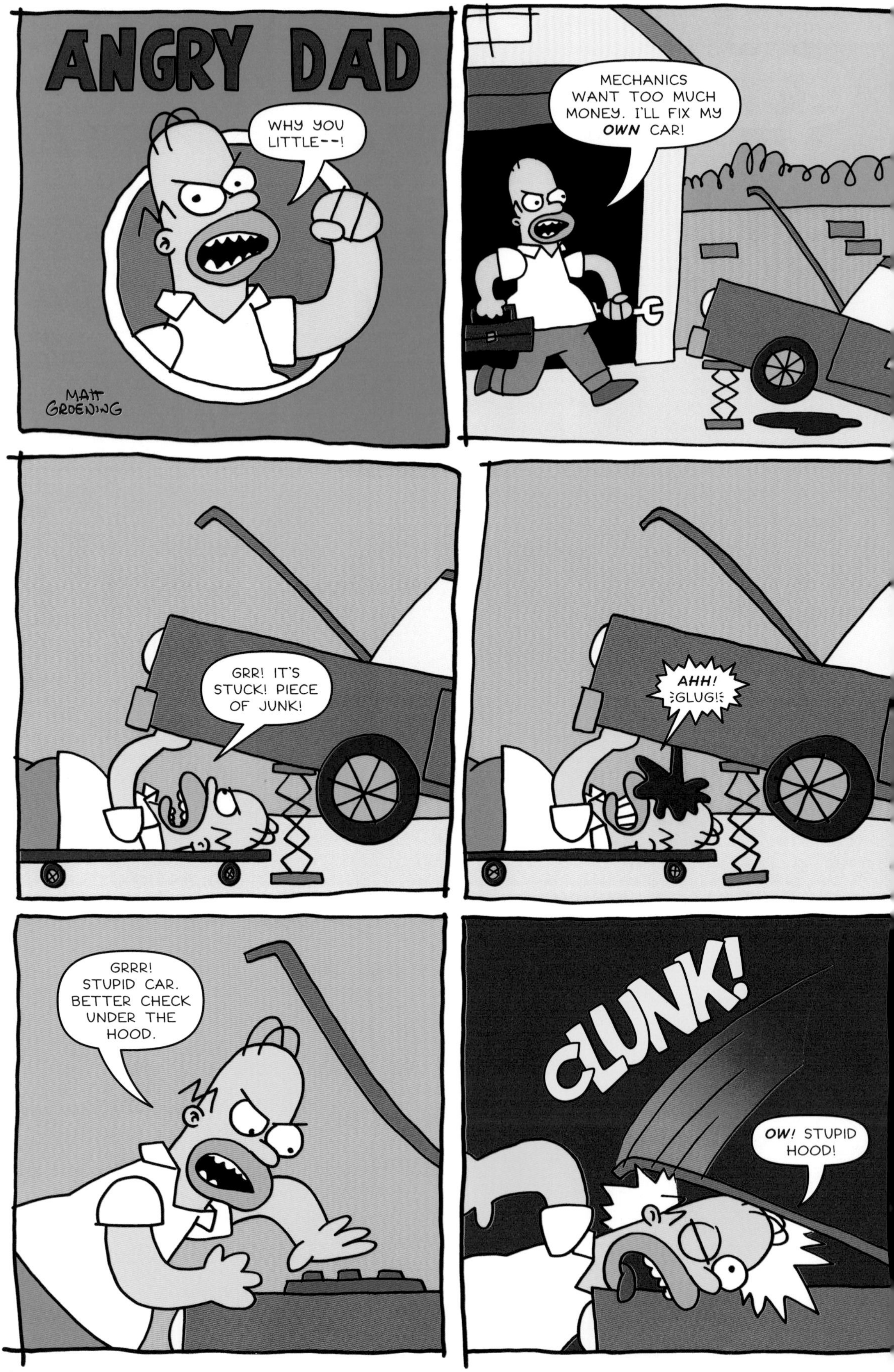
ANGRY DAD
WHY YOU LITTLE--!
MATT GROENING
MECHANICS WANT TOO MUCH MONEY. I'LL FIX MY OWN CAR!
GRR! IT'S STUCK! PIECE OF JUNK!
AHH! GLUG!
GRRR! STUPID CAR. BETTER CHECK UNDER THE HOOD.
CLUNK!
OW! STUPID HOOD!

TONY DIGEROLAMO SCRIPT
JASON HO PENCILS & INKS
NATHAN HAMILL COLORS
KAREN BATES LETTERS
BILL MORRISON EDITOR

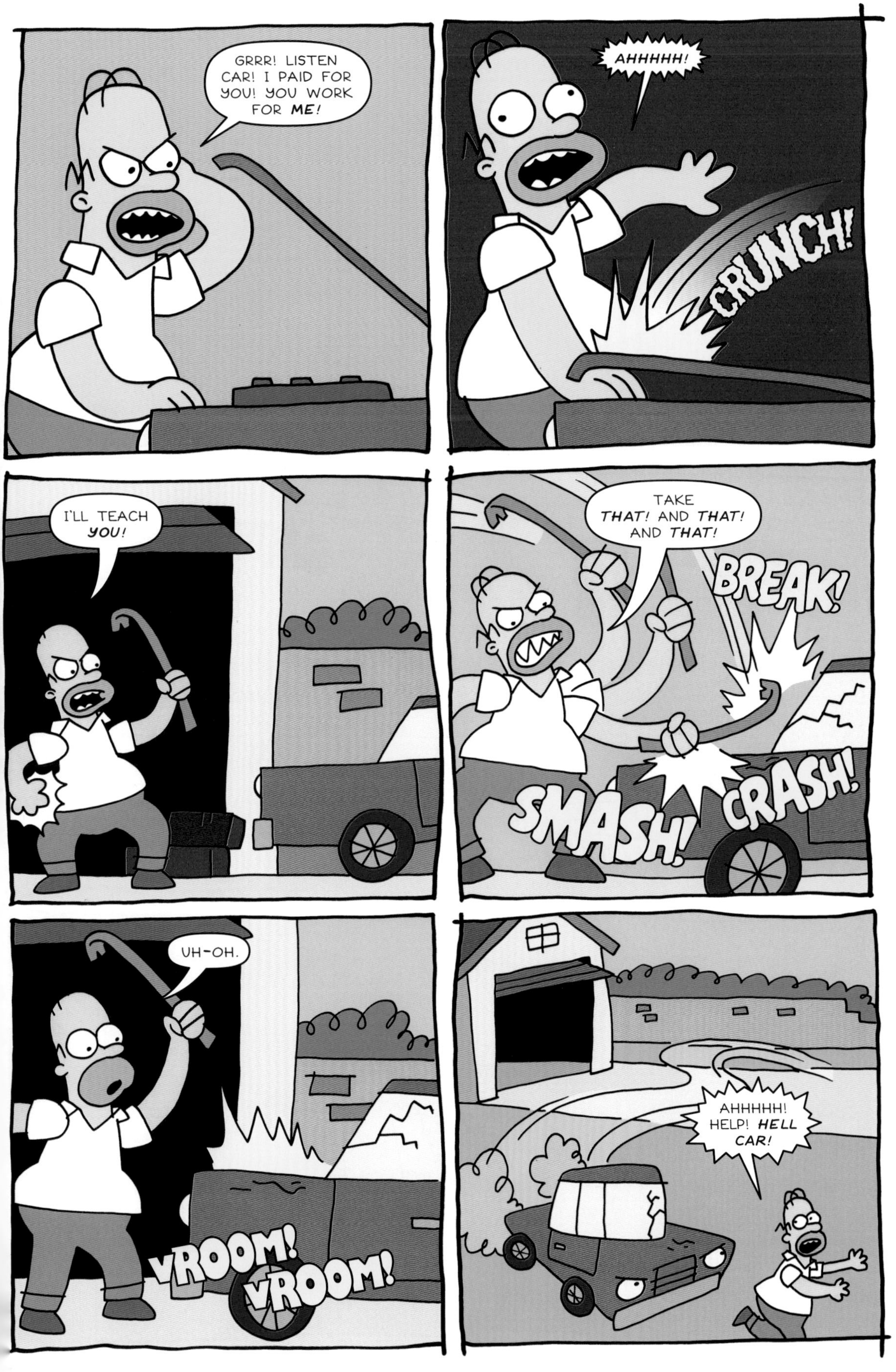
GRRR! LISTEN CAR! I PAID FOR YOU! YOU WORK FOR **ME**!
AHHHHH!
CRUNCH!
I'LL TEACH ***YOU***!
TAKE ***THAT***! AND ***THAT***! AND ***THAT***!
BREAK!
SMASH!
CRASH!
UH-OH.
VROOM!
VROOM!
AHHHHH! HELP! ***HELL CAR***!

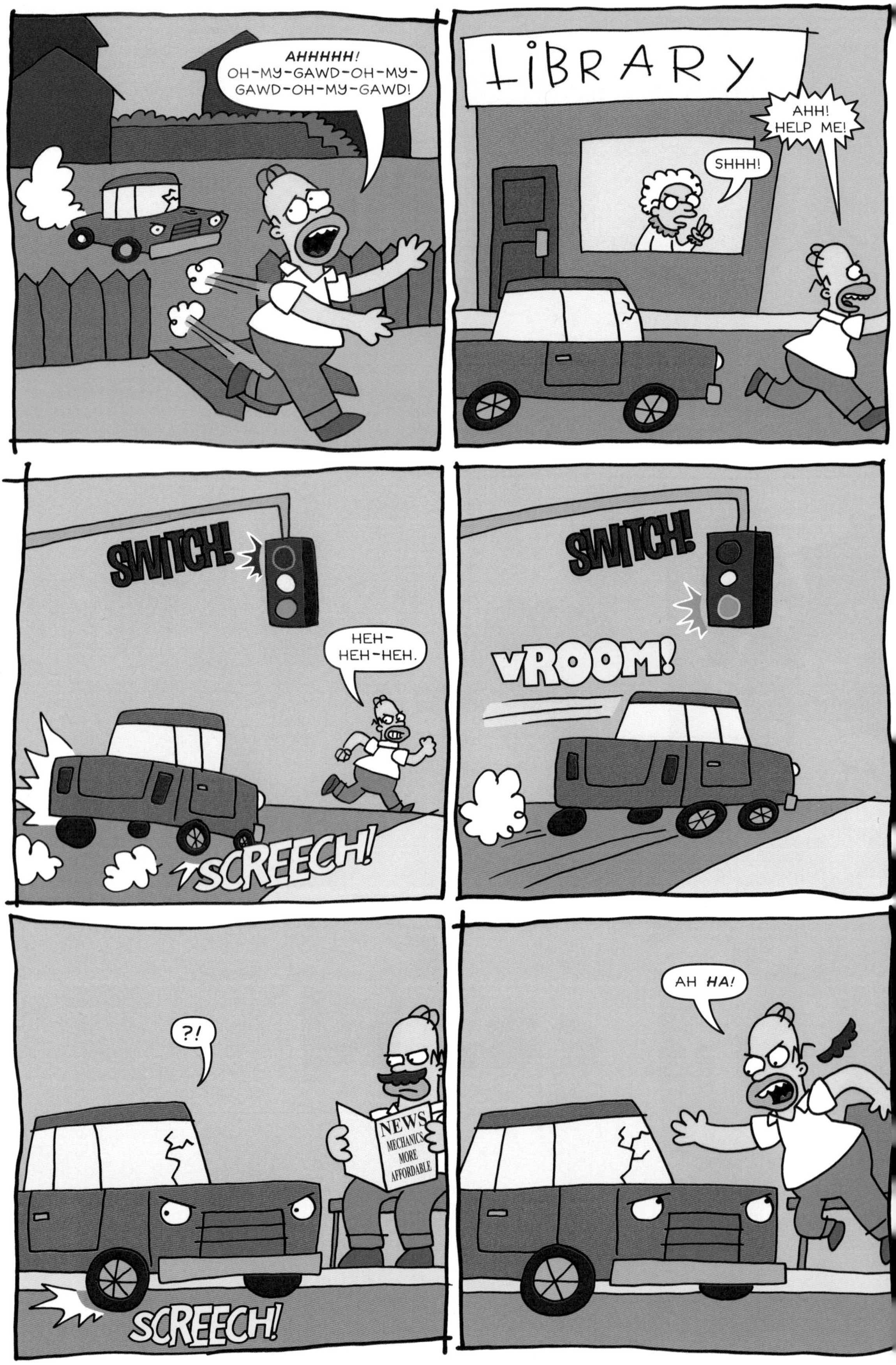
AHHHHH!
OH-MY-GAWD-OH-MY-GAWD-OH-MY-GAWD!
LIBRARY
AHH! HELP ME!
SHHH!
SWITCH!
HEH-HEH-HEH.
SCREECH!
SWITCH!
VROOM!
?!
NEWS
MECHANICS MORE AFFORDABLE
SCREECH!
AH HA!

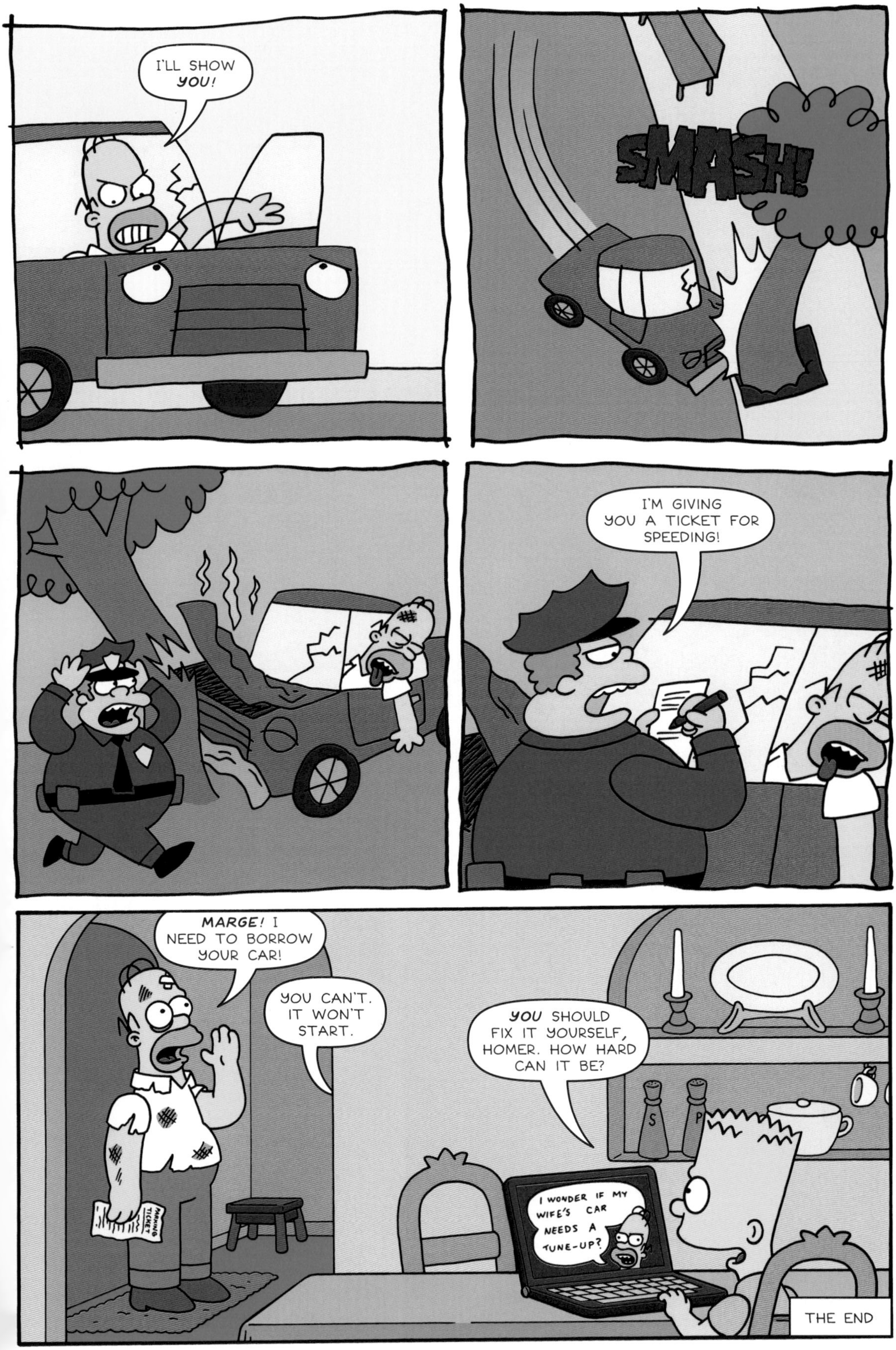
I'LL SHOW *YOU!*
SMASH!
I'M GIVING YOU A TICKET FOR SPEEDING!
MARGE! I NEED TO BORROW YOUR CAR!
YOU CAN'T. IT WON'T START.
YOU SHOULD FIX IT YOURSELF, HOMER. HOW HARD CAN IT BE?
I WONDER IF MY WIFE'S CAR NEEDS A TUNE-UP?
THE END

BART SIMPSON
in
BATTLE OF THE 'PLEXES!

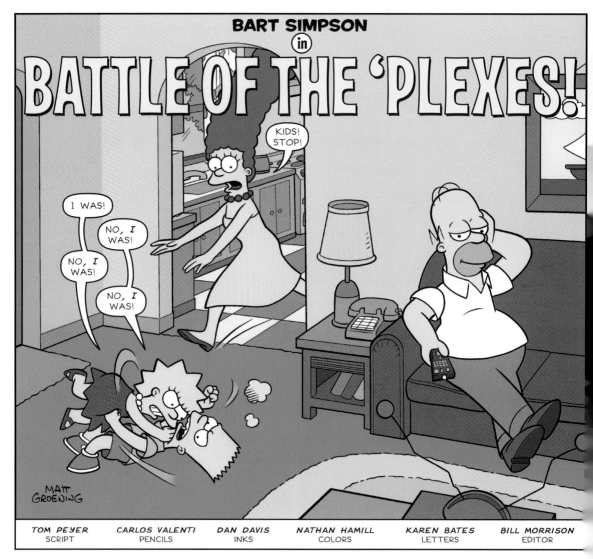

KIDS! STOP!

I WAS!

NO, *I* WAS!

NO, *I* WAS!

NO, *I* WAS!

| **TOM PEYER** SCRIPT | **CARLOS VALENTI** PENCILS | **DAN DAVIS** INKS | **NATHAN HAMILL** COLORS | **KAREN BATES** LETTERS | **BILL MORRISON** EDITOR |

WHAT ARE YOU *FIGHTING* OVER?

WHICH ONE OF US WAS ADOPTED.

I WAS!

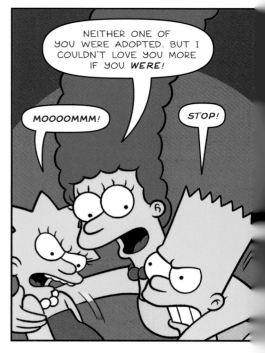

NEITHER ONE OF YOU WERE ADOPTED. BUT I COULDN'T LOVE YOU MORE IF YOU *WERE!*

MOOOOMMM!

STOP!

NOW *LISTEN* TO ME! BROTHERS AND SISTERS SHOULD ALWAYS TRY TO *GET ALONG!*

HOW? BOYS WANT TO PLAY *ROUGH* WHEN GIRLS WOULD RATHER--

AND *GIRLS* NEVER FINISH THEIR *SENTENCES!*

YOU NEVER *LET* US!

YOU *SEE?* IT'S *HOPELESS!*

KIDS, KIDS...

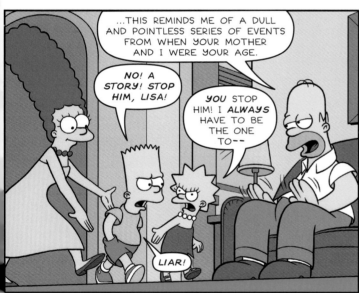

...THIS REMINDS ME OF A DULL AND POINTLESS SERIES OF EVENTS FROM WHEN YOUR MOTHER AND I WERE YOUR AGE.

NO! A *STORY! STOP HIM,* LISA!

YOU STOP HIM! I *ALWAYS* HAVE TO BE THE ONE TO--

LIAR!

YOU'RE RIGHT, HOMIE. THEY'RE JUST LIKE WE WERE.

YES, BACK WHERE IT ALL *STARTED,* IN THAT DECADE LONG AGO...

"...WHEN CARS RAN ON GASOLINE, BIRDS FLEW FREE, AND MILLIONS OF PEOPLE SOUGHT RELIEF FROM THEIR WORRIES IN A MAGICAL PLACE CALLED...*THE MOVIES.*"

THE CANNONBALL RUN
IN COLOR

WHERE'S THE BEEF?

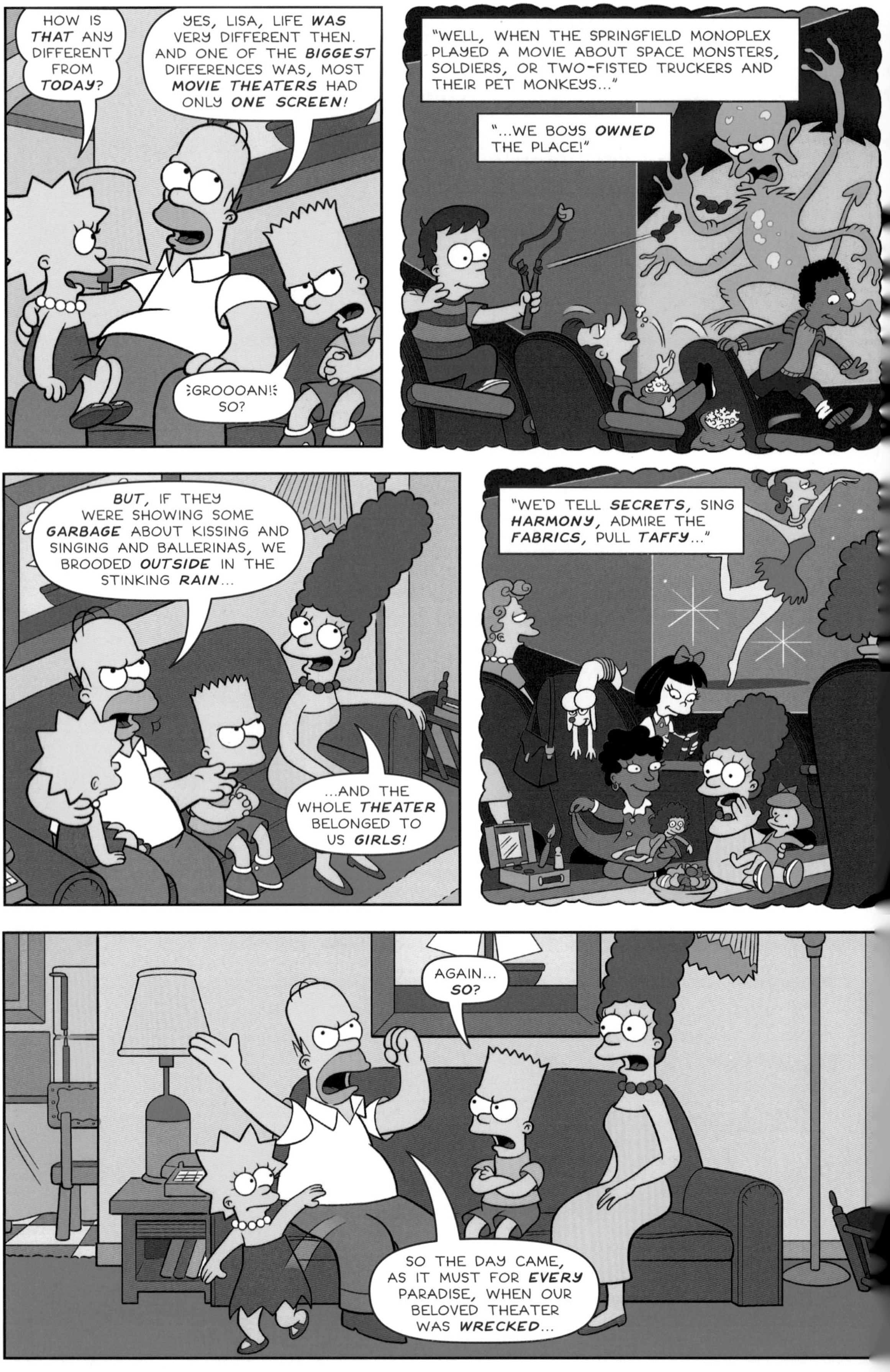
HOW IS THAT ANY DIFFERENT FROM TODAY?
YES, LISA, LIFE WAS VERY DIFFERENT THEN. AND ONE OF THE BIGGEST DIFFERENCES WAS, MOST MOVIE THEATERS HAD ONLY ONE SCREEN!
GROOOAN! SO?
"WELL, WHEN THE SPRINGFIELD MONOPLEX PLAYED A MOVIE ABOUT SPACE MONSTERS, SOLDIERS, OR TWO-FISTED TRUCKERS AND THEIR PET MONKEYS..."
"...WE BOYS OWNED THE PLACE!"
BUT, IF THEY WERE SHOWING SOME GARBAGE ABOUT KISSING AND SINGING AND BALLERINAS, WE BROODED OUTSIDE IN THE STINKING RAIN...
...AND THE WHOLE THEATER BELONGED TO US GIRLS!
"WE'D TELL SECRETS, SING HARMONY, ADMIRE THE FABRICS, PULL TAFFY..."
AGAIN... SO?
SO THE DAY CAME, AS IT MUST FOR EVERY PARADISE, WHEN OUR BELOVED THEATER WAS WRECKED...

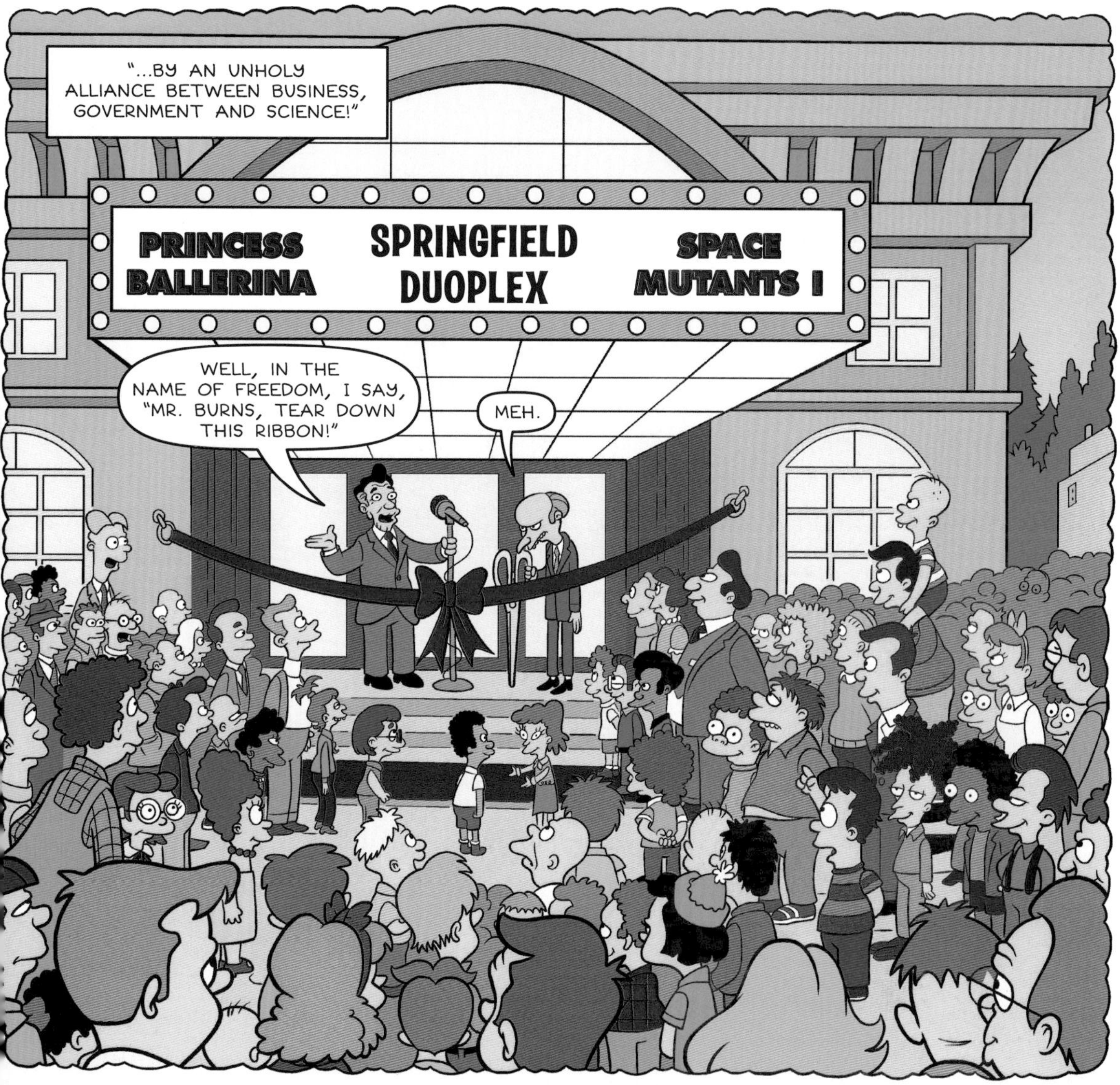
"...BY AN UNHOLY ALLIANCE BETWEEN BUSINESS, GOVERNMENT AND SCIENCE!"
PRINCESS BALLERINA
SPRINGFIELD DUOPLEX
SPACE MUTANTS I
WELL, IN THE NAME OF FREEDOM, I SAY, "MR. BURNS, TEAR DOWN THIS RIBBON!"
MEH.

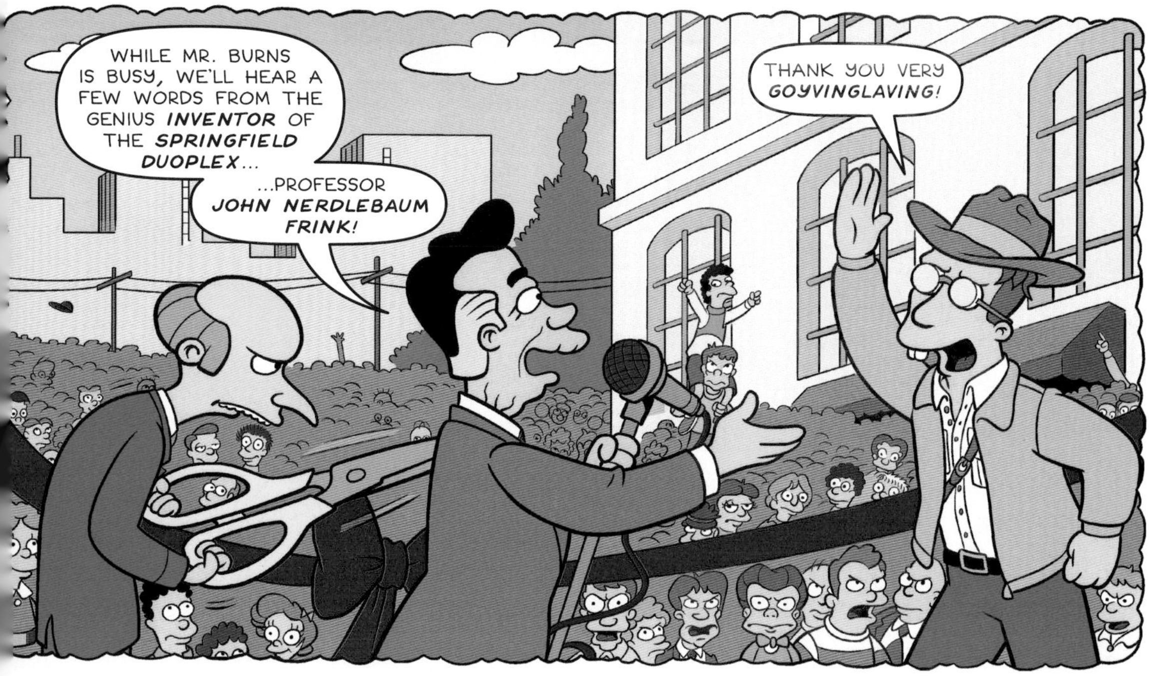
WHILE MR. BURNS IS BUSY, WE'LL HEAR A FEW WORDS FROM THE GENIUS *INVENTOR* OF THE *SPRINGFIELD DUOPLEX*...
...PROFESSOR *JOHN NERDLEBAUM FRINK!*
THANK YOU VERY *GOYVINGLAVING!*

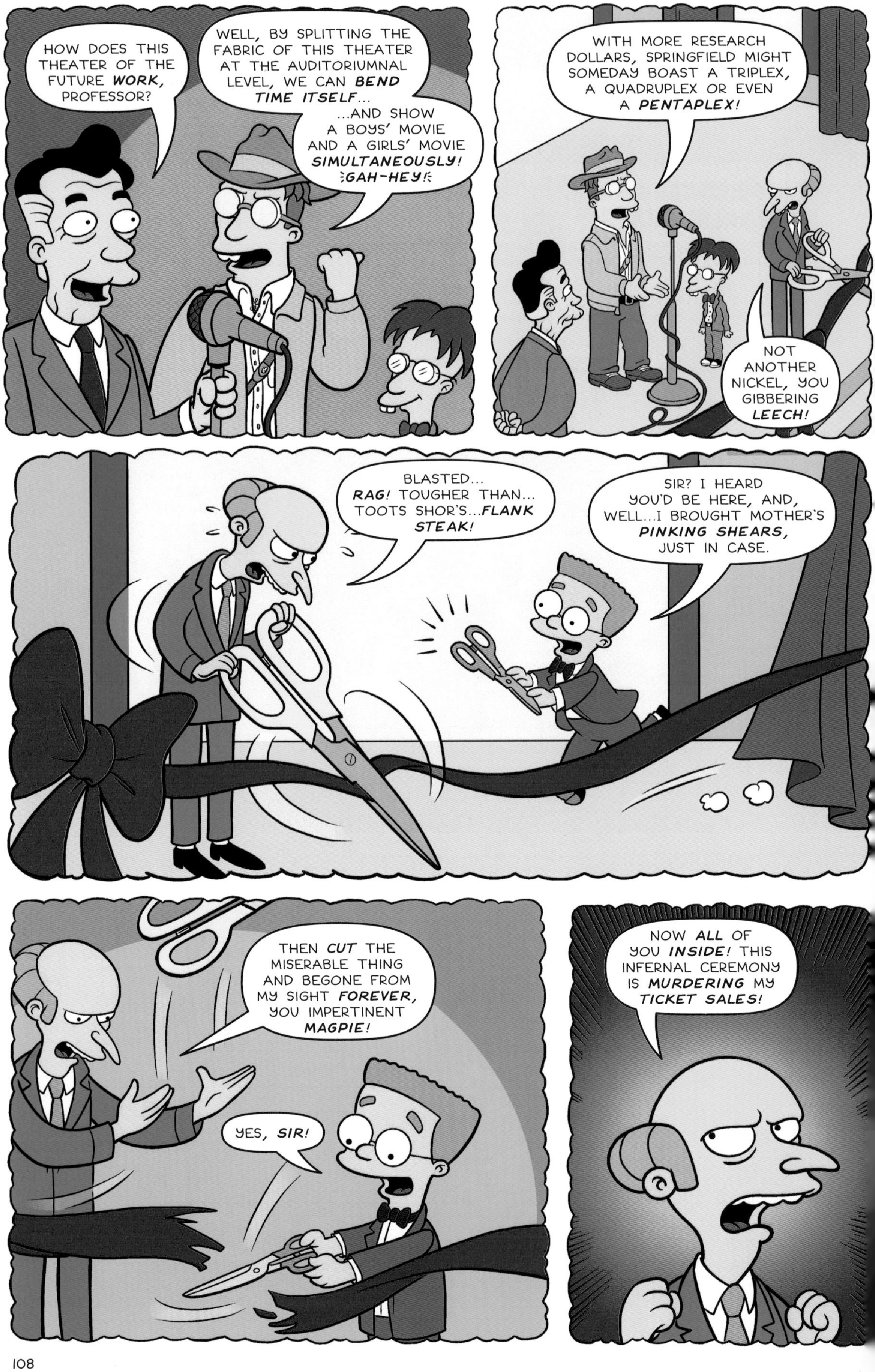
HOW DOES THIS THEATER OF THE FUTURE WORK, PROFESSOR?
WELL, BY SPLITTING THE FABRIC OF THIS THEATER AT THE AUDITORIUMNAL LEVEL, WE CAN BEND TIME ITSELF...
...AND SHOW A BOYS' MOVIE AND A GIRLS' MOVIE SIMULTANEOUSLY! GAH-HEY!
WITH MORE RESEARCH DOLLARS, SPRINGFIELD MIGHT SOMEDAY BOAST A TRIPLEX, A QUADRUPLEX OR EVEN A PENTAPLEX!
NOT ANOTHER NICKEL, YOU GIBBERING LEECH!
BLASTED... RAG! TOUGHER THAN... TOOTS SHOR'S...FLANK STEAK!
SIR? I HEARD YOU'D BE HERE, AND, WELL...I BROUGHT MOTHER'S PINKING SHEARS, JUST IN CASE.
THEN CUT THE MISERABLE THING AND BEGONE FROM MY SIGHT FOREVER, YOU IMPERTINENT MAGPIE!
YES, SIR!
NOW ALL OF YOU INSIDE! THIS INFERNAL CEREMONY IS MURDERING MY TICKET SALES!

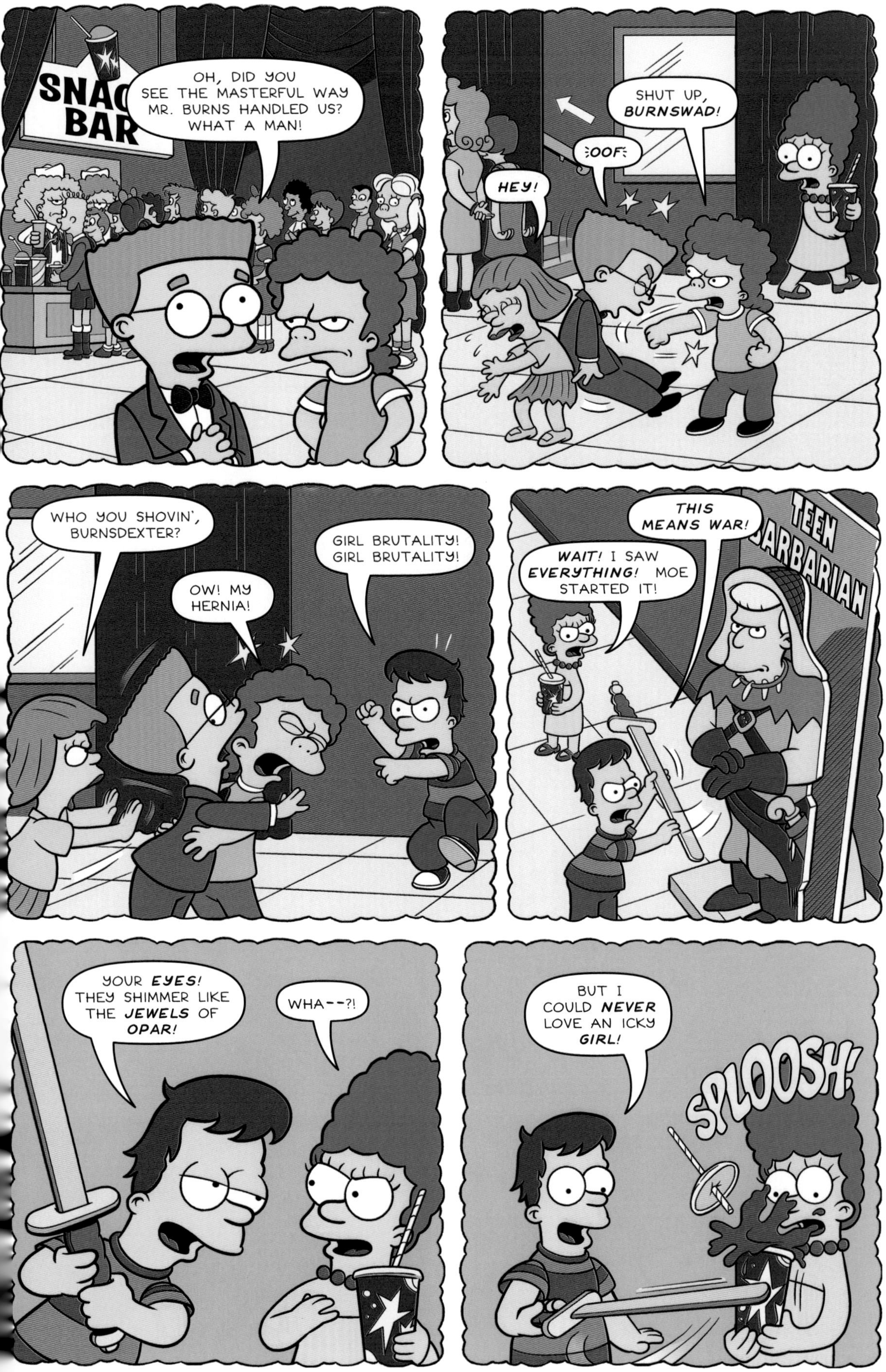
SNACK BAR
OH, DID YOU SEE THE MASTERFUL WAY MR. BURNS HANDLED US? WHAT A MAN!
SHUT UP, BURNSWAD!
OOF
HEY!
WHO YOU SHOVIN', BURNSDEXTER?
OW! MY HERNIA!
GIRL BRUTALITY! GIRL BRUTALITY!
THIS MEANS WAR!
WAIT! I SAW EVERYTHING! MOE STARTED IT!
TEEN BARBARIAN
YOUR EYES! THEY SHIMMER LIKE THE JEWELS OF OPAR!
WHA--?!
BUT I COULD NEVER LOVE AN ICKY GIRL!
SPLOOSH!

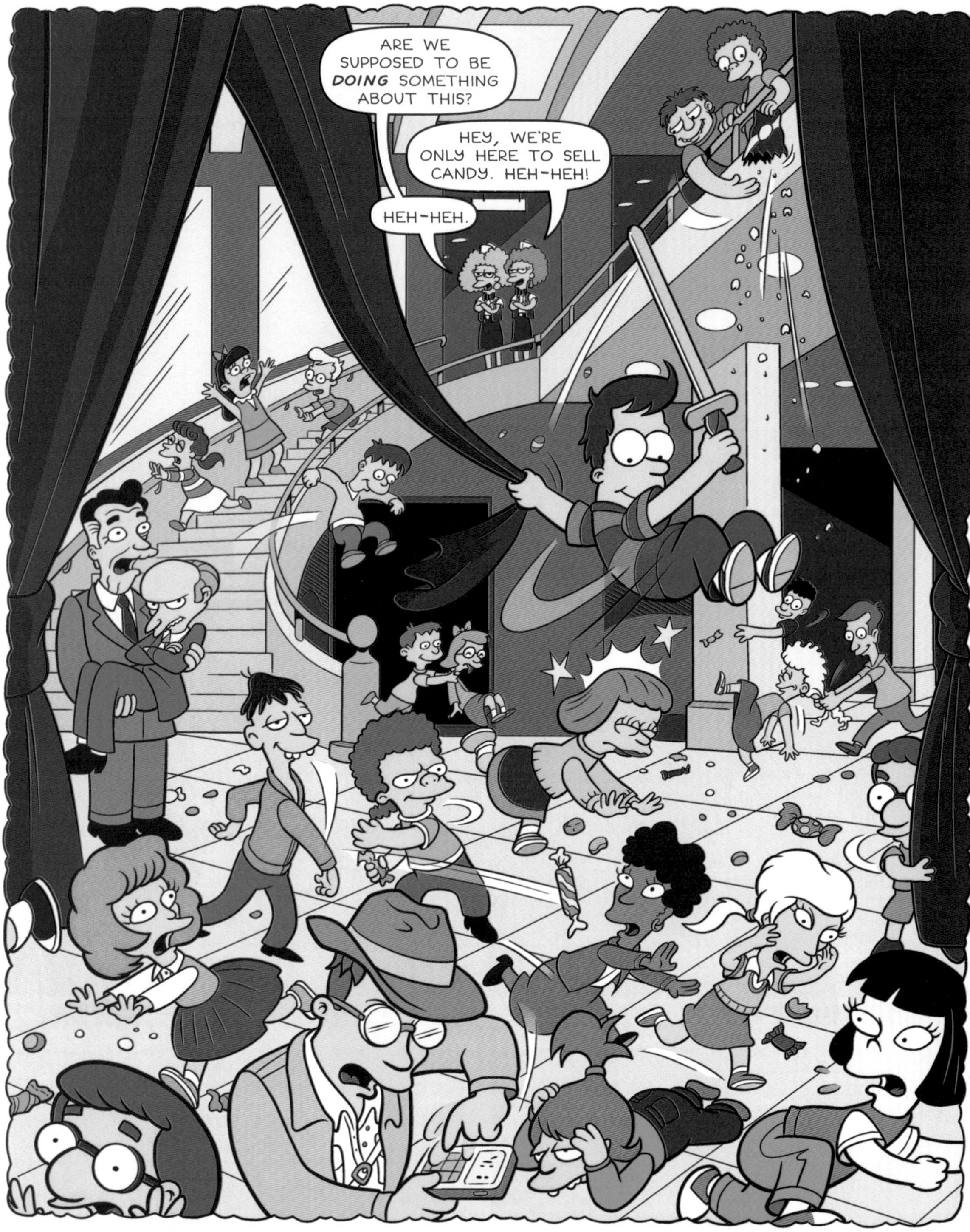
ARE WE SUPPOSED TO BE DOING SOMETHING ABOUT THIS?
HEY, WE'RE ONLY HERE TO SELL CANDY. HEH-HEH!
HEH-HEH.

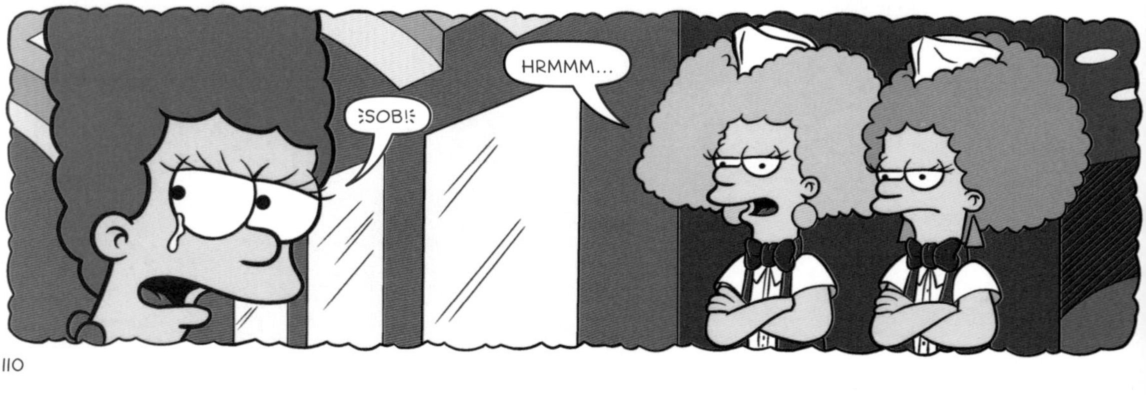
SOB!
HRMMM...

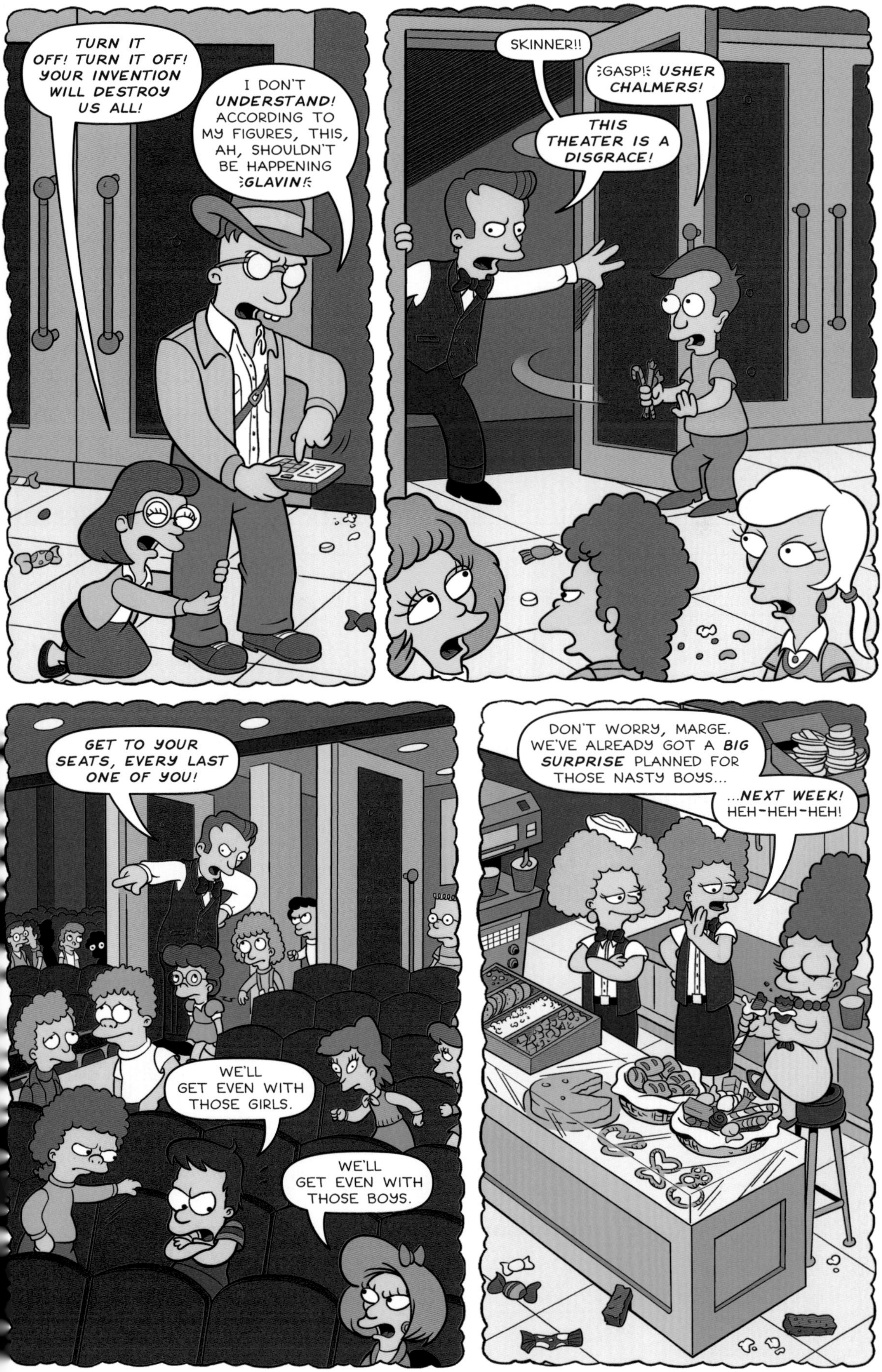

TURN IT OFF! TURN IT OFF! YOUR INVENTION WILL DESTROY US ALL!
I DON'T UNDERSTAND! ACCORDING TO MY FIGURES, THIS, AH, SHOULDN'T BE HAPPENING GLAVIN!
SKINNER!!
GASP! USHER CHALMERS!
THIS THEATER IS A DISGRACE!
GET TO YOUR SEATS, EVERY LAST ONE OF YOU!
WE'LL GET EVEN WITH THOSE GIRLS.
WE'LL GET EVEN WITH THOSE BOYS.
DON'T WORRY, MARGE. WE'VE ALREADY GOT A BIG SURPRISE PLANNED FOR THOSE NASTY BOYS...
...NEXT WEEK! HEH-HEH-HEH!

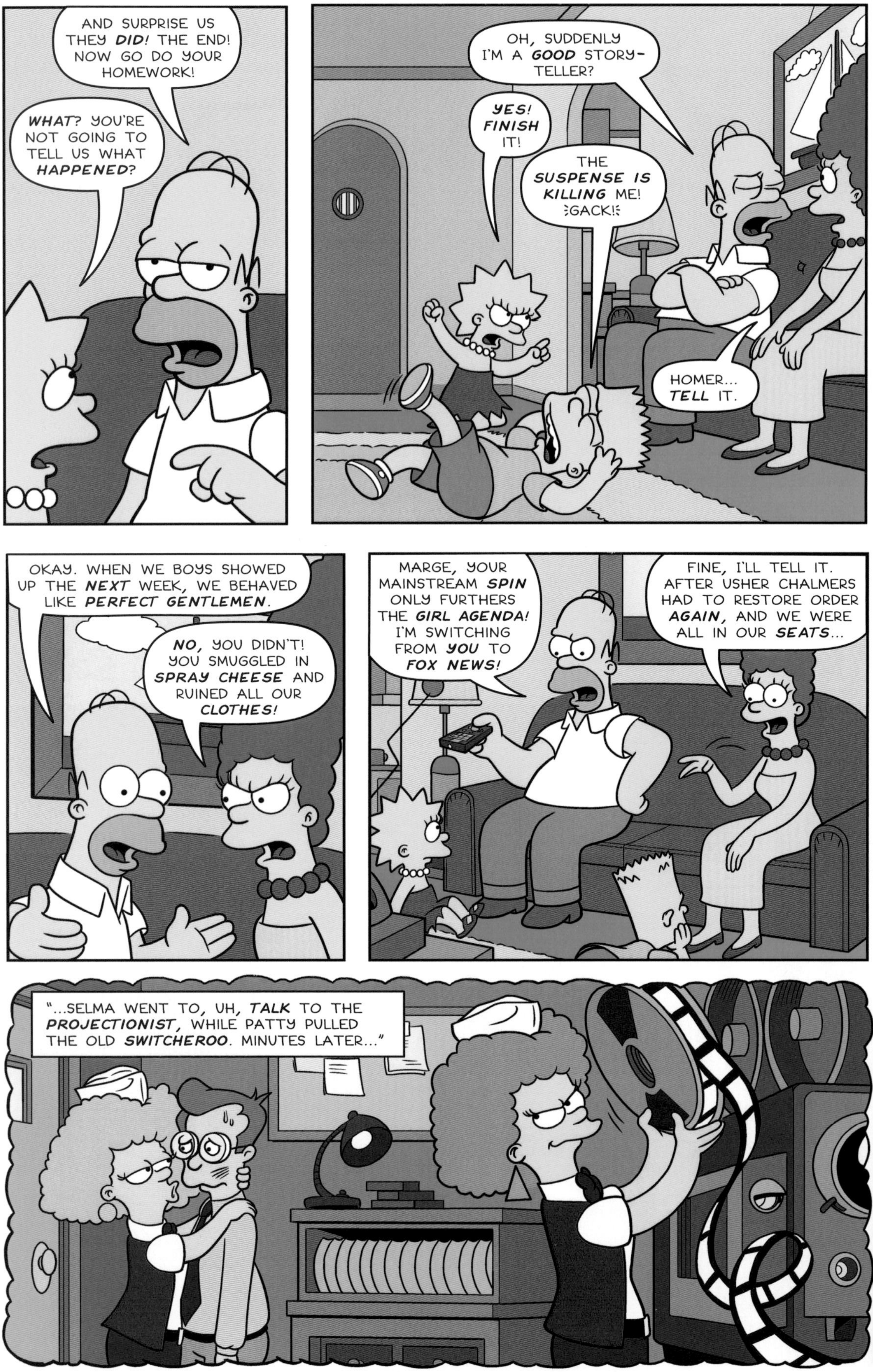
AND SURPRISE US THEY DID! THE END! NOW GO DO YOUR HOMEWORK!
WHAT? YOU'RE NOT GOING TO TELL US WHAT HAPPENED?
OH, SUDDENLY I'M A GOOD STORY-TELLER?
YES! FINISH IT!
THE SUSPENSE IS KILLING ME! GACK!
HOMER... TELL IT.
OKAY. WHEN WE BOYS SHOWED UP THE NEXT WEEK, WE BEHAVED LIKE PERFECT GENTLEMEN.
NO, YOU DIDN'T! YOU SMUGGLED IN SPRAY CHEESE AND RUINED ALL OUR CLOTHES!
MARGE, YOUR MAINSTREAM SPIN ONLY FURTHERS THE GIRL AGENDA! I'M SWITCHING FROM YOU TO FOX NEWS!
FINE, I'LL TELL IT. AFTER USHER CHALMERS HAD TO RESTORE ORDER AGAIN, AND WE WERE ALL IN OUR SEATS...
"...SELMA WENT TO, UH, TALK TO THE PROJECTIONIST, WHILE PATTY PULLED THE OLD SWITCHEROO. MINUTES LATER..."

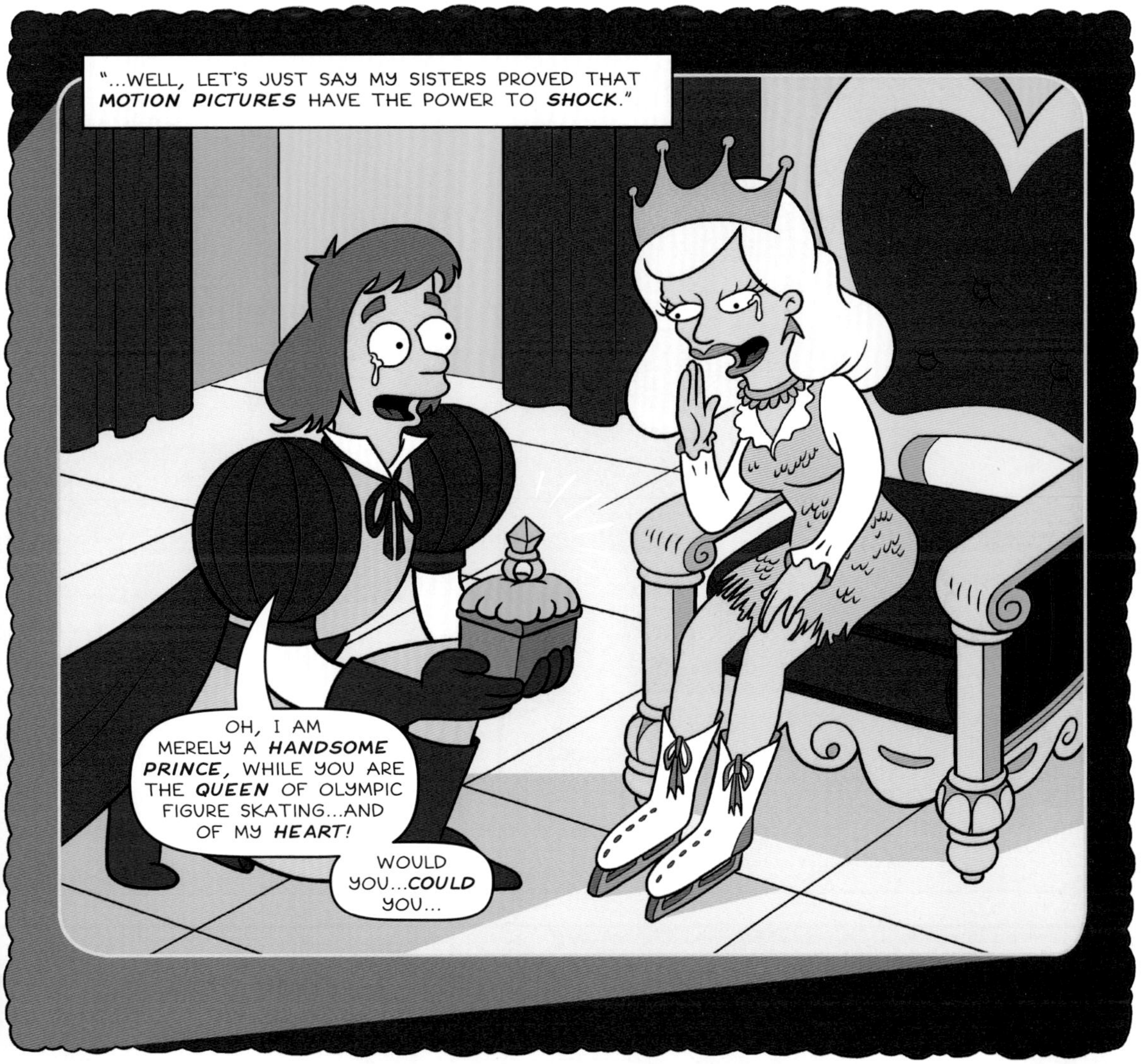
"...WELL, LET'S JUST SAY MY SISTERS PROVED THAT **MOTION PICTURES** HAVE THE POWER TO **SHOCK**."
OH, I AM MERELY A **HANDSOME PRINCE,** WHILE YOU ARE THE **QUEEN** OF OLYMPIC FIGURE SKATING...AND OF MY **HEART**!
WOULD YOU...**COULD** YOU...

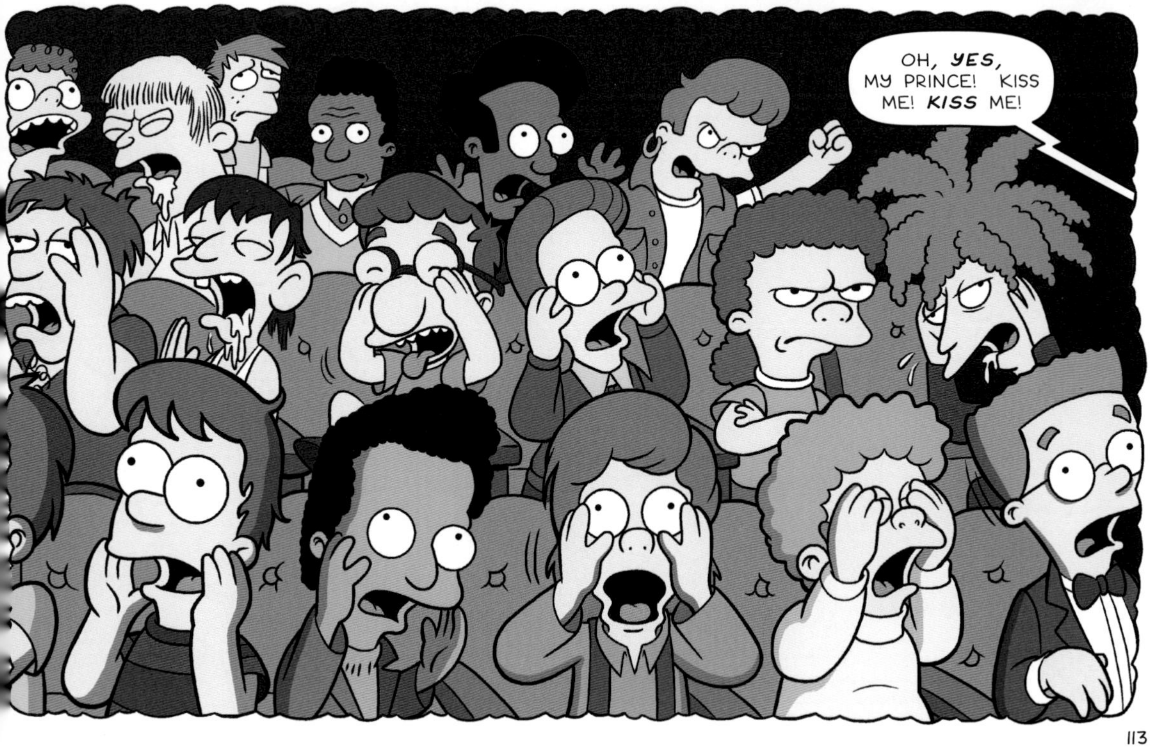
OH, **YES,** MY PRINCE! KISS ME! **KISS** ME!

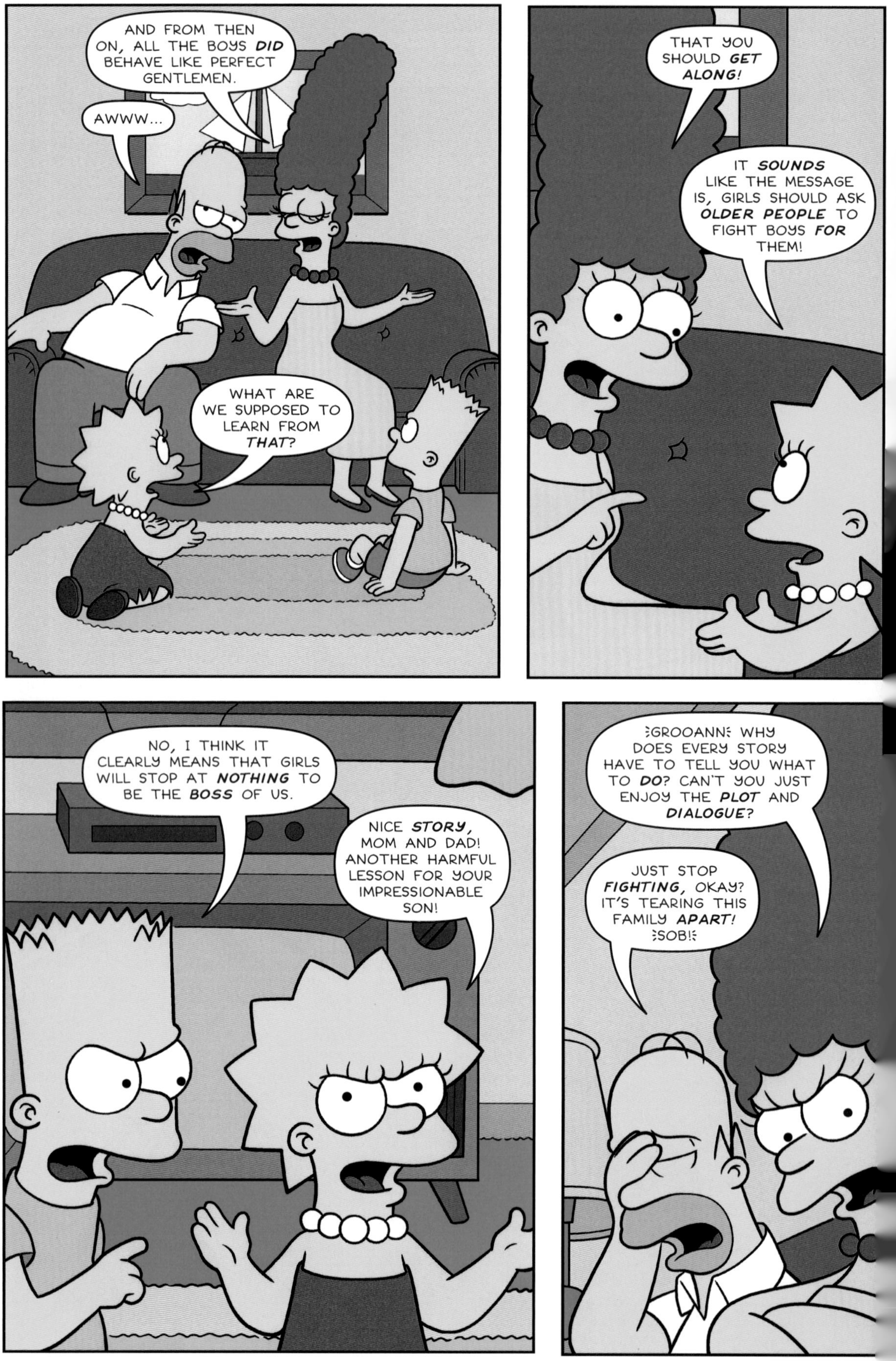

AND FROM THEN ON, ALL THE BOYS *DID* BEHAVE LIKE PERFECT GENTLEMEN.
AWWW...
WHAT ARE WE SUPPOSED TO LEARN FROM *THAT*?
THAT YOU SHOULD *GET ALONG!*
IT *SOUNDS* LIKE THE MESSAGE IS, GIRLS SHOULD ASK *OLDER PEOPLE* TO FIGHT BOYS *FOR* THEM!
NO, I THINK IT CLEARLY MEANS THAT GIRLS WILL STOP AT *NOTHING* TO BE THE *BOSS* OF US.
NICE *STORY*, MOM AND DAD! ANOTHER HARMFUL LESSON FOR YOUR IMPRESSIONABLE SON!
GROOANN WHY DOES EVERY STORY HAVE TO TELL YOU WHAT TO *DO*? CAN'T YOU JUST ENJOY THE *PLOT* AND *DIALOGUE*?
JUST STOP *FIGHTING*, OKAY? IT'S TEARING THIS FAMILY *APART!* SOB!

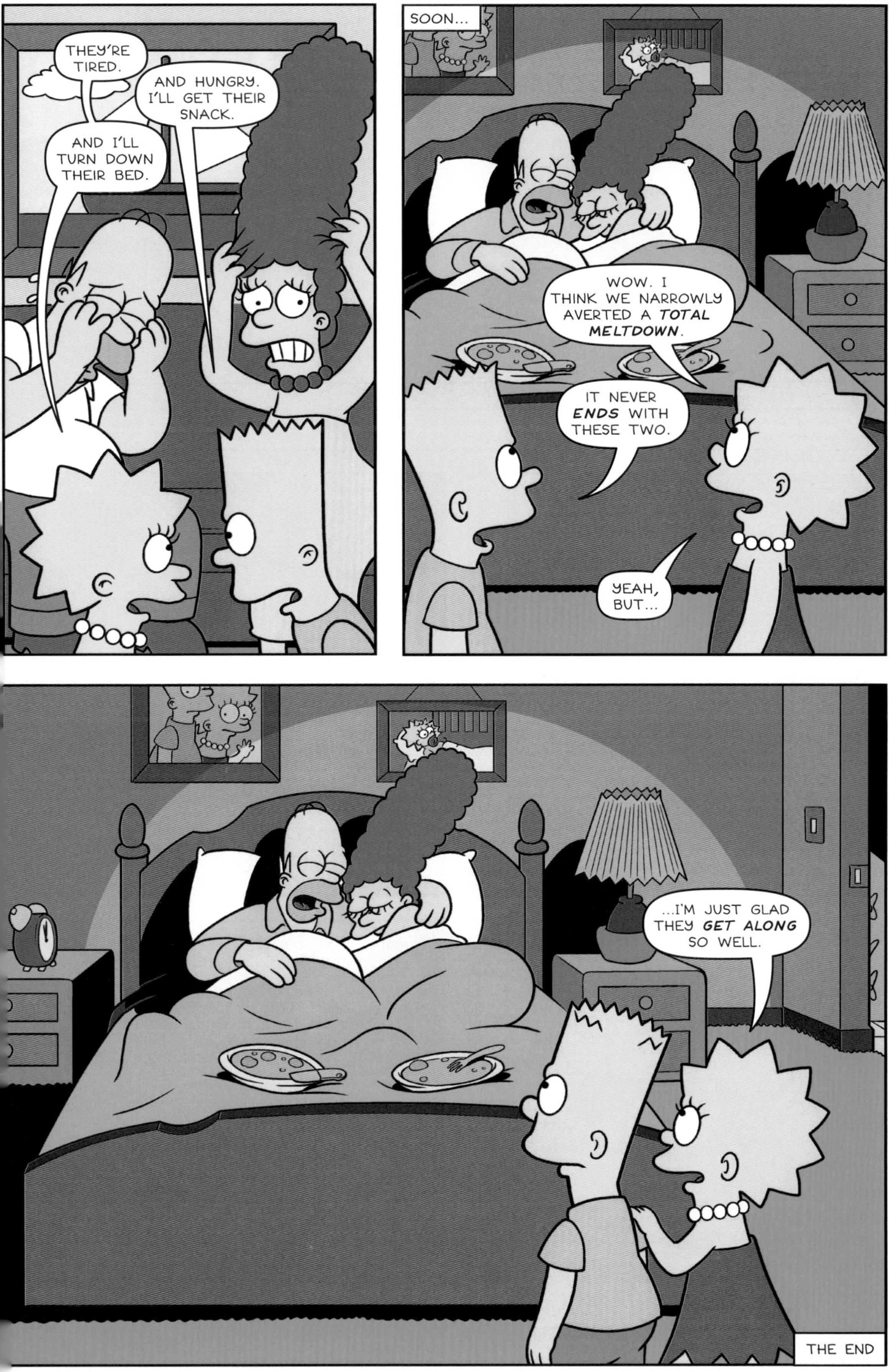
THEY'RE TIRED.
AND HUNGRY. I'LL GET THEIR SNACK.
AND I'LL TURN DOWN THEIR BED.
SOON...
WOW. I THINK WE NARROWLY AVERTED A **TOTAL MELTDOWN**.
IT NEVER **ENDS** WITH THESE TWO.
YEAH, BUT...
...I'M JUST GLAD THEY **GET ALONG** SO WELL.
THE END

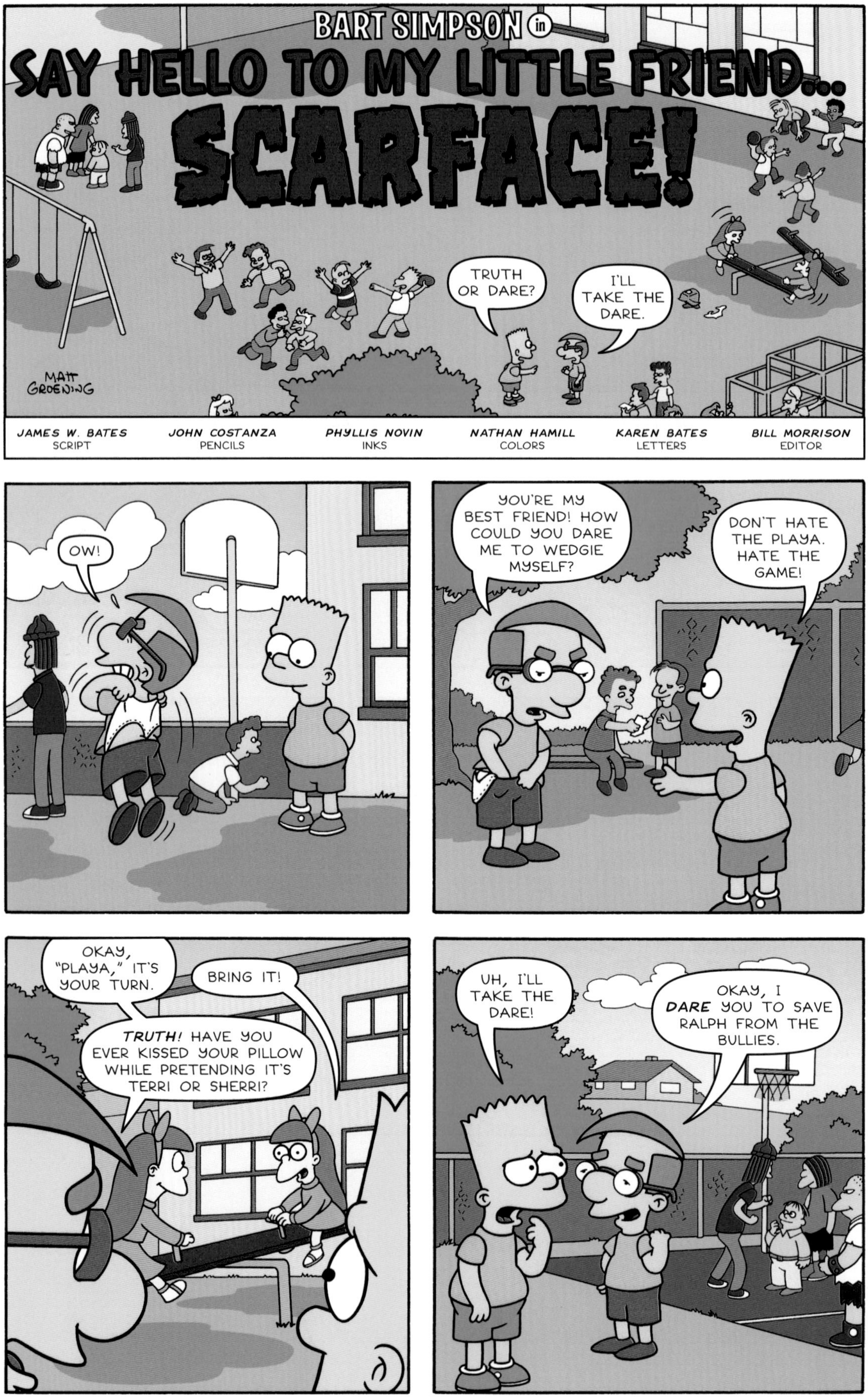
BART SIMPSON in
SAY HELLO TO MY LITTLE FRIEND...
SCARFACE!
TRUTH OR DARE?
I'LL TAKE THE DARE.
MATT GROENING
JAMES W. BATES SCRIPT
JOHN COSTANZA PENCILS
PHYLLIS NOVIN INKS
NATHAN HAMILL COLORS
KAREN BATES LETTERS
BILL MORRISON EDITOR
OW!
YOU'RE MY BEST FRIEND! HOW COULD YOU DARE ME TO WEDGIE MYSELF?
DON'T HATE THE PLAYA. HATE THE GAME!
OKAY, "PLAYA," IT'S YOUR TURN.
BRING IT!
TRUTH! HAVE YOU EVER KISSED YOUR PILLOW WHILE PRETENDING IT'S TERRI OR SHERRI?
UH, I'LL TAKE THE DARE!
OKAY, I DARE YOU TO SAVE RALPH FROM THE BULLIES.

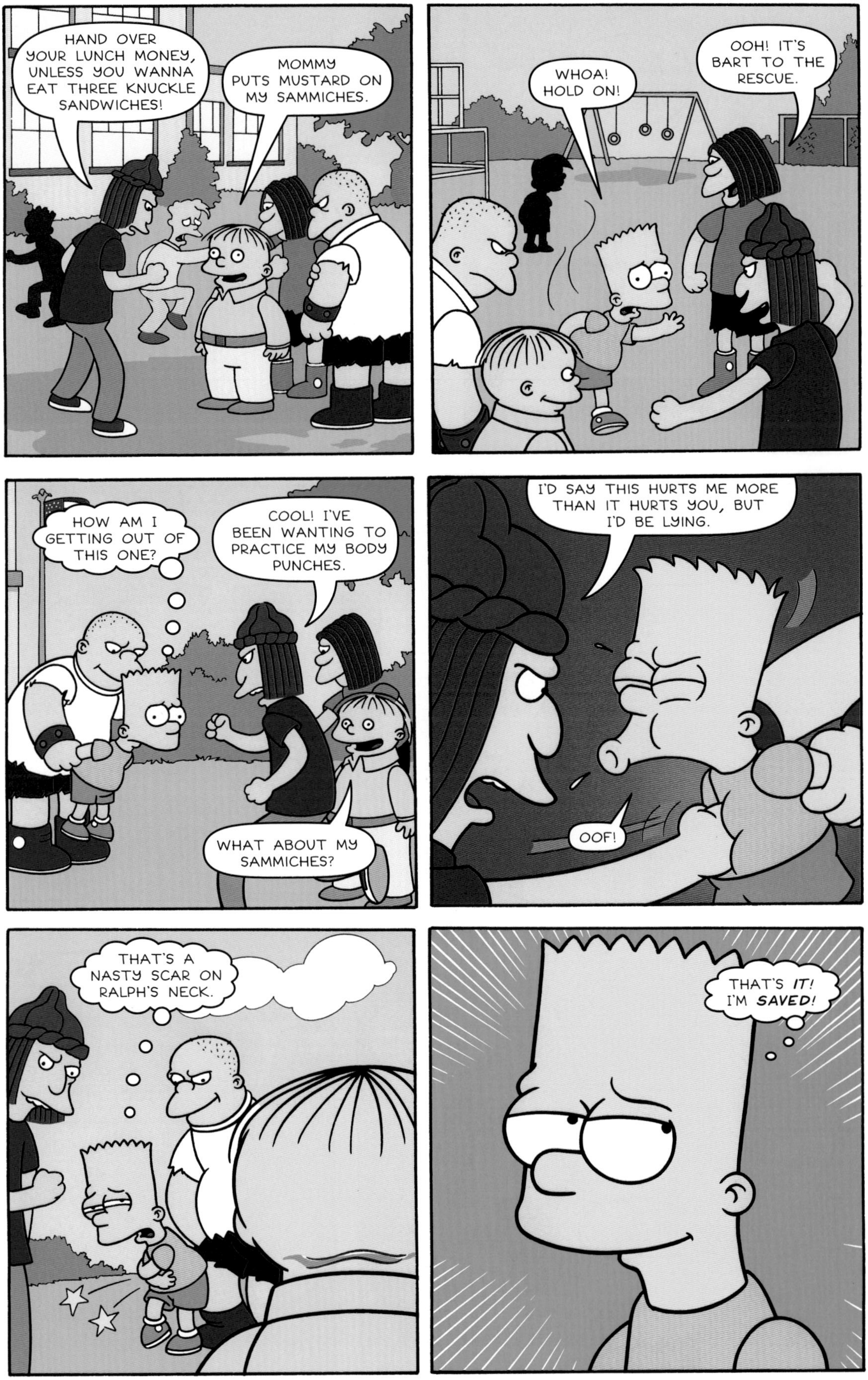
HAND OVER YOUR LUNCH MONEY, UNLESS YOU WANNA EAT THREE KNUCKLE SANDWICHES!
MOMMY PUTS MUSTARD ON MY SAMMICHES.
WHOA! HOLD ON!
OOH! IT'S BART TO THE RESCUE.
HOW AM I GETTING OUT OF THIS ONE?
COOL! I'VE BEEN WANTING TO PRACTICE MY BODY PUNCHES.
WHAT ABOUT MY SAMMICHES?
I'D SAY THIS HURTS ME MORE THAN IT HURTS YOU, BUT I'D BE LYING.
OOF!
THAT'S A NASTY SCAR ON RALPH'S NECK.
THAT'S *IT*! I'M ***SAVED***!

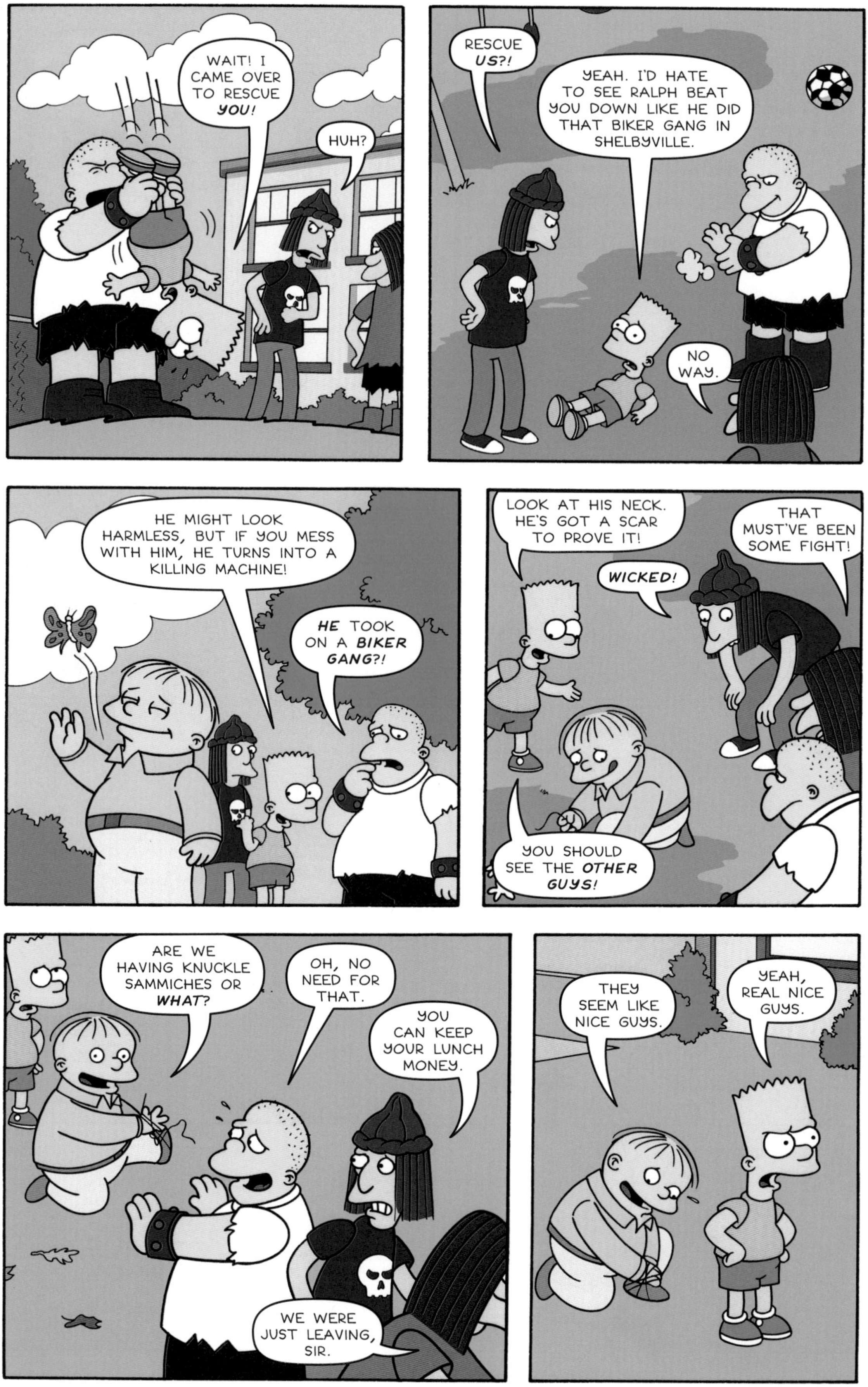
WAIT! I CAME OVER TO RESCUE *YOU*!
HUH?
RESCUE *US*?!
YEAH. I'D HATE TO SEE RALPH BEAT YOU DOWN LIKE HE DID THAT BIKER GANG IN SHELBYVILLE.
NO WAY.
HE MIGHT LOOK HARMLESS, BUT IF YOU MESS WITH HIM, HE TURNS INTO A KILLING MACHINE!
HE TOOK ON A *BIKER GANG*?!
LOOK AT HIS NECK. HE'S GOT A SCAR TO PROVE IT!
WICKED!
THAT MUST'VE BEEN SOME FIGHT!
YOU SHOULD SEE THE *OTHER GUYS*!
ARE WE HAVING KNUCKLE SAMMICHES OR *WHAT*?
OH, NO NEED FOR THAT.
YOU CAN KEEP YOUR LUNCH MONEY.
WE WERE JUST LEAVING, SIR.
THEY SEEM LIKE NICE GUYS.
YEAH, REAL NICE GUYS.

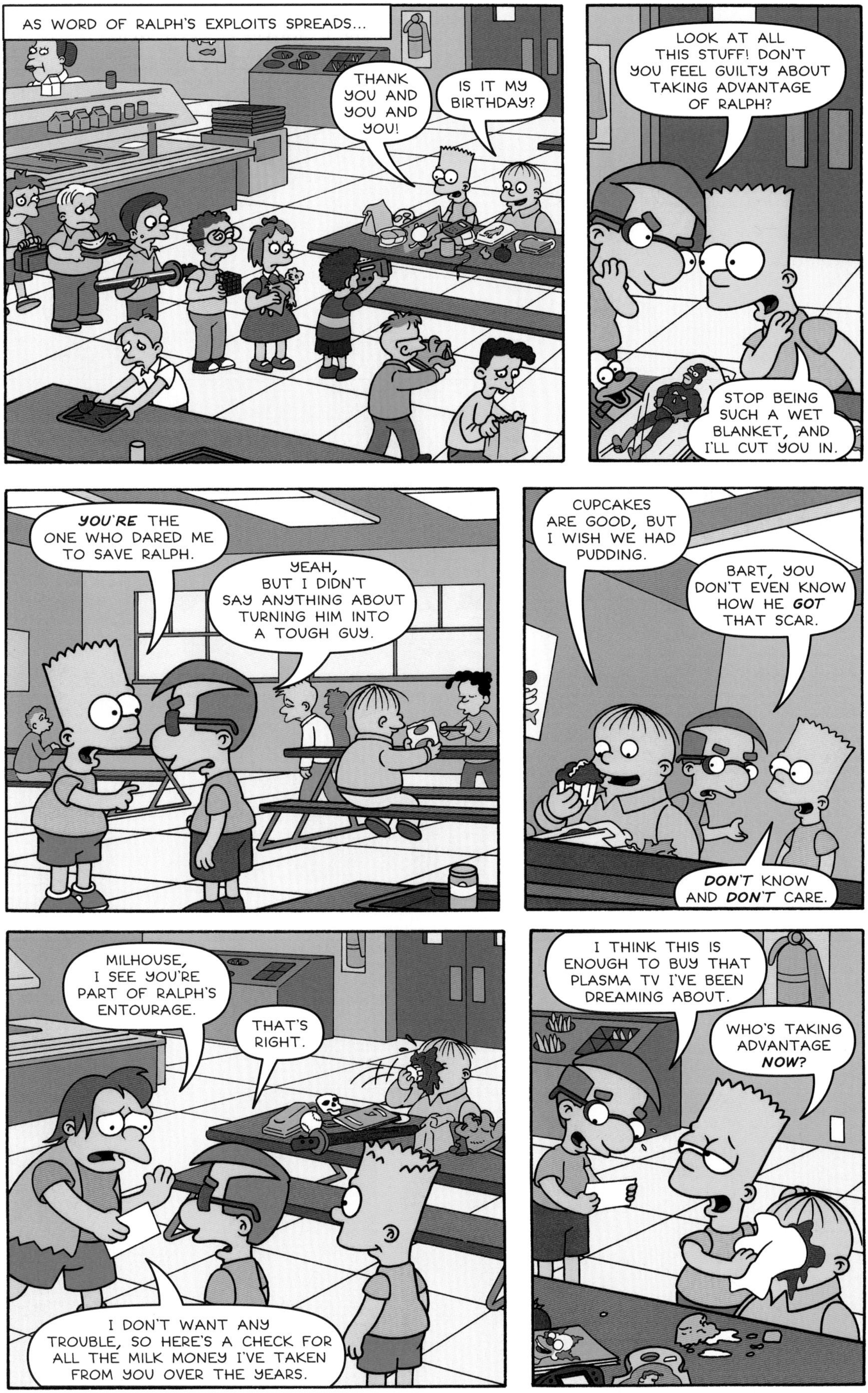
AS WORD OF RALPH'S EXPLOITS SPREADS...
THANK YOU AND YOU AND YOU!
IS IT MY BIRTHDAY?
LOOK AT ALL THIS STUFF! DON'T YOU FEEL GUILTY ABOUT TAKING ADVANTAGE OF RALPH?
STOP BEING SUCH A WET BLANKET, AND I'LL CUT YOU IN.
YOU'RE THE ONE WHO DARED ME TO SAVE RALPH.
YEAH, BUT I DIDN'T SAY ANYTHING ABOUT TURNING HIM INTO A TOUGH GUY.
CUPCAKES ARE GOOD, BUT I WISH WE HAD PUDDING.
BART, YOU DON'T EVEN KNOW HOW HE *GOT* THAT SCAR.
DON'T KNOW AND *DON'T* CARE.
MILHOUSE, I SEE YOU'RE PART OF RALPH'S ENTOURAGE.
THAT'S RIGHT.
I DON'T WANT ANY TROUBLE, SO HERE'S A CHECK FOR ALL THE MILK MONEY I'VE TAKEN FROM YOU OVER THE YEARS.
I THINK THIS IS ENOUGH TO BUY THAT PLASMA TV I'VE BEEN DREAMING ABOUT.
WHO'S TAKING ADVANTAGE *NOW*?

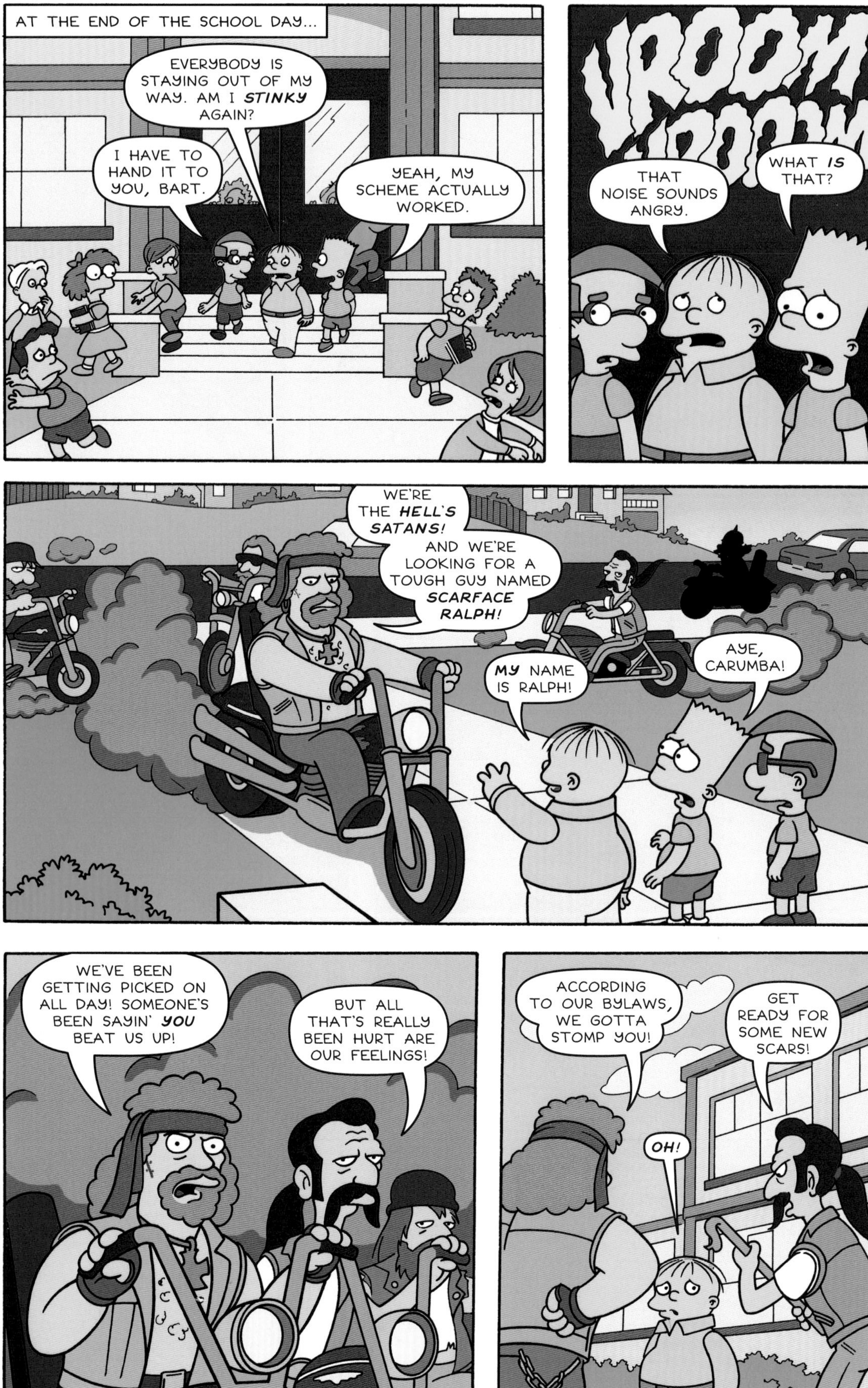
AT THE END OF THE SCHOOL DAY...
EVERYBODY IS STAYING OUT OF MY WAY. AM I STINKY AGAIN?
I HAVE TO HAND IT TO YOU, BART.
YEAH, MY SCHEME ACTUALLY WORKED.
VROOM
THAT NOISE SOUNDS ANGRY.
WHAT IS THAT?
WE'RE THE HELL'S SATANS!
AND WE'RE LOOKING FOR A TOUGH GUY NAMED SCARFACE RALPH!
MY NAME IS RALPH!
AYE, CARUMBA!
WE'VE BEEN GETTING PICKED ON ALL DAY! SOMEONE'S BEEN SAYIN' YOU BEAT US UP!
BUT ALL THAT'S REALLY BEEN HURT ARE OUR FEELINGS!
ACCORDING TO OUR BYLAWS, WE GOTTA STOMP YOU!
GET READY FOR SOME NEW SCARS!
OH!

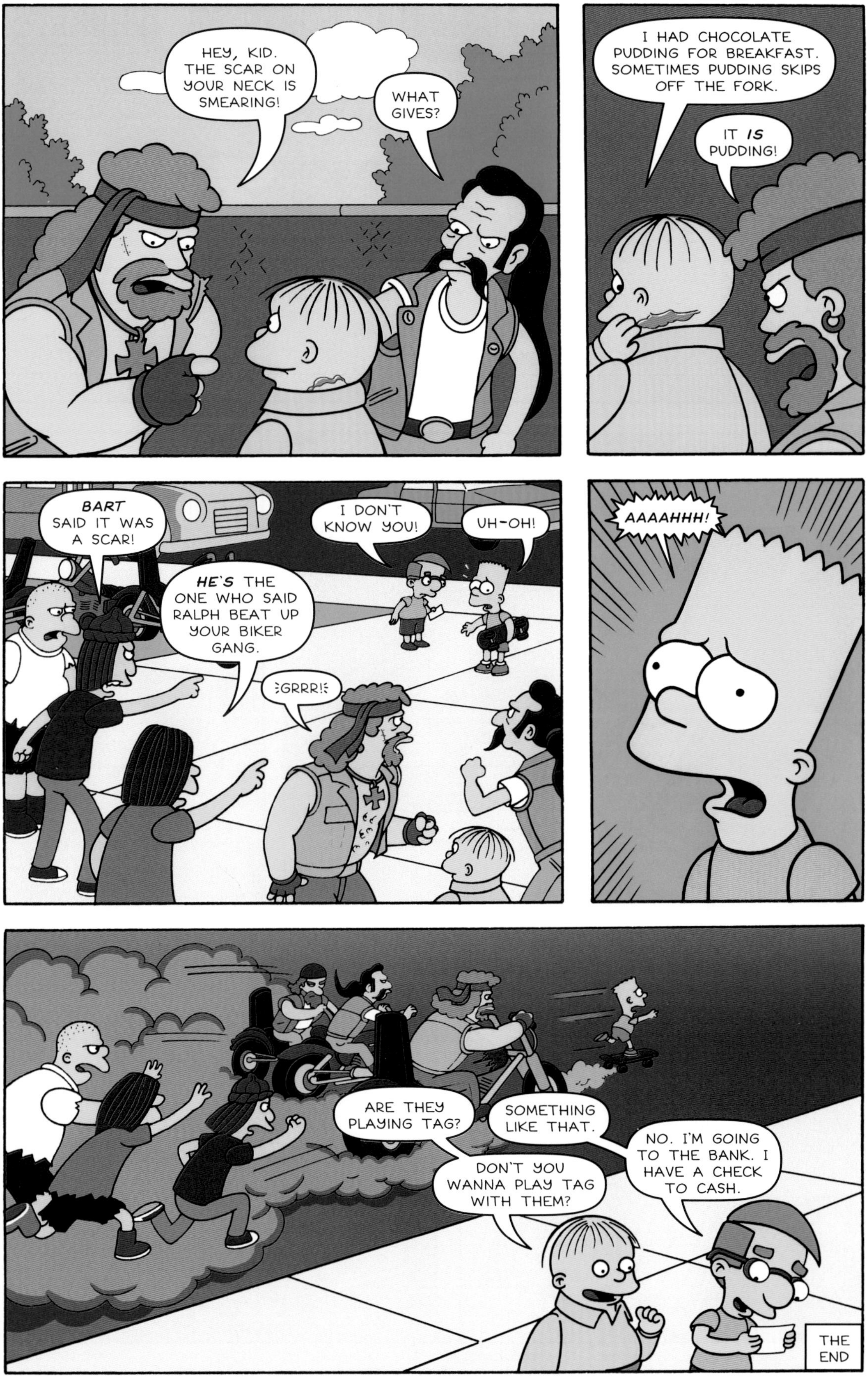
HEY, KID. THE SCAR ON YOUR NECK IS SMEARING!
WHAT GIVES?
I HAD CHOCOLATE PUDDING FOR BREAKFAST. SOMETIMES PUDDING SKIPS OFF THE FORK.
IT *IS* PUDDING!
BART SAID IT WAS A SCAR!
I DON'T KNOW YOU!
UH-OH!
HE'S THE ONE WHO SAID RALPH BEAT UP YOUR BIKER GANG.
GRRR!
AAAAHHH!
ARE THEY PLAYING TAG?
SOMETHING LIKE THAT.
DON'T YOU WANNA PLAY TAG WITH THEM?
NO. I'M GOING TO THE BANK. I HAVE A CHECK TO CASH.
THE END

BART SIMPSON IN PONCE UPON A TIME
♫ SCATTERED PICTURES, ♫ OF THE SMILES WE LEFT BEHIND...LA LA DE-DA DE-DA DAH DA...OF THE WAY ♪ WE WERE... ♪
MOM, DON'T YOU EVER GET TIRED OF LOOKING AT THOSE OLD PHOTOS?
MATT GROENING
OH NEVER, BART! THESE MISTY WATER-COLORED MEMORIES LIGHT THE CORNERS OF MY MIND!
Graduation!
LOOK! HERE'S ONE OF YOU WHEN YOU WERE JUST A TODDLER.
AAH, THE BITTERSWEET DAYS OF MY ILL-SPENT YOUTH!
THAT'S WEIRD... THAT ONE LOOKS LIKE A PICTURE OF ME, BUT IN BLACK AND WHITE.
ACTUALLY, THAT'S A PHOTO OF YOUR FATHER.
Memories

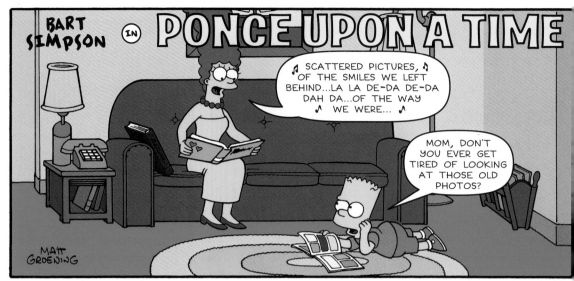

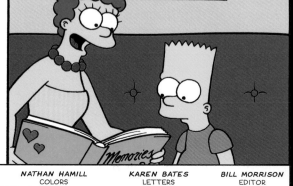

MARY TRAINOR SCRIPT | *NINA MATSUMOTO* PENCILS | *MIKE DECARLO* INKS | *NATHAN HAMILL* COLORS | *KAREN BATES* LETTERS | *BILL MORRISON* EDITOR

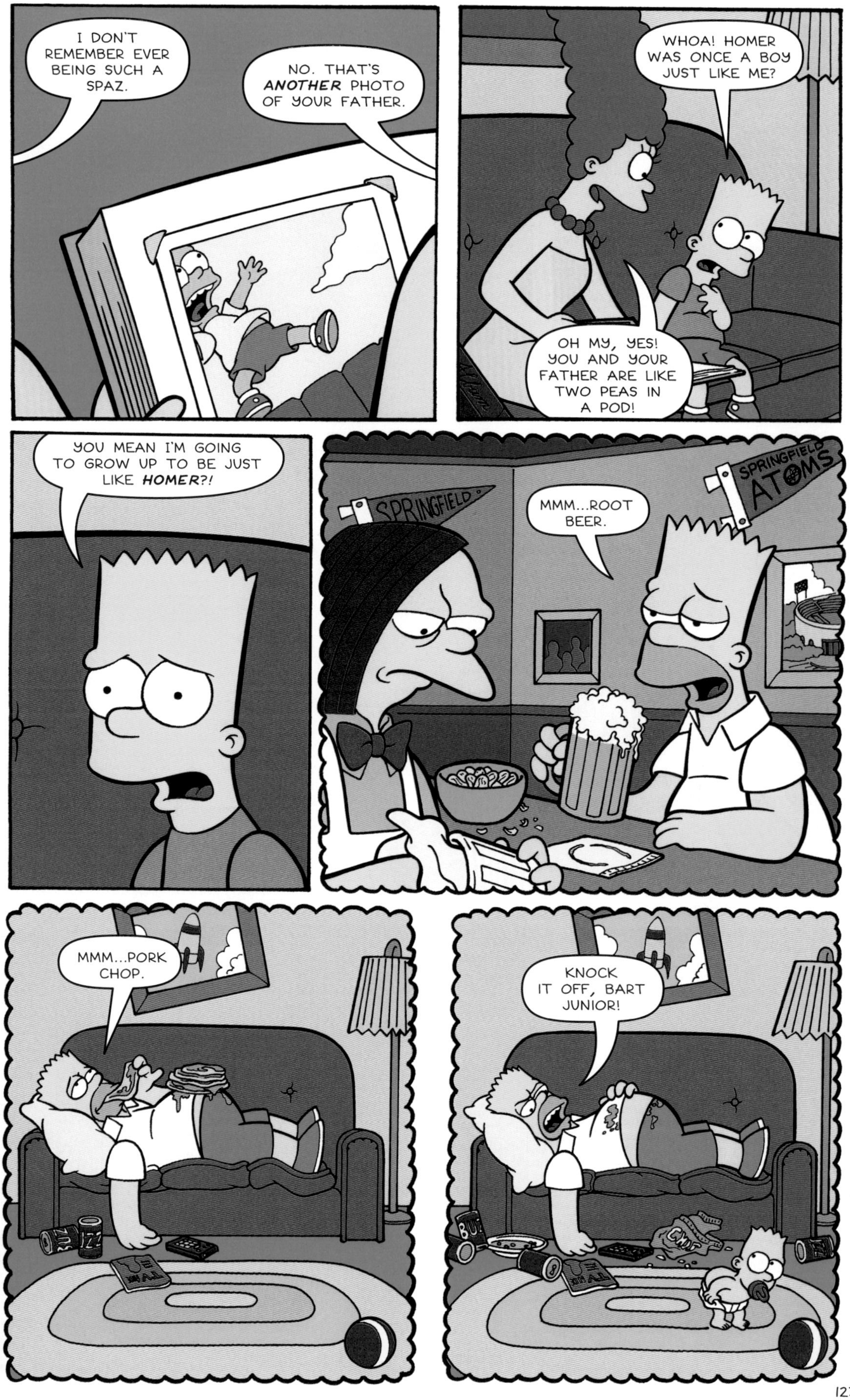
I DON'T REMEMBER EVER BEING SUCH A SPAZ.
NO. THAT'S **ANOTHER** PHOTO OF YOUR FATHER.
WHOA! HOMER WAS ONCE A BOY JUST LIKE ME?
OH MY, YES! YOU AND YOUR FATHER ARE LIKE TWO PEAS IN A POD!
YOU MEAN I'M GOING TO GROW UP TO BE JUST LIKE **HOMER**?!
SPRINGFIELD
SPRINGFIELD ATOMS
MMM...ROOT BEER.
MMM...PORK CHOP.
KNOCK IT OFF, BART JUNIOR!

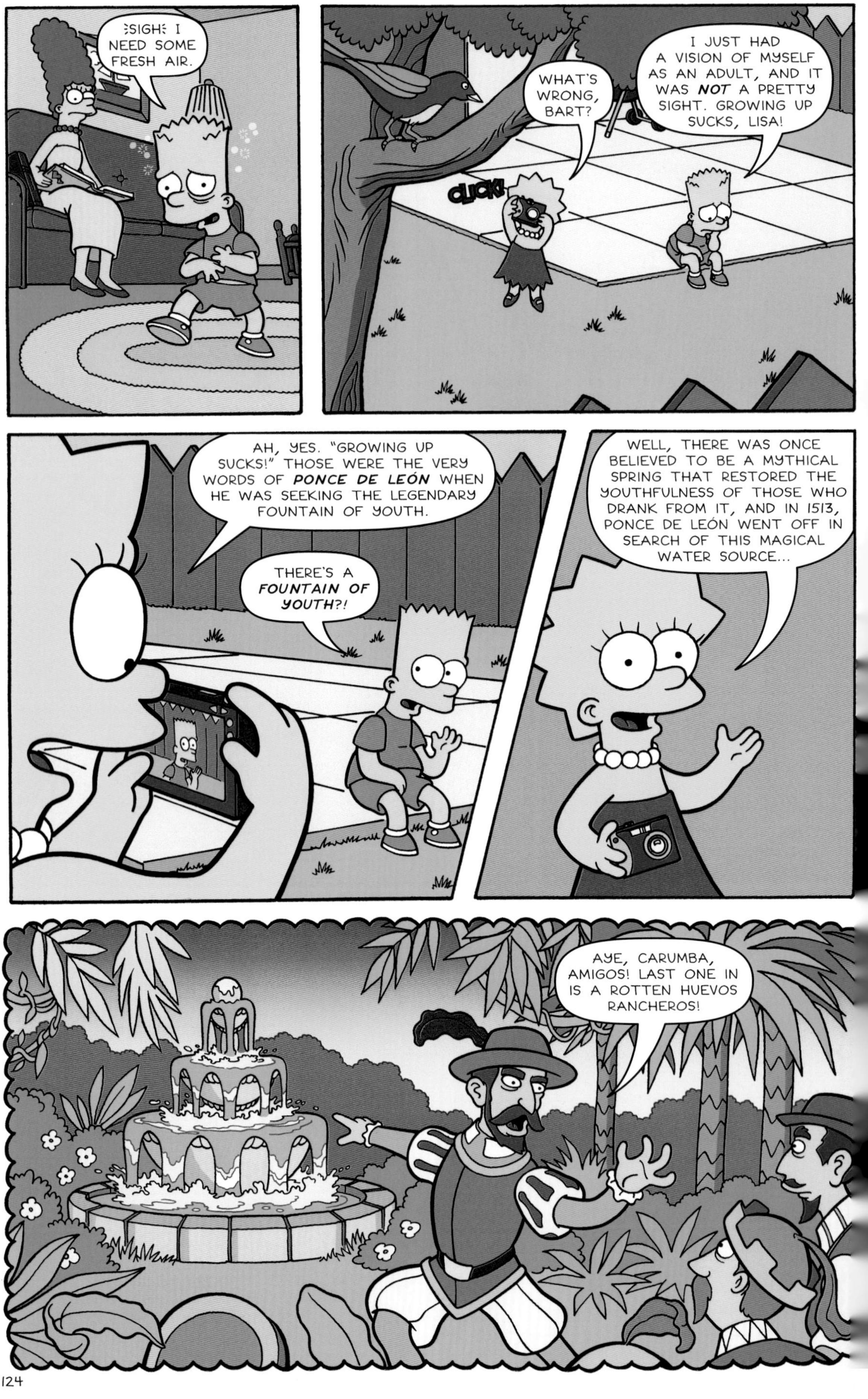
⁝SIGH⁝ I NEED SOME FRESH AIR.
WHAT'S WRONG, BART?
I JUST HAD A VISION OF MYSELF AS AN ADULT, AND IT WAS **NOT** A PRETTY SIGHT. GROWING UP SUCKS, LISA!
CLICK!
AH, YES. "GROWING UP SUCKS!" THOSE WERE THE VERY WORDS OF **PONCE DE LEÓN** WHEN HE WAS SEEKING THE LEGENDARY FOUNTAIN OF YOUTH.
THERE'S A ***FOUNTAIN OF YOUTH***?!
WELL, THERE WAS ONCE BELIEVED TO BE A MYTHICAL SPRING THAT RESTORED THE YOUTHFULNESS OF THOSE WHO DRANK FROM IT, AND IN 1513, PONCE DE LEÓN WENT OFF IN SEARCH OF THIS MAGICAL WATER SOURCE...
AYE, CARUMBA, AMIGOS! LAST ONE IN IS A ROTTEN HUEVOS RANCHEROS!

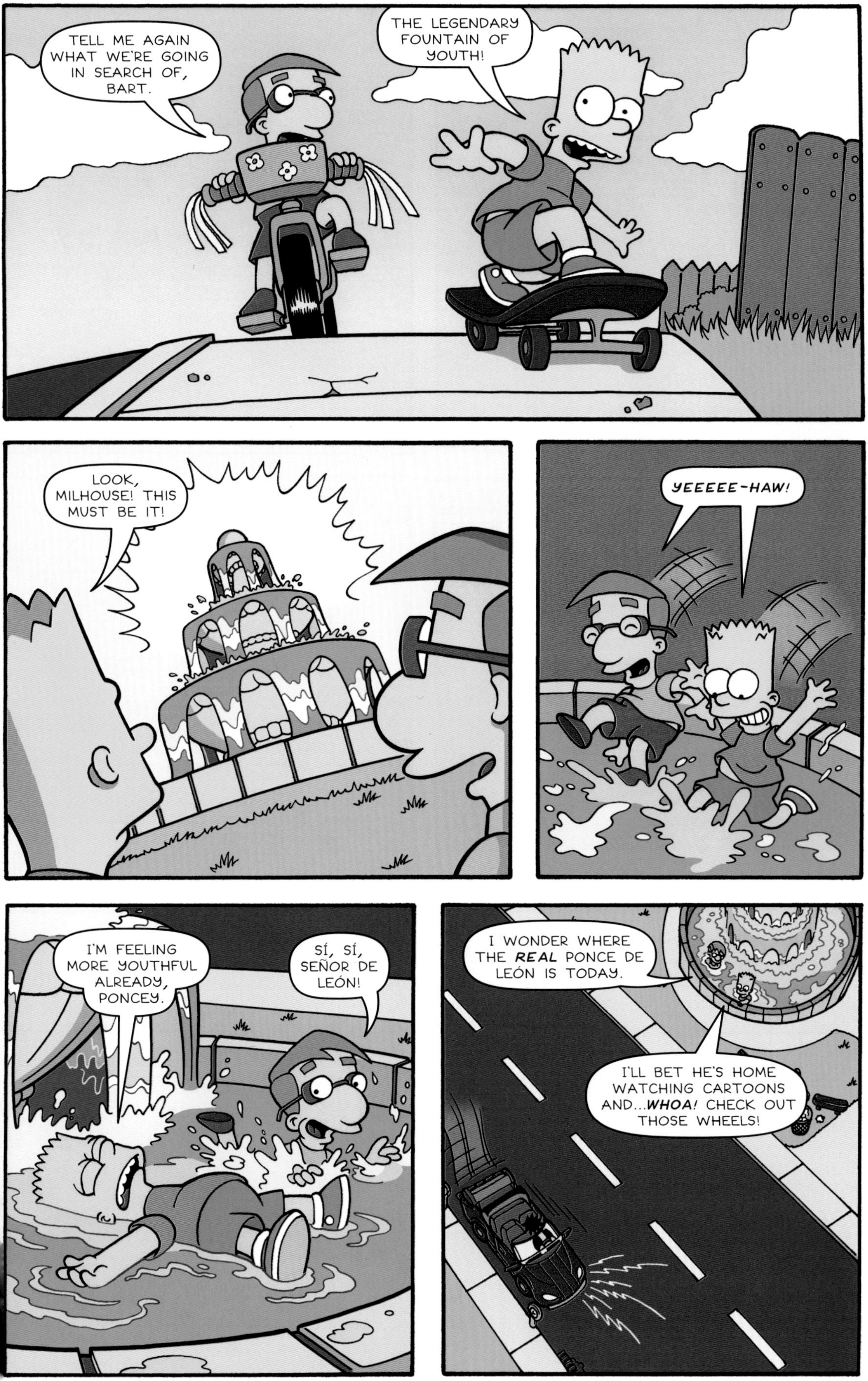
TELL ME AGAIN WHAT WE'RE GOING IN SEARCH OF, BART.
THE LEGENDARY FOUNTAIN OF YOUTH!
LOOK, MILHOUSE! THIS MUST BE IT!
YEEEEE-HAW!
I'M FEELING MORE YOUTHFUL ALREADY, PONCEY.
SÍ, SÍ, SEÑOR DE LEÓN!
I WONDER WHERE THE REAL PONCE DE LEÓN IS TODAY.
I'LL BET HE'S HOME WATCHING CARTOONS AND...WHOA! CHECK OUT THOSE WHEELS!

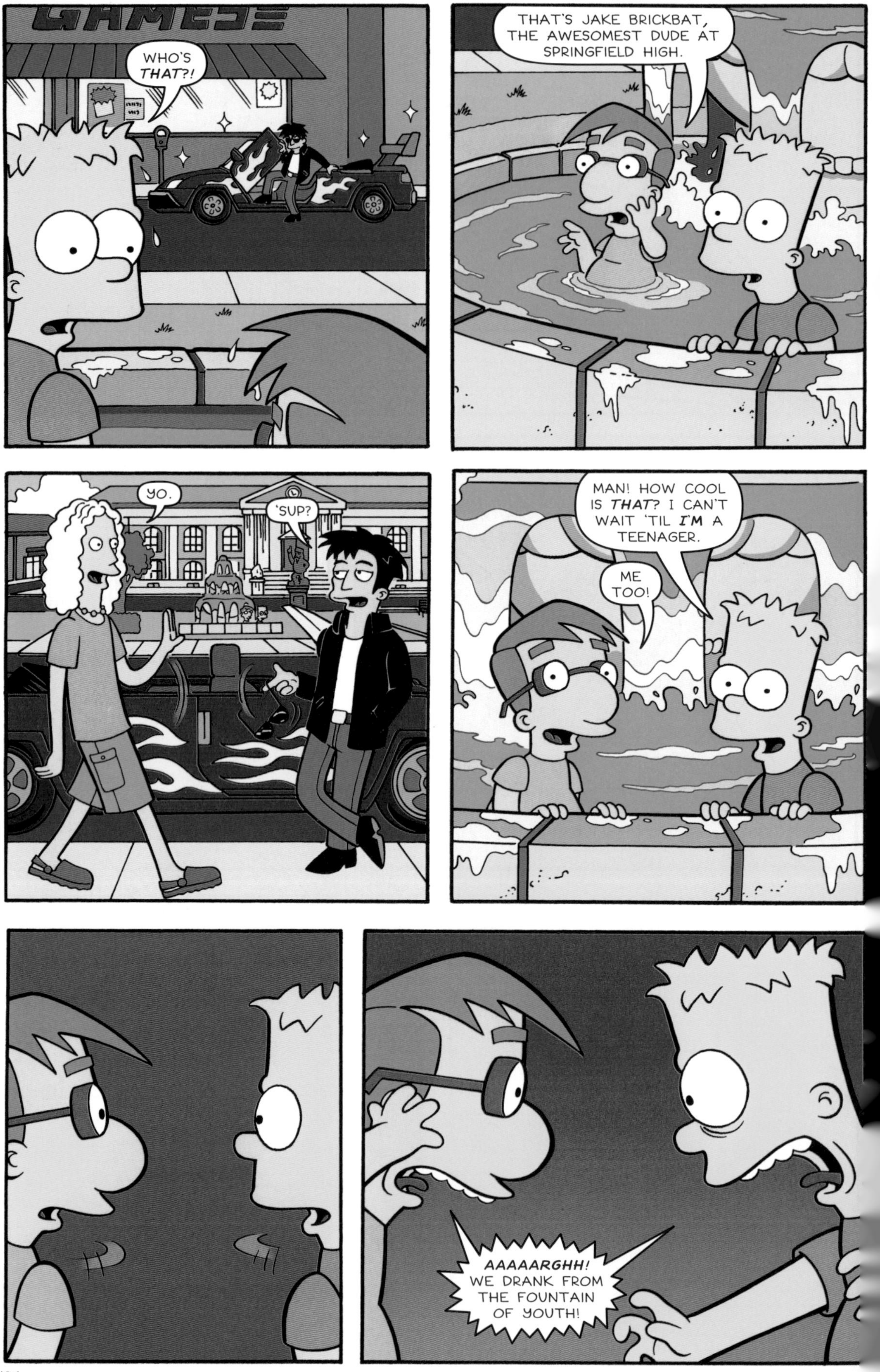
WHO'S THAT?!
THAT'S JAKE BRICKBAT, THE AWESOMEST DUDE AT SPRINGFIELD HIGH.
YO.
'SUP?
MAN! HOW COOL IS THAT? I CAN'T WAIT 'TIL I'M A TEENAGER.
ME TOO!
AAAAARGHH! WE DRANK FROM THE FOUNTAIN OF YOUTH!

SPIT! SPIT!

:GACK!:

PTOOOEY!!

EWWW...*GROSS!* WHAT IS *WRONG* WITH YOU GUYS?

WE DRANK FROM THE FOUNTAIN OF YOUTH, AND NOW WE'LL NEVER GROW UP!

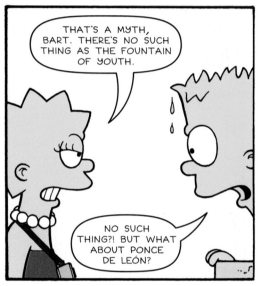

THAT'S A MYTH, BART. THERE'S NO SUCH THING AS THE FOUNTAIN OF YOUTH.

NO SUCH THING?! BUT WHAT ABOUT PONCE DE LEÓN?

PONCE DE LEÓN NEVER FOUND ANYTHING BUT FLORIDA. AND HE LIVED TO BE, LIKE, OVER 60 YEARS OLD!

THEN, PERCHANCE, I MAY GROW UP TO FULFILL MY LIFELONG DREAM!

I NOW PRONOUNCE YOU MR. AND MRS. LISA SIMPSON!

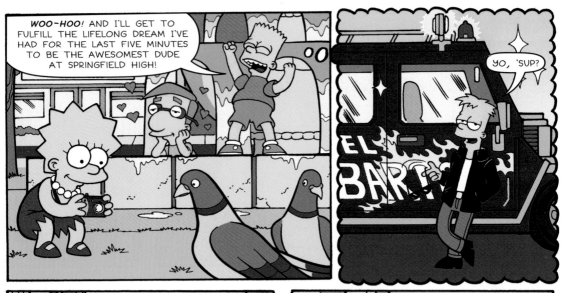

WOO-HOO! AND I'LL GET TO FULFILL THE LIFELONG DREAM I'VE HAD FOR THE LAST FIVE MINUTES TO BE THE AWESOMEST DUDE AT SPRINGFIELD HIGH!

YO, 'SUP?

I DON'T KNOW WHY I WAS SO FREAKED OUT ABOUT GROWING UP ...I'M *NOTHING* LIKE HOMER!

WHOOPS...

CLICK!

YIIII!

THE END